Exploring Sikhism

This volume brings together essays published over four decades by an internationally renowned scholar of Sikh Studies whose interest embraces all aspects of Sikh history, belief, and practice. The essays, trenchant, insightful, and engagingly written, cover a range of subjects—from the nature of the Sikh Panth (the Sikh community) and the Khalsa Rahit (the code of belief and behaviour all initiated Sikhs must promise to obey) to Guru Nanak and the Sikh diaspora. The volume concludes with a spirited answer to some of the criticisms that have been levelled against McLeod over the course of his career. This collection will be invaluable for students and scholars of Sikh studies as well as general readers interested in the work of this important scholar.

Hew Mcleod is Emeritus Professor at the University of Otago, Dunedin, New Zealand.

D1563548

EXPLORING SIKHISM

Aspects of Sikh Identity, Culture, and Thought

W.H. McLeod

OXFORD
UNIVERSITY PRESS

OXFORD
UNIVERSITY PRESS

YMCA Library Building, Jai Singh Road, New Delhi 110 001

Oxford University Press is a department of the University of Oxford. It furthers the
University's objective of excellence in research, scholarship, and education
by publishing worldwide in

Oxford   New York

Auckland   Bangkok   Buenos Aires   Cape Town   Chennai
Dar es Salaam   Delhi   Hong Kong   Istanbul   Karachi   Kolkata
Kuala Lumpur   Madrid   Melbourne   Mexico City   Mumbai   Nairobi
São Paulo   Shanghai   Taipei   Tokyo   Toronto

Oxford is a registered trade mark of Oxford University Press
in the UK and in certain other countries

Published in India
By Oxford University Press, New Delhi

First published 2000
Second impression 2001
Oxford India Paperbacks 2003

ISBN 0 19 565856 6

Printed at Saurabh Printers Pvt. Ltd., Noida
Published by Manzar Khan, Oxford University Press
YMCA Library Building, Jai Singh Road, New Delhi 110 001

To
Jagtar Singh Grewal
an elder brother, better-informed

PREFACE

This collection represents the various aspects of Sikh studies which have interested me during the past thirty-five years. First came Guru Nanak, proclaimed by Sikhs as the founder and formulator of the faith which they profess. Guru Nanak provided me with my first scholarly introduction to the Sikh faith; his life and teachings were the subject of my thesis at the London School of Oriental and African Studies. The life and teachings of Guru Nanak have remained a primary interest and it is entirely appropriate that this collection should begin with three articles about him.

A second interest has been the nature of the Sikh Panth which gathered around him and his successors. In recent years my attention has been increasingly focussed on the Singh Sabha movement and its contribution to the shaping of the contemporary Panth. The third of the articles in this section deals with this subject.

This does not mean, however, that I have lost interest in the eighteenth century. On the contrary, this is where my current interest is concentrated as I seek to understand the historical development of the Rahit (the Khalsa code of belief and discipline). Much research still remains to be done on the Rahit and on the rahit-namas which are its recorded versions.

Definitions of key terms have always been critical to my work on Sikhism. One of the first was the meaning of the word 'Panth'. This work has now been done and the word 'Panth' has been firmly fixed both in my own usage and in the forthcoming edition of the Oxford English Dictionary. 'Sant' was another word which required analysis because of the two widely-divergent meanings attached to it. Yet another is the word 'fundamentalism'. This is a term which has acquired recent prominence by political commentators, imparting to it a meaning which seems, to me, to be astray. In the article dealing with fundamentalism I seek to return to the strictly religious meaning of the word and to ask whether or not there are any areas of the Panth which qualify as fundamentalist.

From key definitions the collection moves on to the question of what sects can be identified within the Panth. Among the several sects one has been singled out for closer analysis. This is the Namdhari sect, the Sikhs commonly known as Kukas.

One question which initially concerned me was whether Sikhs acknowledge caste. There could be no doubt that caste is plainly evident within the Panth, but was its presence admitted and did orthodox Sikhs approve of its presence? An article on the Ahluwalias and Ramgarhias represents some of my conclusions in this area. Further treatment is contained in my published works, particularly in the fifth chapter of *The Evolution of the Sikh Community*.[1]

Sikh migration represents a somewhat different interest from the other articles in this collection. It developed after I had returned to New Zealand and led in particular to the book *Punjabis in New Zealand*.[2]

The short article on Macauliffe which appears in the biographical section does not pretend to be scholarly or to be based upon my own research. It has been included because there is so little available about this very important figure in the history of Sikhism.

Finally there are the reactions to what I have written. Much of what I have done has aroused considerable indignation on the part of many Sikhs. This is entirely understandable, for one cannot investigate a living faith from a strictly academic point of view without arousing strong feelings. In general my policy has been to keep silent when accusations are levelled against me, but I have on one occasion attempted to offer a justification. This appears in the final section.

Hew McLeod
University of Otago
Dunedin, New Zealand

Notes

1. *The Evolution of the Sikh Community*. Oxford: Clarendon Press, 1976. Delhi: Oxford India Paperbacks, 1996.
2. *Punjabis in New Zealand: A History of Punjabi Migration, 1890–1940*. Amritsar: Guru Nanak Dev University, 1986.

CONTENTS

Glossary   xiii

PART I: GURU NANAK

1. The Influence of Islam upon the Thought of Guru Nanak   3
2. Kabir, Nanak, and the Early Sikh Panth   19
3. The Nanak of Faith and the Nanak of History   37

PART II: THE SIKH PANTH

4. The Development of the Sikh Panth   49
5. The Sikh Struggle in the Eighteenth Century   70
   and its Relevance for Today
6. The Contribution of the Singh Sabha Movement   91
   to the Interpretation of Sikh History and Religion

PART III: THE RAHIT AND THE RAHIT-NĀMĀS

7. The Problem of the Panjabi Rahit-nāmās   103
8. The Khalsa Rahit: The Sikh Identity Defined   126

PART IV: DEFINITIONS

9. On the Word *Panth*: A Problem of   139
   Terminology and Definition

10. The Meaning of 'Sant' in Sikh Usage   149
11. Sikh Fundamentalism   162

PART V: CASTES AND SECTS OF THE SIKHS

12. The Kukas: A Millenarian Sect of the Panjab   189
13. Ahluwalias and Ramgarhias: Two Sikh Castes   216

PART VI: SIKH MIGRATION

14. The First Forty Years of Sikh Migration: 237
    Problems and Some Possible Solutions

PART VII: BIOGRAPHY

15. Max Arthur Macauliffe   257

PART VIII: HISTORIOGRAPHY

16. Cries of Outrage: History versus Tradition   267
    in the Study of the Sikh Community

Index   280

GLOSSARY

Ādi Granth	: The Guru Granth sahib (q.v.), the sacred scripture of the Sikhs recorded by Guru Arjan in 1603–04.
Āhlūwālīā	: Sikh caste of the Punjab, by origin distillers but successful in acquiring a greatly elevated status.
Akālī	: Follower of Akal Purakh (q.v.); member of the Akali Dal (Akali Party).
Akāl Purakh	: 'The One beyond Time', God.
Akāl Takhat	: The principal *takhat* (q.v.), located immediately adjacent to the Golden Temple.
amrit	: 'Nectar of immortality'; sweetened initiation water used in *amrit sanskār* (q.v.).
Amrit-dhārī	: A Sikh who has 'taken *amrit*', viz. an initiated member of the Khalsa (q.v.).
amrit sanskār	: The initiation ceremony of the Khalsa (q.v.).
Ardās	: The Khalsa Prayer, a formal prayer recited at the conclusion of most Sikh rituals.
Aroṛā	: A mercantile caste of the Punjab.
Bābā	: 'Father', a term of respect applied to holy men.
Baisākhī Day	: New Year's Day in rural Punjab, the first day of the month of Baisakh or Visakh.
bāṇī	: Works of the Gurus and other poets included in the Sikh sacred scriptures.
baqā'	: The Sufi concept of a continuing existence within the condition of union with God.

barādārī	: Fraternity
baṛā piṇḍ	: The superior big village network of eastern Doaba.
Bhagat	: A contributor to the Ādi Granth (q.v.) who was not one of the Gurus (e.g. Kabir, namdev, &c.).
Bhāī	: 'Brother', title of respect given for piety and/or learning.
Bhakti	: Belief in, adoration of a personal god.
bhorā	: Cave, hole in the ground.
Chamār	: Leather-working outcaste.
Chūhṛā	: Sweeper outcaste.
Chief Khalsa Diwan	: United body formed in 1902 to conduct the affairs of the Amritsar and Lahore Singh Sabhas jointly (q.v.).
darśan	: Audience; appearance before eminent person, sacred object &c.
Dasam Granth	: The scripture attributed to the authorship or times of Guru Gobind Singh.
deg tegh fateh	: 'Cauldron, sword, victory', slogan of the eighteenth-century Khalsa (q.v.).
ḍerā	: Camp; dwelling place of a Sant and his followers.
ḍhāḍhī	: Village bard.
dharma	: Duty to the Panth.
ḍhikr	: The Sufi discipline of remembrance or thinking of God.
dīvān (dewan)	: Court; assembly.
fanā'	: Dying to self; the Sufi concept of merging of the individual self in the Universal Being.
Faringi, Farangi	: Foreigner; European.
Five Ks	: Five items (each beginning with the initial 'k') which Sikhs of the Khalsa (q.v.) must wear. The five are *kes* (uncut hair), *kaṅghā* (comb), *kachh* (breeches which must not extend below the knees), *kirpān* (sword or poniard), and *kaṛā* (steel wrist-ring).
gaddī	: 'Cushion'; seat of authority.
garībī	: Poverty.
got (gotra)	: Exogamous caste grouping within a *zat* (q.v.); sub-caste.
Granth	: The '[Sacred] Volume', the Adi Granth or Guru Granth Sahib (qq.v.).
granthī	: Professional reader of the Granth (q.v.); custodian of a gurdwara (q.v.).
Gujar	: An Agrarian caste.
gurbāṇī	: Compositions of the Gurus.

gur-bilās	: 'Praise of the Guru'; hagiographic narratives of the lives of the sixth and tenth Gurus, stressing their role as warriors.
gurduārā, gurdwara	: Sikh temple.
Gurmat	: The teachings of the Gurus; Sikhism.
Gurmukhī	: 'From the Guru's mouth', the script in which Punjabi is written.
Gurū	: A spiritual preceptor, either a person or the mystical 'voice' of Akal Purakh (q.v.).
Gurū Granth Sahib	: The Adi Granth, specifically in its role as Guru (qq.v.).
Gurū Granth	: The Granth in its role as Guru (qq.v.).
Gur[u]matā	: 'The Guru's intention', a resolution passed by the Khalsa (q.v.) in the presence of the Guru Granth Sahib (q.v.).
Gurū Panth	: The Panth in its role as Guru (qq.v.).
haj	: The pilgrimage to Mecca.
halāl	: Flesh of an animal killed in accordance with Muslim ritual whereby it is bled to death.
haumai	: Self-centredness.
havan jag	: Ritual fire ceremony practised by the Namdhari Sikhs (q.v.). Also called a *hom*.
hukam	: Divine Order; a passage from the Guru Granth Sahib (q.v.) chosen at random.
hukam-nāmā	: 'Letter of command'; document containing a command or a request issued by one of the later Gurus to an individual or a congregation; a similar document issued to the Panth from Akal Takhat (qq.v.).
irāda	: Desire; determination; purpose.
izzat	: Prestige; honour; self-respect.
janam-sākhī	: Hagiographic narrative of the life of Guru Nanak.
Jaṭ	: Punjabi rural caste, numerically dominant in the Panth (q.v.).
jathā	: Military detachment.
jathedār	: Commander of a *jathā* (q.v.).
jhaṭkā (jhaṭakā)	: Flesh of an animal killed with a single blow, approved for consumption by members of the Khalsa (q.v.). Cf. *halāl, kuṭṭhā* (qq.v.).
Julāhā	: Weaver caste.
Kalāl	: Distiller caste.
Kānphaṭ yogī	: 'Split-ear' yogi; follower of Gorakhnath and adherent of the Nath tradition (q.v.).

karāh prasād	: Sacramental food prepared in a large iron dish (*karāhī*).
karma	: The destiny, fate of an individual, generated in accordance with the deeds performed in his/her present and past existences.
kathā	: Homily.
Kes-dhārī	: A Sikh who retains the *kes* (uncut hair).
Khālistān	: 'Land of the Pure', the name adopted by proponents of an independent homeland for the Sikhs.
Khālistānī	: A supporter of the Khalistan movement (q.v.).
Khālsā	: The religious order established by Guru Gobind Singh at the end of the seventeenth century.
khaṇḍe dī pāhul	: 'Initiation with the two-edged sword', the Khalsa (q.v.) initiation ceremony.
khānqāh	: A Muslim religious establishment.
Khatrī	: A mercantile caste of the Punjab.
khauf	: Fear, dread.
kīrtan	: Singing of hymns.
Kūkā	: Member of the Namdhari sect of Sikhs (q.v.).
kurahit	: One of the four cardinal infringements of the Rahit (q.v.). The four *kurahit* today ar: 1. Cutting one's hair. 2. Consuming *kuṭṭhā* meat (q.v). 3. Extra-marital sexual intercourse. 4. Smoking.
kuṭṭhā	: Meat from an animal killed in the Muslim style. Cf. *jhaṭkā, halāl* (qq.v.).
laṅgar	: The kitchen/refectory attached to every gurdwara (q.v.) from which food is served to all regardless of caste or creed; the meal served from such a kitchen.
Lohār	: Blacksmith caste.
mañjī	: Preaching office of the early Panth (q.v.).
mantra	: A verse, phrase, or syllable of particular religious import.
maqāmāt	: Places; stations; halts.
ma'rifat	: Knowledge, learning.
masand	: Administrative deputy acting for the Guru. Inaugurated by Guru Ram Das they served faithfully for some time, but later became corrupt and were disestablished by Guru Gobind Singh.
Mazhabī	: The Sikh section of the Chhuhra or sweeper outcaste group (q.v.); an Outcaste Sikh.
miharāb	: The niche in a mosque which indicates the direction of the Ka bah in Mecca.

mīrī-pīrī	: Doctrine that the Guru possesses temporal *(mīrī)* as well as spiritual authority *(pīrī).*
misal, misl	: A military cohort of the mid-eighteenth century Khalsa (q.v.).
misldār	: Commander of a misl.
mlechchha	: Foreigner; a barbarian.
mullāh	: A teacher of the law and doctrines of Islam.
murāqaba, murāqabat	: Contemplation. The Sufi discipline of meditation.
murishid	: The head of a Muslim religious order.
Nāī	: Barber caste.
nām	: The divine Name, a summary term expressing the total being of Akal Purakh (q.v.).
namāz	: Muslim prayer.
Nāmdhārī	: Member of the Namdhari Sikh sect (also known as Kuka Sikhs, q.v.), followers of Balak Singh and Ram Singh.
nām japan	: Devoutly repeating the divine Name.
nām simaran	: The devotional practice of meditating on the divine Name or *nām* (q.v.).
Nānak-panth	: The community of Nanak's followers; the early Sikh community; (later) members of the Sikh community who do not observe the discipline of the Khalsa (q.v.).
Nāth tradition	: Yogic sect of considerable influence in the Punjab prior to and during the time of the Sikh Gurus.
Nirankārī	: Member of the Nirankari Sikh sect, follower of Baba Dayal (1783–1855) and his successors.
nirguna	: 'Without qualities', formless, non-incarnated.
Nirmalā	: A sect of celibate Sikhs which commanded particular strength in the nineteenth century.
Nit-nem	: The Sikh daily liturgy.
pāhul	: The administration of *amrit* (q.v.) during the Khalsa initiation ceremony. Cf. *khande dī pāhul* (q.v.).
pakkā	: Lit. 'cooked'. Firm, high-class.
pangat	: '[Sitting in] line', the custom whereby equality is maintained in the langar (q.v.).
Pañj Piāre	: The 'Cherished Five' or 'Five Beloved'; the first five Sikhs to be initiated as members of the Khalsa (q.v.); five Sikhs in good standing chosen to represent a sangat (q.v.).
panth	: A 'path' or 'way'; system of religious belief or practice; community observing a particular system of belief or practice.

Panth	: The Sikh community (panth spelt with a capital 'P').
parampará	: Tradition; body of doctrine.
páṭh	: A reading from the Sikh scriptures.
patit	: A Kes-dhari (q.v.) who cuts his hair or an Amritdhari (q.v.) who commits one of the four cardinal sins (the four *kurahit*, q.v.).
pauṛī	: Stanza of a *vār* (q.v.).
pīr	: Spiritual guide; head of a Sufi community.
pothī	: Tome, volume.
Purātan	: One of the extant collections of janam-sakhi anecdotes (q.v.).
qāzī	: A Muslim judge; administrator of Islamic laws.
rāg (rāga)	: Metrical mode.
Rahit	: The code of belief and conduct of the Khalsa (q.v.).
rahit-nāmā	: A manual of the Rahit (q.v.).
Rāj	: Mason caste.
rāj karegā khālsā	: 'The Khalsa shall rule'.
Rāmdāsiā	: The Sikh section of the Chamar or leather-worker outcaste group (q.v.); an Outcaste sikh.
Rāmgaṛhīā	: A Sikh artisan caste, predominantly drawn from the Tarkhan or carpenter caste (q.v.) but also including Sikhs from the Lohar (blacksmith), Raj (mason) and Nai (barber) castes (qq.v.).
śabda (shabad)	: Word; a hymn of the Adi Granth (q.v.).
sabhā	: Society, association.
Sahaj-dhārī	: A non-Khalsa Sikh, one who does not observe the Rahit (q.v.).
sampradāya	: Doctrine, system of beliefs; group holding particular beliefs; sect.
Sanātan Sikhs	: Conservative members of the Singh Sabha (q.v.), opposed to the Tat Khalsa (q.v.).
saṅgat	: Congregation, group of devotees.
sant	: One who knows the truth; a pious person; an adherent of the Sant tradition (q.v.).
Sant	: One renowned as a teacher of Gurmat (q.v.).
Sant Niraṅkārī	: A break-away group from the Nirankari sect (q.v.).
sant-sipāhī	: A 'sant-soldier', the ideal Sikh; a Sikh who combines the piety of the *sant* (q.v.) with the bravery of a soldier.
Sant tradition	: A devotional tradition of North India which stressed the need for interior religion as opposed to external observance.
sardār	: Chieftain; leader of a *misal* (q.v.). 'Sardar' is nowadays

	used as a title of address for all Kesdhari Sikh men (q.v.). The corresponding title for a Sikh woman is 'Sardarani'.
sevā	: Service, commonly to a gurdwara (q.v.).
SGPC	: See *Shiromani* Gurdwara Parbandhak Committee.
shaikh	: A venerable man; the head of a Muslim religious community.
sharī'at	: Muslim religious law.
Shiromani Gurdwara Parbandhak Committee	: The committee which controls the historic gurdwaras (q.v.) of the Punjab and Haryana (commonly referred to as the SGPC).
silsilah	: A lineage. Sufi lineage.
Siṅgh Sabhā	: Reform movement in the Panth (q.v.) initiated in 1873. The Singh Sabha became the arena for a struggle between the conservative Sanatan Sikhs (q.v.) and the radical Tat Khalsa (q.v.).
ślok (shalok)	: A short composition (normally a couplet) from the Adi Granth (q.v.).
Sūfī	: A member of one of the Muslim mysticla orders.
takhat	: 'Throne'; one of the five centres of temporal authority in the Panth (q.v.).
ṭaksāl	: 'Mint'. A group gathered round a Sikh sant.
tālib	: Seeking; a seeker.
tanakẖāh	: A penance for a violation of the Rahit (q.v.).
tanakẖāhīā	: A transgressor against the Rahit (q.v.).
Tarkẖān	: Carpenter caste, Cf. *Ṭhokā* (q.v.).
Tat Khālsā	: The 'true Khalsa' or 'pure Khalsa'. In the early eighteenth century the immediate followers of Banda. In the late nineteenth and twentieth centuries radical members of the Singh Sabha (q.v.).
tauba	: Repentance, recantation; vowing to sin no more.
tawakkul	: Trusting; dependence on the divine will.
tazkira	: Sufi collections of biographical anecdotes.
Ṭhokā	: A carpenter. The carpenter caste. Cf. *Tarkẖān* (q.v.).
Udāsī	: Adherent of the Udasi panth (q.v.), an order of ascetics (normally celibate) who claim as their founder Siri Chand (one of Guru Nanak's sons).
udāsī	: Lengthy tour; missionary journey.
Vāhigurū	: 'Praise to the Guru'; the modern Sikh name for God.
Vaishnava	: Believer in, practitioner of bhakti (q.v.) directed to the god Vishnu in one of his incarnations (either Ram or Krishan).

vār	: A poetic form; an Adi Granth (q.v.) arrangement consisting of stanzas with preceding *śloks* (q.v.).
varṇa	: 'Colour'; the classical caste hierarchy or a division of it. The four sections are Brahman, Kshatriya, Vaisha, and Shudra, with Outcastes placed outside the hierarchy.
yaqīn	: Certainty, assured knowledge.
zāt (jāti)	: Endogamous caste grouping; caste. Cf. *got* (q.v.).

The Ten Gurus

1. Guru Nanak (1469–1539)
2. Guru Angad (1504–52)
3. Guru Amar Das (1479–1574)
4. Guru Ram Das (1534–81)
5. Guru Arjan (1563–1606)
6. Guru Hargobind (1595–1644)
7. Guru Hari Rai (1630–61)
8. Guru Hari Krishan (1656–64)
9. Guru Tegh Bahadur (1621–75)
10. Guru Gobind Singh (1666–1708)

PART I

GURU NANAK

1

THE INFLUENCE OF ISLAM UPON
THE THOUGHT OF GURU NANAK*

'Sikhism', writes Dr. A.C. Bouquet, 'is the fruit of hybridiza-
tion between Islam and Hinduism.'[1] This is the usual interpretation of the religion of Guru Nanak and his successors, a
universal assumption among western writers. According to this interpretation, Sikhism is regarded as a blend of Hindu beliefs and
Islam, 'an outstanding example of conscious religious syncretism,'[2]
a noble attempt to fuse, in a single system, elements drawn from
two separate and largely disparate religions. To quote another metaphor which evidently expresses this same interpretation: 'Sikhism
was born out of wedlock between Hinduism and Islam.'[3]

Is this interpretation correct? Can Sikhism be regarded as a
synthesis of ideas drawn from Hindu beliefs and Islam? In a very
broad sense we can accept the truth of this assessment. Other possible
interpretations must be certainly rejected. Sikhism cannot be located
wholly within the area of Hindu tradition, it cannot be regarded as
a sect of Islam, and we can hardly accept the claim that it was
delivered by direct, unmediated divine inspiration. We must,
however, proceed beyond this general interpretation to a detailed
analysis of what it actually means, and here we should expect a
diversity of opinion. The general interpretation is, in fact, rarely
subjected to a careful scrutiny, but it is clear from the brief

*Originally published in History of Religions, Vol. 7, No. 4, May 1968.

enunciations which we are given that it almost always assumes a mingling of basic components, a genuine syncretism. With this assumption we are bound to disagree. It is based upon misleading English translations of Sikh scripture, particularly the works of Guru Nanak, and to some extent upon an understanding of Persian rather than Panjabi Sufism.

In contrast to this 'mixture' theory, we can postulate an 'admixture' theory, and it is this second interpretation which is advanced in this essay. It affirms a basically Hindu origin and holds that Muslim influence, although certainly evident, is nowhere of fundamental significance in the thought of Guru Nanak. The religion of Guru Nanak, and of Sikhism as a whole, is firmly embedded in the Sant tradition of northern India, in the beliefs of the so-called nirguṇa sampradyā. The categories employed by Guru Nanak are the categories of the Sants, the terminology he uses is their terminology, and the doctrines he affirms are their doctrines.[4] Where we encounter significant exceptions to this rule, they point not to manifest Muslim influence but rather to reinterpretation by Guru Nanak or to the kind of recasting which has endowed his works with their distinctive clarity and coherence. This still leaves open the possibility of Muslim influence having been mediated to Guru Nanak through Sant channels, but here, too, native Indian antecedents almost always appear to be the stronger alternative. In some cases, such trails lead us back through the bhakti tradition; in others they branch off into Nath belief. We are bound to acknowledge a considerable area of obscurity when seeking to survey the background of Sant doctrine, but, insofar as it can be understood, it generally points us back to Indian tradition, not to any version of Islam.

Let it not be supposed, however, that concepts issuing from Muslim sources are totally absent or that the thought of Guru Nanak contains nothing which suggests Muslim influence. This would not be correct. The Muslim contribution to the thought of Guru Nanak is not of fundamental importance, but neither is it to be dismissed as wholly insignificant. This leads us to two specific questions relating to this general question of Muslim influence. First, from what Muslim sources did the influence come? Second, what distinctively Muslim elements, or other evidence of Muslim influence, can be distinguished in the thought of Guru Nanak?

The first question has already been answered many times. The source of such Muslim influence as can be detected in the works of

Guru Nanak has been identified as the thought of the Sufis. Two factors seem to point unmistakably to this conclusion. The first is the evident affinity between much that we find in Sufism and much that is characteristic both of the Sant tradition and of the thought of Guru Nanak. Second, and in evident support of the first assumption, there are Guru Nanak's explicit rejections, or, rather, reinterpretations, of conventional Islam. The conventional Islam of his time obviously impressed Guru Nanak as essentially a religion of external authority and external fulfilment. For Guru Nanak, dependence upon an external authority such as the *shari'at* and upon such exercises as the prescribed *namāz* could be meaningful only if the external authority and practice expressed a vital inner meaning. This they had manifestly, and inevitably, ceased to do, and so we have Guru Nanak's characteristic insistence upon the need to reinterpret external expressions of religion in a manner which amounted to a total denial of their validity.

mihar masīti sidaku musalā haku halālu kurāṇu
saram sunati sīlu rojā hohu musalamāṇu
karaṇī kābā sachu pīru kalamā karām nivaj
tasabī sā tisu bhāvasī nanāk rakhai lāj

Make mercy your mosque, faith your prayer mat, and righteousness your Qur'an.
Make humility your circumcision, uprightness your fasting, and so you will be a [true] Muslim.
Make good works your Ka'bah, Truth your *pīr*, and compassion your creed and your prayer.
Make the performance of what pleases [God] your rosary and, Nanak, he will uphold your honour.[5]

Obviously, there was no affinity with conventional Islam, and any constituents which may have come directly from this source must have come through the power of pervasive influence rather than through any conscious acceptance of its credentials.

This would appear, at first sight, to be the answer to our question concerning the source of Muslim influence in the thought of Guru Nanak, but before accepting this answer let us examine it. This we must do, as it invites misunderstanding in two respects. It implies, in the first place, a direct confrontation between Guru Nanak and various Sufis. Such meetings presumably took place, but we should not assume that this was the only channel of Sufi influence in the case of Guru Nanak. Second, the answer implies a clear-cut distinction between Sufism on the one hand and orthodox Islam on the other. This does not correspond to the condition of Islam in the Panjab of Guru Nanak. We may acknowledge that Sufism was the source which we are seeking, but let us be clear what we mean by Sufism in this context.

The first of these potential misunderstandings can be dealt with briefly. A comparison of the works of Guru Nanak with those of his Sant predecessors will at once reveal that a measure of the discernible Sufi influence in his thought had already entered the thought of the Sants. The traces of Sufi influence which appear in such concepts as the divine immanence are already to be found in the works of Guru Nanak's Sant predecessors and were evidently mediated to him in this manner. This should not mislead us into assuming that the Sufi influence transmitted in this manner was substantial, but it is at least arguable that the Sant works provided the principal channel along which Sufi influences passed into the thought of Guru Nanak.

The second of the potential misunderstandings requires lengthier treatment. Here we are concerned with the possibility of direct influence. The nature and extent of Sufi influence upon Guru Nanak can be appreciated only in the light of an understanding of contemporary Panjabi Sufism, the variety of Sufi belief with which he would have come in contact and which was quite distinct from classical Sufism. For many, the mention of Sufism will evoke thoughts of Junaid, Hallaj, Ghazali, and Jalal al-Din Rumi. These were the great figures of the Sufi movement, and we quite rightly associate them with classical Sufism. They do not, however, serve as representatives of the Panjabi Sufism of Guru Nanak's period. Panjabi Sufism, as distinct from Arabic or Persian Sufism, will suggest the names of Shaikh Faridu'd-din Ganj-i-Shakar, Shah Husain, Bulhe Shah, Varas, and Hasham. Of these, all except Shaikh Farid can be excluded from our discussion, as they came later than Guru Nanak. Shaikh Farid should certainly be considered, but we cannot regard him as a representative of the Panjabi Sufism of Guru Nanak's time, nor can we assume that his teachings had descended unchanged. Indeed, we are not in a position to know with any assurance the full range of Shaikh Farid's teachings[6] and are frequently compelled to fall back upon assumption rather than upon a trustworthy source.

This same conclusion must also apply to our understanding of the Panjabi Sufism which Guru Nanak would have encountered, but the assumptions can be made with a certain cautious assurance. Much depends upon our decision concerning the compositions recorded under the name of Farid in the *Ādi Granth*. There appear to be only two possible interpretations of the four *sabads* attributed to Farid in the *Adi Granth*[7] and of the *sloks* ascribed to him in the collection *Salok Sekh Farid ke*.[8] The first possibility is that they are the work of Shaikh Ibrahim, the incumbent of Shaikh Farid's *gaddī* in Pak Pattan during the lifetime of Guru Nanak and sometimes referred to as Farid the Second. The alternative explanation is that they represent the works of a number of the occupants of the Pak Pattan *gaddi* as they have emerged after a period of oral circulation. Some portions may go back to the original Farid himself, but it is impossible to assume that the purity of any such portion would have survived the period of oral transmission.

The second of these alternative appears to be the more likely, as some of the *sloks* seem to point back to the original Farid.[9] In either case, however, what the *sabads* and *sloks* offer us is not an expression of Farid's own Sufism but illustrations of the Panjabi Sufism of a later period. Whereas Farid was evidently close to the traditions of classical Sufism, the works bearing the name of Farid in the *Adi Granth* represent a marked divergence. They offer us not classical Sufism but a variety which has been strongly influenced by Sant concepts.[10]

This accommodation to Sant belief signifies one development within the Sufism of the Panjab prior to and during the time of Guru Nanak.[11] A concurrent and much more widespread development was a movement toward orthodox Sunni Islam, matched by a movement within orthodox Islam toward the Sufism of the period. The dominant pattern seems to have been a considerable interchange of theory and practice between Sufi and Sunni Islam, and the result was a popular Islam which combined characteristic features of both, though frequently in a debased form. Guru Nanak indicates this condition in references which place the Sufis under the same condemnation as other Muslims.

kājī sekh bhekh fakīrā
vade kahāvahi haumai tani pīrā
kālu na chhodai binu satigur kī dhīrā

Qāzīs, shaikhs, and those who wear the *faqīr's*
robe call themselves great, but within their
bodies is the pain of *haumai*. Without the aid
of the True Guru they cannot evade Death.[12]

The leaders of the orthodox, the Sufi masters, and those who claimed to be followers of the Sufi way—all are astray.[13]

Both of these developments are significant in the context of a discussion concerning the influence of Islam upon the thought of Guru Nanak. The significance of the first, which relates to the more refined variety of Panjabi Sufism, is that insofar as this particular type of Sufism exercised an influence upon Guru Nanak it would tend to have been a mediated Sant influence rather than a distinctively Sufi contribution. Its accommodation to Sant belief, together with its decline from earlier greatness, would have deprived it of much that we regard as characteristically Sufi. The second development bears testimony to a variety of popular Sufism which, because of its compromise with the external emphases of conventional Islam, could not have brought any strong influence to bear on Guru Nanak. This does not mean however, that it had no influence. Its pervasive quality makes it at least possible that, in terms of direct influence, this popular Sufism was actually a more important source than personal contacts between Guru Nanak and representatives of the more refined variety of Sufism.

Let us carry this question of personal contact and direct influence further and attempt to understand something of the manner in which the contact took place. In seeking to answer this aspect of our question, we can work from what purports to be external evidence, from the internal evidence provided by Guru Nanak's own works, and from reasonable assumption. The external evidence is provided by the *janam-sākhīs*[14] and must be rejected as almost wholly unreliable. We have, for example, the *janam-sākhī* record of a period of instruction from a *mullāh* during Guru Nanak's childhood.[15] This does not mean that we can accept such a period as a proven event, for the *janam-sākhīs* do not possess the necessary authority, particularly as far as the Guru's childhood is concerned. The same must be said concerning the *janam-sākhī* records of Guru Nanak's travels. The one point at which the *janam-sākhīs* do appear to record an acceptable instance of contact with a Sufi is in their accounts of Guru Nanak's meeting with Shaikh Ibrahim.[16] In this case, however, the meeting must have taken place after the substance of Guru Nanak's thought had been definitively formulated. Moreover, the *janam-sākhīs* probably offer an essentially correct interpretation of the contact when they project it as a case of Guru Nanak giving rather than taking.

The *janam-sākhīs* provide us with little reliable assistance, and we must accordingly turn to the internal evidence. The evidence offered by Guru Nanak's own works is open to a variety of interpretations, and what follows is tentative rather than assured. We may begin by affirming that Guru Nanak's works testify to the fact that he certainly knew the terminology of the Sufis. The following *slok* makes this clear:

hukamu rajāī sākhatī daragah sachu kabūlu
sāhibu lekhā mangasī dunīa dekhi na bhūlu
dil daravani jo kare daravesi dilu rasi
isak muhabati nānakā lekhā karate pāsi[17]

We must, however, add that this *slok* is an isolated exception to the general pattern of Guru Nanak's style. There appears to be little doubt that it represents a direct address to a Sufi audience, but the fact that it is an exception suggests that his direct contacts with the kind of Sufis who would use this language cannot have been frequent. It may be argued that the general absence of such expressions is a result not of infrequent contacts but of a conviction on Guru Nanak's part that this kind of Sufi was already on the right path and in little need of assistance. This is difficult to accept, for, had his direct contacts with them been both frequent and friendly, we should surely have found more evidence of Sufi influence, both in terms of their beliefs and of the small portion of traditional terminology which had been carried over into Panjabi. If, on the other hand, his contacts had been frequent and unfriendly, we should have expected several *sabads* and *sloks* of a manifestly dialectic character directed against the Sufis. We have compositions of the kind which are obviously directed against Nath yogis, but only occasional references aimed at the Sufis.

The evidence of Guru Nanak's own works seems to indicate, not a regular direct contact with members of Sufi orders, but, rather, the kind of informal contact with ordinary Muslims which would have been inevitable in his circumstances. Among those Muslims, there would certainly be some strict Sunnis, and we can assume that there would also be a number who might correctly be described as Sufis. The majority would, however, represent in varying degrees the dominant blend of modified orthodoxy and debased Sufism. Contacts of this kind would explain the expressions in Guru Nanak's works which sound like echoes of the Qur'an, they would explain the grouping of Sufi and Sunni in his criticisms of external religions, and they would explain the paucity of references which point to direct Sufi influence.

The answer to our first question—the question concerning the sources of Muslim influence—can now be summarized. The source of this influence was Sufism, but the influence was communicated in two ways, and by differing varieties of Sufism. The primary influence appears to have been indirect. Sufism had already exercised a limited influence upon Sant belief, and such influence was subsequently mediated to Guru Nanak as a part of the Sant synthesis. The secondary influence was communicated by means of direct contact. In some small measure this direct influence may have come through contact with exponents of a relatively refined Sufism, but the principal source of the direct influence appears to have been the popular variety which had blended with orthodox Islam and was to some extent indistinguishable from it.

We turn now to our second question. What distinctively Muslim elements can be distinguished in the thought of Guru Nanak, and what other evidence is there of Muslim influence? At first sight these elements appear to be numerous and the influence to be strong, for we find in his works many features which have obvious affinities with Sufi concepts. There is an emphasis upon the unity of God, a revelation in creation, the paradox of God transcendent as well as immanent, an expression of God in terms of light, a perverse human organ[18] which requires purification, a doctrine of grace, an emphasis upon the suffering involved in separation from the Beloved, a concept of *nām simaran*[19] which appears to combine elements of both the *dhikr* and *murāqabat* of the Sufis, an ascent to union through a number of stages, and a purging of self and an ultimate union which, although they are nowhere explicitly defined, do not appear to be inconsistent with the Sufi notions of *fanā'* and *baqā'*. He also shares with many Sufis a belief in the needlessness of asceticism on the one hand and in the snare of worldly wealth on the other. To these evident parallels with Sufi belief and expression we should also add the references which appear to be obvious echoes of the Qur'an.[20]

This is an impressive list and one which seems to suggest that Sufism must certainly have exercised a considerable influence in the formation of Guru Nanak's beliefs. Before we draw this conclusion, however, we must consider a number of features which point in the opposite direction. In the first place, there is the conspicuous lack of Sufi terminology in the works of Guru Nanak. Characteristic Sufi terms such as *dhikr khauf, tawakkul, yaqīn, murāqaba, irāda, ma'rifat, tālib,* and *tauba* are either rare or totally absent. Even when such words make an occasional appearance they are not generally used in a sense implying the precise meaning which they would possess in Sufi usage,[21] and in some cases they are introduced with the patent intention of providing a reinterpretation of their meaning.[22] In contrast with this relative absence of Sufi terms, we find a wealth of Sant terminology and imagery derived from Hindu sources. Almost all of his basic terminology is of native Indian derivation. In choosing names of God, his preference is strongly for Hindu names, and, when dealing with a concept which has obvious affinities with Sufi belief, he will almost always use a non-Sufi term.[23]

Second, we must observe that, although there are certainly strong resemblances to Sufi thought, almost all of the evident affinities can, with equal cogency, be traced back to native Indian sources. This is not to affirm that we must in all cases seek an Indian source but merely that an apparent affinity need not necessarily point to a Sufi source. Moreover, we must bear in mind the complex interchange of influences which had affected Sufism, particularly in India. Notions which at first sight might appear to be traceable to Sufi sources may in some cases have pedigrees which carry them back through Sufism to an earlier Indian source.[24]

An illustration of this point is provided by the figure of the bride awaiting the divine Spouse, a conventional image which expresses the soul's yearning for God and which symbolizes the mystical union crowning the soul's ascent to God. Guru Nanak inherited the image from the Sant tradition and used it frequently in his works.[25] This same figure is to be found in Sufi compositions. In classical Persian Sufism the devotee is generally cast in the male role, but Indian Sufism had reversed the roles, and as a result we find a Sufi usage in striking consonance with Sant usage. This does not, however, mean that the Sants received the image from the Sufis. The figure has a lengthy history in native Indian tradition, and there seems to be little doubt that it was from this source that the Sant tradition received it. Sufi usage may well have provided some encouragement, but in doing so it would have been mediating, in some measure at least, the native Indian original. The fact that Indian Sufism had reversed the roles of male and female strongly suggests a response to its environment.

A third reason for exercising caution in our comparisons with Sufi belief is the fact that in some fundamental respects Guru Nanak's thought is in direct conflict with that of the Sufis. The obvious example of this is his acceptance of the doctrines of *karma* and transmigration.[26] We should also observe his denial of the need for esoteric perception,[27] the contrast between the human preceptors of the Sufi orders (*shaikh, pīr,* or *murshid*) and Guru Nanak's understanding of an inner voice of God (the *gurū*), and the differing roles ascribed to divine grace.

Fourth, we should note once again the evidence which Guru Nanak himself offers of his own opinion concerning the leaders of the Sufi orders. As we have already seen, the *shaikhs* and *pīrs* suffer the same condemnation as the *qāzīs* and *mullāhs.*[28]

These four considerations must restrain us from any hasty acceptance of significant Sufi influence, although in themselves they do not necessarily rule it out. There remains the possibility that such influence has been communicated through Sant channels after having been assimilated to the total Sant pattern and to the terminology of the Sants. There also remains the possibility that although distinctively Muslim terms are relatively uncommon some of them may nevertheless express borrowings of fundamental importance.

To test these possibilities we shall consider the more important points which are offered as instances of Muslim influence. The first such instance is the claim that Guru Nanak's monotheism represents a debt to Islam.[29] In this respect we can certainly acknowledge the likelihood of strong encouragement from Islam, but it is surely going too far to identify Islam as the actual source.[30] Theism extends far back in the religious history of India, and the monotheistic strain is already evident within Hindu bhakti before the weight of Muslim influence came upon it. The antecedents of the Sant movement are to be found primarily in the bhakti tradition, and this would seem to be the true source of its monotheism. Sant antecedents also include the Nath tradition, and the Nath emphasis upon unity would presumably have strengthened the bhakti inheritance at this point. Islamic insistence upon the Divine Unity can certainly be accepted as another strengthening influence but not as the actual source.

A second obvious possibility would appear to be Guru Nanak's doctrine of the *hukam.* Here we have an Arabic word expressing a concept which seems to reflect a distinctively Muslim doctrine. The actual word must obviously be accepted as a borrowing from the terminology of Islam but not the doctrine which it expresses. Translators of the works of Guru Nanak have encouraged misunderstanding at this point by rendering *hukam* as 'Will' and so implying, whether intentionally or not, that we have here a concept modelled on the Islamic doctrine of the Will of God. The *hukam* of Guru Nanak is best translated as 'Divine Order' and may be defined as the divinely instituted and maintained principle governing the existence and movement of the universe. It is a constant principle, and to the extent to which it can be comprehended it functions according to a predictable pattern. This pattern of regularity and consistency distinguishes it from the Islamic concept.[31] In Islam the Divine Will, if not actually capricious, is at least 'unpledged,' whereas the *hukam* of Guru Nanak's usage is definitely pledged and dependable. The word has obviously come from Islamic sources, but not the basic doctrine which it covers.[32] As in the case of our first instance, the most we can allow at this point is a measure of encouragement.

Other instances can be dealt with summarily. We may observe without comment that Guru Nanak's doctrine of *nām simaraṇ* does not correspond to the Sufi technique of *dhikr* and that the five *khaṇḍs* or 'realms,' of *Japjī*[33] do not correspond even remotely to the *maqāmāt* of the Sufis.[34] A distinct resemblance can be perceived between Guru Nanak's descriptions of the actual climax of the spiritual ascent and the Sufi concepts of *fanā'* and *baqā'*, but the comparison is difficult to draw, as the descriptions concern what both Guru Nanak and the Sufis would regard as indescribable. The terms used by Guru Nanak to express this condition are from Hindu sources,[35] and we do not find in his works the characteristic Sufi emphasis upon visible ecstasy.

This process will eliminate much that has been regarded as evidence of Muslim influence, but we should not press it to the point of denying *all* such influence. Occasionally one encounters in the works of Guru Nanak an expression or an image which clearly seems to have been borrowed from Muslim sources. An example of this is provided by the 'veil' which conceals the Truth from man's perception.[36] A more important, though much less direct, instance of Muslim influence may possibly be the weight attached to the equality of all men in matters religious. If we allow the egalitarian emphasis of Islam as a significant influence upon the bhakti movement, we may perhaps allow it as a mediated influence in the case of Guru Nanak, although it is difficult to imagine his having omitted this teaching under any circumstances.

Almost immediately we seem to be moving away from the obvious to the merely possible, and to the 'merely possible' we may add an issue which concerns Guru Nanak's doctrine of God. In his works we find a strong emphasis upon the absolute sovereignty of

God and statements to the effect that if God chooses to withold his gracious glance from a particular person there can be no hope of salvation for that person. These statements may amount to no more than a natural corollary of Guru Nanak's concept of divine grace, but it seems reasonable to assume that the measure of stress which he lays upon this negative corollary may be a result of Sufi influence. Elsewhere in his works we find the emphasis laid upon the positive corollary, namely, that God in his grace chooses to impart enlightenment to men who would otherwise fail to perceive the divine self-revelation in the created world around them and in their own inward experience. This accords much more naturally with his total theology than does the negative corollary. The most likely explanation for the latter appears to be that the weight of Muslim emphasis upon the absolute nature of the divine authority has led to the ingrafting into Guru Nanak's theology of a distinctively Muslim expression of that divine authority.

Beyond this, it is impossible to proceed with firm assurance. It seems intrinsically probable that the Sufis must have at least encouraged latent tendencies, but it is not possible to identify these with complete certainty. Guru Nanak's doctrine of the unity of God we have already acknowledged as a strong candidate in this respect, and it seems safe to grant the same recognition in the case of the characteristic Sant emphasis upon the divine immanence, a feature of basic importance in the thought of Guru Nanak. Another example may perhaps be his stress upon the formless quality of God (*nirankār*).

The conclusion to which our examination points is that Sufi influence evidently operated upon the thought of Guru Nanak but that in no case can we accord this influence a fundamental significance. Sufi and Qur'anic imageries have certainly made their impress, and there must have been encouragement of tendencies which accorded with Sufi teaching; but no fundamental components can be traced with assurance to an Islamic source. Guru Nanak's principal inheritance from the religious background of his period was unquestionably that of the Sant tradition, and evidence of other independent influences is relatively slight. We must indeed acknowledge that the antecedents of Sant belief are by no means wholly clear and that within the area of obscurity there may be important features which derived primarily from Sufi sources. The complexity of the subject leaves appreciable room for doubt, and we are accordingly bound to own that at least some of our conclusions must be regarded as tentative, not as definitively established. It appears, however, that Sant belief owes none of its basic constituents to the Sufis. For Sant belief, the major source is to be found in the bhakti movement, with Nath theory entering as a significant second source of some significance.

This stress upon Guru Nanak's Sant inheritance should not lead us into a variety of misunderstanding which commonly occurs in discussions relating to antecendents and influences. It should not imply any denial of the originality of Guru Nanak's thought. The fact that a man works with elements which have been provided by others should not necessarily suggest that the product of his labours is not peculiarly his own. Others will supply the threads, but the pattern which he weaves with them may be a design of singular originality. In the case of Guru Nanak, this was certainly the result. We may trace the threads to a variety of sources; the ultimate pattern remains uniquely his own.

Notes

1. A.C. Bouquet, *Sacred Books of the World* (Harmondsworth: Penguin Books, 1954), p. 313.

2. John B. Noss, *Man's Religions* (New York: Macmillan, 1956), p. 272.

3. Khushwant Singh, *A History of the Sikhs*, Vol. I (Princeton, N.J., and London: Princeton University Press, 1963), p. 17.

4. For a treatment of Sant doctrine, see C. Vaudeville's introductions to *Kabir Granthavali* (*Doha*) (Pondicherry: Institut Français d'Indologie, 1957) and *Au cabaret de l'amour: paroles de Kabīr* (Paris: Gallimard, 1959). See also her article 'Kabir and Interior Religion' in *History of Religions*, Vol. 3, No. 2 (Winter, 1964), pp. 191–201.

5. *Vār Mājh, slok* 1 of *pauṛī* 7, pp. 140–1. Cf. also *Sirī Rāgu* 28, p. 24; *Vār Sirī Rāgu, slok* 1 of *pauṛī* 4, p. 84; *Vār Mājh slok* 3 of *pauṛī* 7 and *slok* 1 of *pauṛī* 8, p. 141; *Vār Āsā, slok* 1 of *pauṛī* 6, p. 465; *Dhanāsarī* 7, p. 662. In this and subsequent footnotes, page numbers which are not otherwise identified refer to the standard printed editions of the *Ādi Granth*. It should be noted that Guru Nanak's criticisms are directed, not at Muslims as such, but at the dominant interpretation of Islam with its considerable stress upon external religion. In the works of Guru Nanak, Brahmans, yogis, and various kinds of ascetics are criticized with even greater frequency for precisely the same reason.

6. Khaliq Ahmad Nizami, *The Life and Times of Shaikh Farid-u'd-din Ganj-i-Shakar* (Aligarh: Department of History, Muslim University, 1955), p. 87.

7. Two *sabads* in *Rāg Āsā*, p. 488, and two in *Rāg Sūhī*, p. 794.

8. *Ādi Granth*, pp. 1377–84.

9. This cannot be affirmed with complete assurance. The *sloks* which seem

to carry us back to Farid may be the work of successors or may represent legends which have come to be attached to his name. For discussions of the authorship question, see Khaliq Ahmad Nizami, *op. cit.*, pp. 121–2, and Lajwanti Rama Krishna, *Panjabi Sufi Poets* (Calcutta: Oxford University Press, 1938), pp. 6–7.

10. The characteristic Sufi terminology has not completely disappeared, as we do meet such expressions as *dilahu muhabati* and *iśak* (*'ishq*) *khudāī*, the names Allah and Sahib, and a single example of erotic imagery (*ślok* 30). Most of the terms which we associate with Sufi theory and practice are, however, totally absent, and with the exception of the words *darveś* and *sabr* none recur with the frequency we should expect. In contrast to this lack of typical Sufi expression we find, in these same *śabads* and *śloks*, several examples of Sant terminology used in senses which accord completely with Sant doctrine. *Man* is a common word, and other Sant terms are *nām*, *sach* and *sachiā*, *gurū*, and *sādh saṅgh*.

This aspect of Panjabi Sufism cannot be explained by the fact that our sources for this period are in Panjabi instead of Persian. In the first place, there are fundamental features of classical Sufism which are covered by neither Panjabi words nor borrowed Persian terms. Second, there are Sant terms which represent Sant concepts and not mere translations of corresponding Sufi concepts. It must be stressed that we are here dealing with Panjabi Sufism. The movement toward Hindu concepts in general and Sant belief in particular was evidently more pronounced in the Panjab than in other parts of India. See Aziz Ahmad, *Studies in Islamic Culture in the Indian Environment* (Oxford: The Clarendon Press, 1964), pp. 136–7.

11. Subsequent developments, particularly toward the end of the seventeenth century, carried Panjabi Sufism even further toward Hindu beliefs (Lajwanti Rama Krishna, *op. cit.*, pp. xvii–xix).

12. *Gauṛī aṣṭ.* 14 (7), p. 227.

13. Cf. also *Sirī Rāgu aṣṭ.* 17 (3), p. 64; *Vār Mājh, śok* 1 of *pauṛī* 13, p. 143; *Basant* 3, p. 1169; *Basant Hiṇḍol* 8, p. 1191. Note also *Vār Malhār, pauṛī* 9, p. 1282, where the *pīrs* share in the same condemnation as Naths, ascetics, and Siddhs.

14. Hagiographic accounts of the life of Guru Nanak.

15. *Miharbān Janam-sākhī, goṣṭ* 6; *Purātan Janam-sākhī, sākhī* 3; *Gyān-ratanāvalī, sākhī* 45. The location in the *janam-sākhīs* of the *Bālā* tradition varies with the different versions.

16. *Miharbān Janam-sākhī, goṣṭs* 147–9; *Purātan Janam-sākhī, sākhī* 32; *Gyān-ratanāvalī, sākhīs* 36–7.

17. *Vār Mārū, ślok* 1 of *pauṛī* 12, p. 1090.

He who lives in harmony with the divine Order wins acceptance in the court of the True One.

Do not be led astray by the world's deceptive appearance, for the Lord will demand the record [of your deeds].

He who sets a watch upon his heart is the one who follows the way of the [true] *faqīr*, [he who directs] his heart [in the way of] rectitude. Nanak, the Lord has the record [of our deeds and in that record is inscribed the measure] of our love [for Him].

18. Guru Nanak's *man* and the *dil-rūh-sirr* complex of the Sufis.

19. 'Remembrance of the Name,' meditation upon the divine Name.

20. Cf. *Japjī* 2, p. 1.

21. *Dil* is the most common example.

22. E.g., *faqīr* and *darveś*. The description of Guru Nanak himself as a *faqīr* is to be ascribed to the *janam-sākhīs* and oral tradition, not to his own works. In the *janam-sākhīs* and oral tradition it is, of course, used in its popular sense as a synonym for *sādhū* or *sant*, not in its strict Sufi sense.

23. *Sat* or *sach*, not *haqīqat*; *joti*, not *nūr*; *man*, not *sirr*; *haumai*, not *nafs*; *bhāu*, *piār*, or *prem*, not *'ishq*.

24. S.M. Ikram, *Muslim Civilization in India*, ed. Ainslie T. Embree (New York: Columbia University Press, 1964), p. 123.

25. Cf. *Āsā* 10, 14, 26, 27, and 35, p. 351-9, and *Sūhī Chhant* 1, 2, 3, 4, pp. 763-6. For examples of usage by earlier Sants, see Kabir, *Gaurī* 23, 50, and 65, pp. 328, 333-4, 337-8; *Āsā* 24 and 30, pp. 482, 483; *Sūhī* 2, p. 792; Namdev, *Bhairau* 4, p. 1164; and Ravidas, *Sūhī* 1, p. 793. See also *Kabīr-granthāvalī* (*dohā*), *aṅg* 3, 11, 36, and 52 (C. Vaudeville edition).

26. These doctrines eventually penetrated Panjabi Sufism (Lajwanti Rama Krishna, *op. cit.*, p. xviii), but there is no evidence to suggest that they had done so by the time of Guru Nanak.

27. Cf. *Dhanāsarī Āratī*, pp. 13, 663:

    sabh mahi joti joti hai soi
    tis dai chānaṇi sabh mahi chānaṇu hoi

    Within all there is Light, and the Light is Thine.
    By its illumination, all are enlightened.

28. Cf. also Guru Arjan's *Mārū Solahā* 12, pp. 1083-4.

29. 'Its [Sikhism's] basic conviction—monotheism—is drawn from Mohammedanism' (Noss, *op. cit.*, p. 272).

30. Aziz Ahmad, *op. cit.*, p. 142.

31. It is significant that the law of *karma* is regarded as an expression of the *hukam*. The concept of the *hukam* provides a clear illustration of the manner in which Guru Nanak's thought transcended that of his predecessors. The term is to be found in the works of Kabir and in a sense which points toward Guru Nanak's meaning (cf. Kabir, *Mārū* 4, pp. 1103-4). It is, however, only in the works of Guru Nanak that we find the developed doctrine occupying a position of fundamental importance.

32. If we are to seek an Islamic parallel to Guru Nanak's doctrine of the *hukam*, the closest would probably be the notion of 'the reality of Muhammad' (*al-Haqīqat al-Muhammadīya*) or 'the Reality of Realities' (*Haqiqat al-haqā'iq*). Cf. A.J. Arberry, *Sufism* (London: Allen & Unwin, 1950), p. 100.

33. *Japjī* 34–7, pp. 7–8.

34. A much closer resemblance is to be found in the stages enunciated in the *Yoga-vāsiṣṭha*. See S. Dasgupta, *A History of Indian Philosophy*, Vol. II, (Cambridge: Cambridge University Press, 1922–65), p. 264.

35. *Sahaj, param pad, chauthā pad, turīā pad*, and *amar pad*. His usage of the Nath term *dasam duār* also relates to this condition. Note also the term *sach khaṇḍ*.

36. *Japjī* 1, p. 1. Guru Nanak's application is, however, distinctively his own, for he endues the 'veil' with the meaning of *haumai* (Vir Singh, *Santhyā Srī Gurū Granth Sāhib*, Vol. I [Amritsar: Vir Singh, Khalsa Samachar, 1958], 48). We should also note that the popular Sufi metaphor of intoxication is not common in Guru Nanak's works, although the apocryphal saying *nām khumārī nānakā chaṛī rahe din rāt* has enjoyed wide circulation.

2

KABIR, NANAK, AND THE EARLY SIKH PANTH*

•

L egends die hard, and the belief that Nānak was a disciple of
Kabir has been no exception. In recent years, however, this
particular legend has all but disappeared and predictably, there
has been a tendency to swing towards the other extreme, one which
would imply total independence. A more balanced view sees them
as independent of each other, but manifestly within a common
tradition. Although they plainly differed in terms of locality and
social status, the compatible nature of their poetic styles and religious
beliefs indicates a shared inheritance of doctrinal influence.

In this essay we shall be concerned with the general question of
Muslim religious influence in North India during the period
extending from the late fifteenth century through to the middle of
the eighteenth century. This influence we shall endeavour to identify
in works associated with the name of Kabir and those which, with
substantially greater assurance, can be attached to Guru Nanak.
The examination of Sikh doctrine and religious behaviour will
not terminate, however, with the first Guru. Developments of
transforming significance take place within the community during
the period of continuing Muslim influence in the Panjab, and for
this reason our analysis must be carried forward into the eighteenth
century. This analysis will be specifically directed to the question of

*Originally published in David N. Lorenzen, ed., *Religious Change and Cultural Domination*, El Colegio de Mexico, Mexico City, 1981.

the degree to which the teachings associated with Kabir or Nanak and with the evolving traditions of the latter's followers can be properly described as examples of syncretism. Any conclusions which emerge will primarily concern Kabir, Nanak and the Sikhs, but it is to be hoped that they will also assist, in a more general sense, our understanding of Muslim influence in North India.

Definition of key terms
A. *Conversion*

We begin with a brief series of definitions, the first of which can be quickly despatched. Most would readily agree that the word *conversion* designates a process whereby allegiance is consciously transferred from one belief to another, and the formal definition of the word therefore presents no problems. The actual process, however, merits a closer scrutiny if we are to move beyond the somewhat vague generalizations which still serve as explanations for the emergence of a Muslim community in India. Although it receives little attention in this essay, it deserves a passing reference because it forms such a significant part of the background against which the present discussion must take place. With or without an understanding of the doctrines of Islam, and for whatever variety of motivation, many people in North India had affirmed that there is but one God and that Muhammad is his Prophet. Clearly one cannot even begin an examination of Kabir without taking account of this fact. The fact itself is plain enough. Less evident is the manner in which it came about and, more significantly, the actual substance of the fact. Although an examination of Kabir provides an excellent point of entry for such a study, the temptation is one to which we shall succumb only insofar as our scrutiny of his alleged syncretism demands.

B. *Syncretism*

Syncretism demands more careful attention in terms of a preliminary definition. It demands this attention because of the broad spectrum covered by varying usages of the word and, in consequence, because of the need to make it clear where one stands in spectrum. At one end of the scale, there is to be found an understanding which, because it assumes blending and synthesizing of a deliberate and conscious nature, necessarily renders syncretism a phenomenon of great rarity. The opposing extreme would have us take account of all forms of cultural influence, however unconscious and however insignificant. This, in effect, produces a definition which embraces *all* systems of belief. The totally insulated tradition is nowhere to be found. In the sense implied by this view, all religious belief will prove, upon simple analysis, to be syncretic.

One means of ameliorating the problem is to qualify one's actual use of the term. 'A syncretist' writes J.D.Y. Peel, 'is a man who sees some good ... in his traditional religious practices and beliefs, *identified* as such, and attempts to synthesize them with new beliefs in a harmonious religious system.'[1] This 'stock notion of syncretism' he identifies as 'explicit' syncretism, contrasting it with 'implicit' syncretism or with the variety of personal pluralism which comprises an illogical juxtaposition of inconsistent beliefs.[2]

These simple distinctions are useful in that they provide us with three separate categories in place of one. The problem, however, remains. Explicit syncretism is easily defined and so too is personal pluralism understood as an inconsistent bracketing or conglomerate of mutually contradictory beliefs. If the range of religious teachings embraced by our title took us no further than either or both of these categories, the problem would, for present purposes, be at an end. The fact that the discussion will carry us beyond these two into the much hazier territory of implicit syncretism means that assuredly the problem is not yet at an end. Others who have found themselves confronted by this situation have avoided a firm definition in the preliminary stages of the discussion. Instead, they have sought a greater measure of clarity through the analysis of a particular example or range of implicit syncretism.[3] This is the method which we shall follow.

C. *Sampradaya* and *Panth*

Our third definition involves two words closely allied in meaning and sometimes used interchangeably. Both designate the distinctive range of ideas which emerged from the teachings of men such as Kabir and Nanak, and both (particularly the latter) have also served to demarcate the followings which, having gathered around such teachers, acquired a sufficient coherence to sustain a continuing existence. The former (*sampradaya*) tends to be used in a more generalized sense and to emphasize doctrinal content. The latter *(panth)* normally implies a measure of formal organization and thereby assumes a more specific connotation.

Both terms deserve a brief examination in that, to the best of my knowledge, they bear meanings perceptibly different from any

Western term. They do so for the obvious reason that they reflect a distinctively different cultural context, one which permits variable modulation as opposed to fixity and precise definition. Islam tends strongly to affirm the latter. In the Indian environment, however, it encountered a contrasting emphasis and any analysis of its impact and difference within that environment must take account of this fundamental distinction. If we are examining syncretic influence rather than positive conversion, it is to the concepts of sampradaya and panth that we must briefly direct our attention.

The first of the two terms is commonly translated by that over-worked word 'tradition'. As I understand it, sampradaya designates an area of general doctrinal conformity, but one which possesses no clearly-defined boundaries and which permits within its recognizable territory a host of variant forms. The range of variant forms is by no means unlimited in that direct contradiction of certain essential ideas would, *ipso facto*, place a person outside even the shadowy borderland of the sampradaya. There remains, however, a substantial freedom within its ill-defined bounds.

Three such areas will appear in the discussion which follows. Central to our intention is the *Sant* sampradaya. Less significant for present purposes, but unavoidable because of both overlap and explicit rivalry, is the Nath Sampradaya. The third is not customarily described as a sampradaya, but will here be treated as one for the reason that it was so plainly envisaged in these terms by many affected by it and by many more who observed it from without. This is the *Sūfī* sampradaya.

A common feature of the sampradaya is that it exalts the role of the spiritual guide (the guru or the *pīr*) and that, within the generalized sampradaya, there are to be found many such masters, each with his cluster of disciples. As these informal groups acquire coherence, they qualify for the designation 'panth'. This may happen many years after the death of the eponymous 'founder' of the emergent group and may give expression to beliefs which differ radically from those which he actually propounded. The Kabir-panth certainly demonstrates the latter feature and, if it does not actually exemplify the former, one can only conclude that the links between acknowledged master and self-proclaimed disciples must be exceedingly tenuous. Indeed, they are so tenuous that the Kabir-panth can be largely excluded from our discussion. The same cannot be said, however, of the Nanak-panth. Here the links are immediate and firm.

The panth thus serves to sharpen the clarity of definition which in the case of the sampradaya must necessarily remain blurred. In one celebrated instance this sharpening process has been particularly marked. The Nanak-panth may initially have looked very much like others of its kind, but this was to change within the period which interests us. In its later developed form, the Nanak-panth assumed a pronounced clarity of definition, one which entitles it to be regarded as a distinct religious system in its own right. The old term is still used by its adherents, but with a clearly-defined and exclusive meaning. The followers of Nanak and his successors now form what the English convention of capital letters enables us to style as the 'Panth'.

Kabir

We proceed to the first of our three examples of syncretic influence and begin by noting a problem of identification. Kabir, it has been suggested, never existed. Although I am not one of those who positively support this extreme point of view, I should certainly be prepared to affirm that the actual man has been largely screened from our view by the evolved corpus of works attributed to him. Two related processes seem plainly to have operated upon this material during the period of oral transmission which preceded their eventual emergence in three distinct traditions. The first served to amplify the range of beliefs and actual works attributed to Kabir by attaching to his name a fund of homely proverbs and popular wisdom. Kabir had acquired a reputation as a pungent enunciator of simple truths and, as such, served as a magnet for concepts of a like character. The second influence was the normal process of assimilation which continues to function throughout a period of oral transmission if the material thus transmitted is not protected by effective controls.[4]

There can be no doubt that processes of this kind have operated extensively upon works attributed to Kabir. A comparison of the regional traditions represented by the *Bījak*, the *Ādi Granth*, and the *Kabir-granthāvalī* makes this abundantly clear. The result, needless to say, is a significant complicating of any analysis, including the present attempt to observe evidence of Muslim influences operating on native Indian tradition. Detailed Kabirian analysis properly involves separate examination of each of the three regional traditions as well as of the 'authentic' Kabir himself—or such of him as we are able to discern. The importance of this problem is pointed out within the terms of the discussion by a famous couplet from the *Ādi Granth* collection of Kabir *bāṇī*:

nā ham hīndū nā musalamān
alah rām ke piṇḍ parāṇ

I am neither Hindu nor Muslim.
[The One] Allah-Ram is the breath of my body.[5]

These lines spell out, with unequalled clarity, a doctrine which attaches itself firmly to the name and reputation of Kabir. They may indeed represent a point of view which the authentic Kabir actually affirmed, but we must nevertheless take account of the fact that, whereas the *pada* containing this couplet has distinct echoes in the Rajasthani *Kabir-granthāvalī*, the couplet itself is to be found only in the Panjabi tradition. At all times one must retain an awareness that the Panjabi and Rajasthani traditions have elements unique to themselves; that both are, to an even greater degree, distinct from the eastern tradition of the Kabir-panth and the *Bījak*; and that all three are distinct from the authentic Kabir himself.[6]

The authentic Kabir provides us, however, with a relevant and well-established fact to serve as a convenient starting-point. Kabir was himself a Muslim and, as such, delivers a personal testimony to the most obvious of all the results associated with the presence of Muslim influence in India. Kabir-panthi traditions which represent him as the offspring of a Brahman found and brought up by Muslim parents must surely be numbered the most transparent of legends. Kabir's name is inescapably Muslim, and the works attributed to him make sufficient reference to his Julaha identity to set the issue beyond all reasonable doubt.

In the context of the present discussion, however, this single fact carries little weight, in any positive sense. If we are endeavouring, with the crude instruments at our disposal, to measure Muslim influence in terms of resultant syncretism, the poet's name counts for little in comparison with the contents of his verse. Here we must stress once again the distance which separates us from the authentic Kabir, and the consequent difficulty involved in determining the actual nature of his beliefs. The available evidence, nevertheless, seems strong enough to withstand this qualification. The actual content of his beliefs seems clearly to have had little to do with the doctrines of Islam, and influence of a direct or substantial nature emerges in a negative rather than a positive form.

Negative, as opposed to positive influence, is perhaps best illustrated by the couplet from the *Ādi Granth* quoted above. Although this particular expression is limited to one of the regional traditions, and although that tradition demonstrates a particular interest in the doctrine which it expresses, the doctrine itself finds sufficient support elsewhere to encourage the view that it should be traced to Kabir himself. If this is correct, it serves to illustrate a negative impact. The credentials of *qāzī* and *mullāh*, the exclusive authority of the Qur'an, or the very title of 'Musalman' are scarcely likely to attract attention, if they command little weight or significance. The Kabirian denunciation of exclusive claims and the specific reference, in such contexts, to Muslim ideals or authorities plainly signifies that within the society of Kabir's own time and that of the period of subsequent oral transmission these concepts and authorities really mattered. This, of course, merely states the obvious. The point of stating it is to make clear the essentially negative quality of this particular influence.

When we move from negative influences to the search for those of a more positive character, we encounter little that is substantial. It is evident that Kabir himself was largely ignorant of the doctrines of Islam, other than the simple variety which amounted to common knowledge. If that is incorrect, we must necessarily affirm either that he chose to omit reference to them in his utterances or, alternatively, that authentic utterances which incorporated evidences of this understanding were subsequently suppressed in all the regional traditions. The intrinsic improbability of these two latter theories leaves us free to agree with the view that Kabir knew little of Islam beyond such patently obvious facts as their custom of attending mosques, calling upon God in a particular manner, and proceeding as opportunity afforded upon the *haj*.

An obvious rejoinder to this accusation of ignorance is that Kabir was, after all, a Julaha and that humble weavers are seldom enrolled in the rank of the theologically learned. This would suggest that humble weavers are incapable of theological understanding of any style or colouring and that Kabir, whatever his skill as a homely maxim-maker, was ignorant *per se*. The response to any such rejoinder would be that, having expressed all the usual qualifications concerning access to the authentic Kabir, we are still able to affirm that in one significant area of doctrine and religious practice he was far removed from ignorance. Kabir's apparent innocence of Muslim theology must be contrasted with an extensive knowledge of a radically different religious tradition.

Although it is now forty years since P.D. Barthwal demonstrated the close links connecting the Nath and Sant sampradayas, it is only now that most of us in the West are being forced to acknowledge this fact by the works of Dr Charlotte Vaudeville. Of the connection there can be no doubt, and in no instance is it revealed with greater clarity than in the works attributed to Kabir. Once again we can argue that agreement on the part of all three regional traditions entitles us to attach a particular characteristic to the authentic Kabir. The characteristic in this particular case is an extensive understanding of Nath theory and terminology. Kabir cannot be called a Nath, but the Nath imprint upon his understanding seems proven beyond all doubt.[7]

Where does this leave us as far as the authentic Kabir is concerned? It indicates that he embodied Muslim influence, as the offspring of Julaha converts, but that in doctrinal terms the influence was strictly subordinate to others more powerful and that the only overt acknowledgement of its importance takes the form of an explicit rejection. There are, it is true, present in the works attributed to Kabir those features of medieval devotional doctrine which have traditionally been ascribed to Muslim influence. These include the unity of God, affirmations of religious equality, and a stress upon the role of the religious preceptor. In all three instances one could, with equal credibility, declare the result to be a debt to Nath ideals, and to these three one could add other fundamental beliefs or practices such as their use of the vernacular for religious purposes.

None of this can be held either to demolish claims to significant Muslim influence upon Kabir or to erect Nath influence as a proven substitute. It does, however, suggest a direction for our enquiry. Given the substantial Nath content of his thinking, as opposed to the elementary nature of his Muslim understanding, one is at least inclined to question claims of substantial Muslim influence apart from the mere fact of conversion. The regional traditions tend, if anything, to push Muslim influence still further into the background by the great stress which they lay upon features of traditional Vaishnava devotion.

If we are to judge from the authentic Kabir or the Kabirian corpus we must, I submit, be impressed by the strength of both Nath and Vaishnava concepts and the comparative weakness of those which it seems reasonable to ascribe to Muslim influence. Because of the Nath and Vaishnava influences, although both native traditions are themselves so far apart, one is certainly entitled to speak of a Kabirian synthesis or (in the sense already indicated) an example of implicit syncretism, and to accommodate this within the wider range of Sant belief. Nath and Vaishnava elements seem clear. Muslim influence and elements seem much less conspicuous.

Guru Nanak

Nanak has, it seems, been a great favourite with many teachers of religious studies who, confronted by the apparent need to provide clear-cut case of deliberate syncretism, fastened upon a welcome pronouncement in early editions of J.B. Noss's *Man's Religions* with relief. The chapter on Sikhism, in this much-used textbook, was subtitled 'A Study in Syncretism' and the religion of Nanak described therein as 'an outstanding example of conscious syncretism.'[8]

For such teachers, Noss' subsequent amending of this useful sentence must have been a disappointment only partially relieved by more recent work on West African cults.[9] Indeed, there is reason to suspect that some of them have failed to notice the change. Judging by comments which followed the publication of *Gurū Nānak and the Sikh Religion*, the notion that Nanak's teachings represent a synthesis incorporating substantial and direct borrowings from Islam is one that will not be easily dispelled. Although such words as 'deliberate' and 'conscious' may be treated with rather more caution than previously, the essentially syncretic nature of Nanak's thinking seems still to be a part of accepted wisdom. The components are generally declared to comprise a blending of elements drawn from an entity know as 'Hinduism' and ideals derived from Sufi doctrine and practice.[10]

The arguments which have been offered (or implied) in support of the Hindu/Muslim or Hindu/Sufi claim can be grouped in three categories. The first variety of argument apparently derives from the notion that Guru Nanak himself made pronouncements or performed symbolic actions which indicated a conscious attempt to draw Hindu and Muslim together. This, one suspects, is the origin of the belief that Nanak manifests syncretism of an explicit rather than a merely implicit variety. One such statement is the celebrated formula said to have been uttered by the Guru following his emergence from the experience of enlightenment in the waters of the Vein River: *nā ko hindū hai nā ko musalāman*, 'There is neither Hindu nor Muslim.'[11] Another is his alleged custom of dressing in a combination of Hindu and Muslim sartorial styles.[12]

The second range of arguments might be designated the 'must have been' or 'intrinsic likelihood' variety of argument. This begins from the undoubted presence in fifteenth-century Panjab of a host of Muslims (both immigrant and convert) and of the distinguished presence amongst them of representatives of Sufi *silsilahs*. Prominent amongst these were the descendants of the renowned Baha al-Din Zakariya of Multan and Farid al-Din Ganj-i-Shakar of Pak Pattan. Plainly, there was a substantial Muslim following in the Panjab of this period, much of it attached to the prestige and spiritual influence of the Sufi *khānqāhs*.

Numbers and the influence of the order evident in the Panjab of this period must assuredly have had a substantial impact upon the culture of the Panjab in general. This was the culture inherited by Guru Nanak, the very air that he breathed. If it was indeed impregnated with Muslim ideals, whether in a general sense or of a more specifically Sufi nature, it must inevitably have affected his outlook and therefore his teachings. Two assumptions are implicit in this argument. The first is that the entire culture of the Panjab was in fact shot through with Muslim influence. The second is that the presence of such cultural influence must inescapably and significantly affect all who live within the society which gives it expression.

The third category of argument concerns features of Nanak's recorded works which offer evident parallels to Muslim doctrine or custom, the emphasis once again being laid on Sufi beliefs and example. These I have listed elsewhere[13] and other writers have likewise compiled their own catalogues.[14] In them we feature such elements as a doctrine of God at once transcendent, formless, and immanent; and Nanak's concept of *nām simaran* (to which are compared the Sufi *dhikr* and *murāqabat*). With these lists of apparent similarities, we should also associate Nanak's obvious acquaintance with Sufi terminology and his occasional use of it.

Of these three categories, the first can be summarily dismissed. Neither the quoted utterance nor the symbolic dress (nor any other such examples) can be attached to the historical Nanak. They are to be found not in his own works but in the *janam-sākhīs*, the hagiographic narratives which emerge after his death and which, having passed through several expanding phases, provide us with practically all that passes as the 'biography' of Nanak. Enough has already been said on the *janam-sākhīs* as mediators of the historical Nanak. Here we shall merely note that their manifest lack of reliability in this particular area renders their testimony to Nanak's peacemaking symbolism highly suspect. Nanak must be judged on the basis of his own words and nothing in his actual *bāṇī* supports the notion of explicit syncretism or of bringing Hindu and Muslim together on the basis of a mutual acceptance of their distinctive doctrines.

As revealed by his own works, Nanak's attitude amounts to neither acceptance nor to necessary rejection. The key to understanding his teachings at this particular point is his clear distinguishing of the 'true Hindu' and the 'true Muslim' from all the rest. In Nanak's terms both the former are accepted, whereas the remainder, whether Hindu or Muslim, are reprobated if they exercise conventional religious authority and pitied if they respond to its dictates. The emphasis for Nanak must be laid firmly and exclusively upon inner devotion as opposed to external observance. The person who accepts the inner way will achieve salvation, be he Hindu, Muslim or anything else. All others, again without reference to their formal allegiance, will suffer the consequences of the *karma* earned by their hypocrisy or by their fatal application of erroneous convictions. The difference between Hindu and Muslim is irrelevant. Truth lies beyond both and is to be appropriated by a transcending of both.[15]

The second category (the 'intrinsic likelihood' range of argument) poses questions of a rather more complex nature and assuredly cannot be dismissed with the same ease and expedition. On theoretical grounds, the claim that sensitive members of any given society are bound to be affected by its mores is unexceptional to the point of being axiomatic. Given the strength of Muslim numbers and evident influence one would also expect that by the late fifteenth century these mores would in some measure reflect that influence. Let it therefore be acknowledged that, in theoretical terms, there is considerable force in the 'intrinsic likelihood' argument.

The problem with this argument, when applied to the works of Nanak, is not its theoretical basis, but its data content. In order to establish a syncretic case on Hindu/Muslim lines, one must identify within the works of Nanak those features which manifest unmistakeable Muslim origin or influence. We are led directly into the third range of arguments, those which claim to answer the need by providing the actual evidence.

This particular issue has been treated at some length in an earlier article and summarily in *Gurū Nānak and the Sikh Religion*.[16] It therefore seems reasonable to limit the present discussion to an acknowledgement of review comments on the latter, which struck home, and a brief restatement of those elements in the earlier treatment, which seem to me to have survived the attack. At one particular point I am bound to acknowledge the need for explicit modification. In my earlier treatment I drew a distinction between 'classical' Sufism and a popular 'debased' form, suggesting that insofar as a limited influence operated on Nanak's thinking it derived form the latter. Without wholly renouncing the distinction, I acknowledge that it was grossly overdrawn.[17]

This admission, however, concerns the specific origin of any such influence, not the weight and impact which it bore upon the thought of Nanak. In this latter area (which is what really concerns this discussion), I am bound to own that my interpretation has been little modified. The attention which has been drawn to the parallels subsisting between Sufi doctrine and the works of Nanak seem to me to leave the principal answer largely unaffected. This I expressed in the following terms:

The conclusion to which our examination points is that Sufi influence evidently operated upon the thought of Guru Nanak but that in no case can we accord this influence a fundamental significance. Sufi and Qur'anic imageries have certainly made their impress, and there must have been encouragement to tendencies which accorded with Sufi teaching; but no fundamental components can be traced with assurance to an Islamic source. Guru Nanak's principal inheritance from the religious background of his period was unquestionably that of the *Sant* tradition, and evidence of other independent influences is relatively slight. We must indeed acknowledge that the antecedents of Sant belief are by no means wholly clear and that within the area of obscurity there may be important features which derived primarily from Sufi sources. The complexity of the subject leaves appreciable room for doubt, and we are accordingly bound to own that at least some of our conclusions must be regarded as tentative, not as definitively established. It appears, however, that Sant belief owes none of its basic constituents to the Sufis. For Sant belief, the major source is to be found in the bhakti movement, with Nath theory entering as a significant secondary source.[18]

I see no reason to modify this conclusion in any significant degree, and I am therefore constrained to look once again at the 'intrinsic likelihood' theory. If, as our analysis of Nanak's teaching seems to suggest, Muslim influences distinctly project less evidence than one might have anticipated, it presumably follows that we have been tending to overemphasize the impact of those influences. Because there seems to be little doubt concerning Muslim numerical strength or the strength of the cultural influence borne by many of its representatives, one is driven by default to seek explanations in the resilience of those cultural features which we can identify as pre-Muslim or patently non-Muslim.

The example of Kabir and his diverse followers has already pointed in this direction and Nanak's legacy of poetic composition seems plainly to enhance its claims. Neither Kabir (as far as we can determine his authentic beliefs) nor Nanak manifest in their works influences which are at once unmistakably Muslim in origin and fundamental to the structure of their thought. The Sant sampradaya, within which each occupies a distinguished place, likewise presents a range of devotional belief and practice which derives its principal ideals from native Indian sources and which offers only doubtful or peripheral evidence of significant Muslim influence.

In these circumstances it appears safe to dismiss the possibility of conscious, deliberate syncretism. Nanak's own words, like those attributed to Kabir in all regional traditions, seem plainly to exclude this interpretation. Does this still leave open the possibility of implicit syncretism? If there is meaning in the term 'implicit syncretism', it can certainly be applied in both instances, provided that the dominant sources utilized in the process are located within native Indian traditions. The pattern of belief which they represent does not appear to be one which draws substantially from distinctively Muslim sources.

The Early Sikh Panth

It will be observed that in passing judgement on the Sant synthesis we stopped short with the person of Nanak. We can, however, proceed somewhat further with the judgement, gathering into the same fold those of his successors whose works appear in the *Ādi Granth*. The *Ādi Granth*, compiled in 1603–04, carries us through to the fifth of the Sikh Gurus, and in the process sustains the teachings already spelt out by the first Guru. Of the remaining Gurus only the tenth, Guru Gobind Singh, has left evidence of extensive personal compositions and, insofar as we are able to identify these, they too imply confirmation of our judgement. Significant evidence of direct and positive Muslim influence will be difficult to find in the works which can, with reasonable assurance, be attributed to Guru Gobind Singh and, in terms of explicit attitudes, the message is the same. It is, indeed, in one such work that we find the most famous of all

Sikh declarations concerning the essential irrelevance of the differences separating Hindus and Muslims, and of the need to transcend both in order to attain truth.[19]

The compositions which may reasonably be attributed to Guru Gobind Singh occur in the later collection of semi-canonical writings known as the *Dasam Granth*, and if we were to push our analysis in this particular direction we should soon find ourselves moving even further from evidences of Muslim influence than anything we have covered so far. The substantial bulk of the *Dasam Granth* comprises materials drawn directly from the *Puranas*. The general tenor of the *Dasam Granth* is distinctly Puranic, with powerful Shakti overtones.[20] Once again we need have little difficulty in detecting syncretic impulses at work, but not impulses which betray any willingness to incorporate Muslim ideas.

If, however, we turn away from the direction indicated by the *Dasam Granth* and look instead at the other major development in the Sikh literature of the seventeenth and eighteenth centuries, we shall observe a rather different emphasis, one which would appear to carry us closer to positive Muslim influence than anything we have noted hitherto. The early Sikh Panth evidently responded to Muslim influence in both positive and negative terms. It is in this literary development that we observe the signs of positive response, though whether or not it produces results which may properly be labelled syncretic is a question which will bring us back to our problem of definition.

The literary development which thus demands our brief attention is that of the *janam-sākhīs*, to which passing reference was made when questioning the reliability of statements and symbolic actions attributed to Nanak. The reliability issue is one which requires two answers. If we are concerned with the historical Nanak, then the testimony of the *janam-sākhīs* must be regarded with the greatest of caution. The *janam-sākhīs* are strictly hagiographic and must therefore be used with care in any approach to the authentic Nanak. If, however, they are used as a means of access to the understanding of the post-Nanak Panth then, needless to say, one can attach to them a much greater degree of trust. For the image of Nanak, as seen through Sikh eyes during the seventeenth century and later, they are sources of unequalled value.[21]

At first sight, the early *janam-sākhīs* may seem to confirm a trend away from Muslim influence. This conclusion could conceivably be suggested by the obvious emphasis which they lay upon confrontations between Baba Nanak, on the one hand, and sundry Sufi pirs, on the other. The recurrent confrontations of the *janam-sākhīs* serve to identify all whom the compilers viewed as rivals, the method being to contrive a pattern of discourse leading to inevitable triumph by Nanak. Because Sufi pīrs figure prominently in such discourses, they must necessarily be understood as rivals in the eyes of the compilers and presumably of the Panth in more general terms. The inclusion of triumphs wrought in Mecca, Medina, and Baghdad strengthen this impression.

There are, however, other features of the *janam-sākhī* presentation which should substantially qualify this impression. The first is the even greater emphasis which is laid upon confrontations with representatives of the Nath sampradaya in anecdotes which suggest considerably less *janam-sākhī* sympathy for Naths than for Sufis. Hostility towards the former has not prevented the Panth from retaining within its range of beliefs those which can be traced to Nath origins.

The answer to this claim could, of course, be that the compilers were quite unaware of any debt which the Panth, with its Sant inheritance, might owe to the Naths; and also that a parallel in terms of *janam-sākhī* roles need imply nothing in terms of positive influence. A second feature is, however, more difficult to dismiss. If one moves from the *janam-sākhīs* to the Sufi *tazkiras*, one is at once struck by the remarkable identity of the anecdotal approach in each case. The correspondence extends, moreover, well beyond mere narrative forms into actual content. Several anecdotes have obviously been borrowed in toto, and because the Sufi versions are chronologically earlier, there is never any doubt who is borrowing from whom.

The influence of Sufi models can thus be seen in a major literary form and in some of the stories which it relates. This alone does not amount to syncretism, but if the *janam-sākhī* presentation is analysed with greater care, it will, I suggest, become evident that the impress of the model has affected the image of Bāba Nanak projected therein. The trend is towards the image of a Sufi pir.[22] If this hypothesis is sustained, it must convincingly demonstrate direct influence from a recognizably Muslim source; and if the theory of implicit syncretism is viable, it must surely accommodate influence of this kind.

Any trend thus established within the Panth was, however, soon deflected. In the confused circumstances of the eighteenth century the Panth became involved in struggles which assumed an increasingly anti-Muslim colouring. This greatly strengthened other tendencies already powerfully present within it and produced, in terms of doctrine and religious behaviour, an outcome which in part, at least, represents a negative response to Muslim influence. The Khalsa conventions which emerge as a militant tradition and which are embodied in the evolving *rahit* (or Khalsa 'code of discipline') incorporate elements which seem plainly to express a vigorous and self-conscious reaction against Muslim ideals.[23] Once again, we are confronted by an instance of development in response to external influence, a development of great interest and importance. It is, however, one which draws its principal components from areas of Panjab society distinct from those which we can identify as Muslim. The Muslim contribution, important though it be, has been communicated in terms which provide an effective counter-reaction.

Conclusion

There are, I suggest, two varieties of conclusion which emerge from this approach to Kabir, Nanak, and the early Sikh Panth. The first concerns the theoretical form within which the argument has been cast, and specifically the term *syncretism*. Having tentatively acknowledged a distinction between 'explicit' and 'implicit' syncretism we have argued that the former is not to be found within the area which concerns us, and we have strongly hinted that the latter usage provides us with terminology of highly questionable value. It is, in my opinion, an expression which should be discarded in favour of the terms, *influence, assimilation* and *synthesis*. These words are less confusing. They are more clearly distinct from notions of deliberate intention and they lack the pejorative connotation which, for some at least, is attached to *syncretism*.

I therefore suggest that we dismiss the term *syncretism* from Indo-Muslim studies. The distinction between 'explicit' and 'implicit' syncretism seems to me to be valueless, in that the latter category is essentially without meaning. If *syncretism* is to be retained unqualified as a means of designating a conscious and deliberate process, it will describe a phenomenon of great rarity and one which we are unlikely to encounter in the territory which interests us.

The second conclusion is at once more practical and more hesitant. It has been suggested in this paper that Muslim influence of a clear and fundamental kind is difficult to detect in the ideals of the Sant sampradaya. Although its two most distinguished representatives have been commonly cited as prime examples of the impact of Muslim cultural influence (particularly in its Sufi expression), a careful analysis of their works seems likely to reveal that this is, at best, a questionable assumption. It would appear to be an assumption which can still retain claims to possibility, but which should no longer be used with the carefree ease and assurance too often evident in the past. When we move forward into the history of the post-Nanak Panth, we encounter conflicting tendencies, one of which (the development of the *janam-sākhīs*) suggests a certain degree of effective Sufi influence. It is, however, a tendency which is largely overwhelmed by another (the ascendancy of Khalsa ideals). This latter manifests clear signs of Muslim influence, but in terms which signify an effective counter-response.

If, from the last of these developments, we deduce the religious consequences of militant but increasingly ineffective Muslim political power, we shall scarcely be offering anything original or surprising. The paucity of earlier evidence could, however, bear an import of greater significance. One is sometimes inclined to suspect that such dramatic phenomena as the glories of Mughal architecture and the twentieth-century emergence of Pakistan may cause us to exaggerate the impact of earlier Muslim influence. This, in turn, may persuade us to view developments within the fifteenth and sixteenth centuries with a bias which, if it applies at all, should be properly confined to the century which follows. One could never claim that an analysis of the Sant sampradaya will alone confirm this suspicion beyond all shadow of doubt. It may, however, proffer a warning. The fact of Muslim influence can never be in dispute. What *can* be disputed is the extent of that influence and the right to make easy generalizations without careful scrutiny of their justification.

Notes

1. J.D.Y. Peel, 'Syncretism and Religious Change.' *Comparative Studies in Society and History*, Vol. X, p. 129.
2. Ibid., pp. 129, 134, 139.
3. Helmer Ringgreen, 'The Problems of Syncretism' in *Syncretism*, ed. S.S. Hartman (Stockholm: Almqvist & Miksell, 1969), p. 7.
4. The two processes sketched in this paragraph are treated more fully in a review of Charlotte Vaudeville's *Kabīr*, Vol. I, (Oxford: Clarendon Press, 1974), in *South Asia* 5 (1975), pp. 101–4.
5. *Ādi Granth*, p. 1136.
6. For the recensions and published editions of the *Kabīr-granthāvalī*, see Charlotte Vaudeville, *Kabīr*, Vol. 1, pp. 70–80.

7. Ibid., chap. 5.

8. John B. Noss, *Man's Religions*. (New York: Macmillan, 1956), p. 275. See also Aziz Ahmad, *Studies in Islamic Culture in the Indian Environment* (Oxford: Clarendon Press, 1964), p. 152.

9. In recent editions 'conscious' has been changed to 'working': *Man's Religions* (New York, 1974), p. 225.

10. For examples, see J.S. Grewal, *Guru Nanak in History* (Chandigarh: Panjab University, 1969), pp. 198–99; W.H. McLeod, 'The Influence of Islam upon the Thought of Guru Nanak.' *History of Religions*, Vol. 7, No. 4 (May: University of Chicago Press, 1968), p. 302. See chapter 1, this volume.

11. Vir Singh, ed., *Purātan Janam-sākhī* (Amritsar: Khalsa Samachar, 1959), p. 16.

12. Ibid., p. 25.

13. *History of Religions* Vol. 7, No. 4 (May: University of Chicago Press, 1968), pp. 310–11.

14. M. Mujeeb, *Islamic Influence on Indian Society* (Meerut: Meenakshi Prakashan, 1972), p. 175.

15. This aspect of Nanak's doctrine is discussed in W.H. McLeod, 'Religious Tolerance in Sikh Scriptural Writings,' in *Guru Tegh Bahadur* ed. G.S. Talib (Patiala: Punjabi University, 1976), pp. 228–42.

16. McLeod, 'Influence of Islam', pp. 302–16. See above pp. 3–18.

17 I owe this and other perceptive comments to Mr. Simon Digby.

18. McLeod, 'Influence of Islam', pp. 315–16. See above pp. 14–15.

19. *Akal Ustat 86, Dasam Granth*, p. 19.

20. Niharranjan Ray, *The Sikh Gurus and the Sikh Society* (Patiala: Punjabi University, 1970), pp. 27–28; W.H. McLeod, *The Evolution of the Sikh Community* (Delhi: Oxford University Press, 1975), pp. 13–14, 79–81.

21. Ibid., chap. 2.

22. Simon Digby offers an interesting example. The *janam-sākhī* juxtaposing of graciousness and apparent heartlessness is, he convincingly suggests, a reflection of the Sūfi pairing of *jalāl* and *jamal* in its hagiographic image of the pīr: *Indian Social and Economic History Review*, Vol. 7, No. 2 (June, 1970), pp. 308–9.

23. McLeod, *Evolution*, pp. 50–52.

3

THE NANAK OF FAITH AND THE NANAK OF HISTORY*

For more than half a century much theological scholarship in the West has been absorbed in the movement commonly referred to as 'the quest of the historical Jesus.' The name is taken from the English title of a celebrated book by Albert Schweitzer which appeared in its original German edition in 1906,[1] and the antecedents of the movement can be clearly traced back through such nineteenth century works as Renan's *Vie de Jesus*[2] and D.F. Strauss's *Leben Jesu*.[3] The basic assumption has been that the Jesus of history must be, in some measure at least, distinguished from the Christ of faith. There has been no agreement concerning the precise nature of the distinctions which must be drawn, but the basic affirmation has long since been accepted and some exceedingly valuable insights have been developed during the course of the debate.

The quest of the historical Jesus is obviously an issue of considerable importance to Western countries with cultures which owe so much to the Christian tradition. It is of appreciably less significance to India, but should not be discarded as totally irrelevant. Its importance lies not so much in the results which it has produced (although these may certainly be interesting) as in the nature of the basic assumption which underlies these results and in the methods which have been used to elicit them.

*Originally published in J.C.B. Webster ed., *History and Contemporary India*, Asia Publishing House, Bombay, 1971.

The purpose of this paper is to suggest that a similar assumption is necessary in the case of Guru Nanak and to maintain that without it our understanding of subsequent Punjab history must be to some extent distorted. It is true that the situation is not the same as that involved in the search for the Jesus of history. One significant difference is that we are much nearer the time of Guru Nanak and must bear the burden of only five centuries of tradition instead of twenty. A second difference is that the quest of the historical Nanak permits a convenient distinction between canonical scripture and non-canonical tradition, and thus avoids the considerable problems arising from the necessity of drawing distinctions within a canon. Thirdly, we are nowhere presented with problems of the magnitude of those arising from the resurrection narratives of the Gospels and from the doctrinal adjustments required by a rejection of these narratives as accounts of an historical event.

These differences, and others, mean that the quest is less complicated than that of the historical Jesus and that the same effort should not be needed in order to discover what may be known of the figure of history. The basic assumption is, however, necessary and efforts should certainly be made to distinguish one figure from the other. There can be no denying that there is a Nanak of faith as well as a Nanak of history. This should not suggest that the two figures are wholly distinct. They are, on the contrary, closely related and it would be altogether mistaken to deny that the figure of faith communicates much that relates to the Guru Nanak of history. On the other hand, it cannot be affirmed that the two are identical and our concern must be to draw, wherever possible, the necessary distinctions.

There appear to be at least three important reasons for applying the procedure to Guru Nanak. In the first place, a failure to do so must inevitably cloud our understanding of Guru Nanak himself. Many examples can be given of the manner in which a measure of distortion must persist if we ignore this basic distinction between the Nanak of faith and the Nanak of history. Most are relatively insignificant, but some are important. They occur with particular frequency in the accounts covering the years of Guru Nanak's travels, the most obscure of all the periods in his lifetime. For this period we are bound to depend almost exclusively upon the *janam-sākhīs*. As historical records the *janam-sākhīs* are largely unreliable and this condition applies with particular force to the years which intervene between Guru Nanak's early manhood in the Punjab and the final period of settled existence in the village of Kartarpur. Within the corpus of *janam-sākhī* traditions there are frequent contradictions, and the examination of such incidents as are subject to historical analysis almost invariably lead to either radical modification or, more commonly, to its complete rejection. There can be no doubt that Guru Nanak must have spent several years in travel beyoñd the Punjab, and its seems likely that this period would have covered the first two decades of the sixteenth century, but there is little we can add to this general statement. Where he went, and in what sequence, cannot be affirmed with any assurance.

This condition of radical uncertainty raises questions of two kinds. In the first place there is the question of the purpose of the travels. At this point there is conflict between the two most important *janam-sākhī* traditions. The *Miharbān Janam-sākhī* explicitly states that the purpose was to find a *guru*[4] whereas the *Purātan Janam-sākhīs* clearly imply that the *udāsīs* were missionary tours. It is the latter interpretation which has been accepted and which has dictated the biographical pattern for this period. Miharban's comment has received no attention and would doubtless be summarily rejected as an illustration of sectarian polemic. The rejection may well be warranted, but questions of this kind demand more than summary treatment.

Secondly, there must be questions relating to particular places which Guru Nanak is said to have visited. Much has, for example, been made of the *janam-sākhī* traditions that Guru Nanak visited Mecca, Medina, and Baghdad. These have been introduced into discussions relating to his attitude concerning religion in general and Islam in particular, and introduced in a manner which assumes their historicity. This is a procedure which runs a considerable risk of misunderstanding. We cannot affirm with complete assurance that Guru Nanak did *not* visit Mecca, Medina, and Baghdad, but nor can we affirm that he did visit these places. The balance of likelihood strongly favours the former possibility and we should accordingly proceed with considerable caution in any issue which claims support from such incidents.[5]

In some cases the use of incidents of this kind has involved significant alterations in order to bring the tradition into line with rational possibility and with the conclusion which the incident is supposed to exemplify. The Mecca *sākhīs* provide the material for an illustration of this in the story of the miraculously moving *miharāb*.[6] By terminating this story at the point where Guru Nanak tells the offended qazi to turn his feet in a direction where God is not, modern writers have avoided a miracle and produced an extremely neat story. It does not, however, accord with what the *janam-sākhīs* say and there is no evident justification for any claim that the *janam-sākhīs* subsequently added a miracle to an earlier story which was both rational and authentic. The only *janam-sākhī* which approaches this modern rationalized version is *Pothī Sach-khand* of the *Miharbān Janam-sākhī*. In this version we do not find the miraculously moving *miharāb*, but then nor are we given the conclusion which is drawn by modern writers.[7]

Another *janam-sākhī* reference which has been extensively used in discussions relating to the religion of Guru Nanak and to the nature of his mission is the celebrated sentence which he is said to have uttered after he had emerged from three days of submersion in the Vein river: 'There is no Hindu; there is no Mussulman.'[8] The saying is one which may well be authentic, but we must not overlook the fact that it is to be found only in the *janam-sākhīs* and that it receives no explicit confirmation in any *śabad* or *ślok* by Guru Nanak. There will be an understandable reluctance to abandon such a striking aphorism, and there may in fact be no need to do so. The question must, however, be raised. The utterance may be interpreted to accord with certain authentic compositions recorded in the *Ādi Granth*, but the inescapable fact remains that the utterance itself is recorded in notably unreliable sources.

Other points at which the *janam-sākhīs* have evidently led us astray in their accounts of Guru Nanak's period of travels are their versions of visits to Assam, Ceylon, and Mount Sumeru, and their descriptions of Guru Nanak's alleged contacts with Babur. The first three of these have been held to establish, or at least imply, a spread of influence which probably never occurred. *Sākhīs* dealing with the Guru's early life must also be examined with the same caution. Conclusions have, for example, been drawn from the *janam-sākhī* records of instruction by both pandit and mullah. One such conclusion is that the Guru was an educated man, a point which requires no support as it is established beyond all doubt by his compositions. A second is that he was provided at an early age with coherent expositions of both conventional Hinduism and orthodox Islam. This is much more questionable. The period which is best served by the *janam-sākhīs* is that of the years in Kartarpur between the conclusion of his travels and his death, for they are here dealing with a period spent in or near the Punjab and as close as possible to the time of their composition. They do not in fact tell us much about the events of the period, but this is understandable and significant, for it suggests that authentic knowledge and memory may have acted in some measure as checks upon the proliferation of legend.

The necessary distinction between the figure of faith and the man of history must lead us to examine the *janam-sākhī* accounts with a cautious scepticism. The examination will soon reveal the limited extent to which the *janam-sākhīs* reveal the Nanak of history. They have, as we shall see, their own importance, but it is in only small measure a biographical importance. It is not sufficient to omit the miracle stories of the *janam-sākhīs* and accept the rest. This is a method which has been commonly adopted by writers during this century, but it is not nearly radical enough. It involves no more than a modification of the traditional view that the *janam-sākhīs* can be accepted as basically reliable biography. This view must not be simply modified but positively rejected, and the distinction between the figure of faith and of history can help us to appreciate the need for this rejection.

In the *janam-sākhīs* what we find is the Guru Nanak of faith, the image of the Guru seen through the eyes of popular piety seventy-five or a hundred years after his death. It is an important image, but its real importance cannot be appreciated if it is identified with the figure of history. Of this figure the *janam-sākhīs* provide only glimpses and by their inadequacy force us back to the works preserved in the *Ādi Granth*. This presents a more difficult task, for Guru Nanak's *śabads* and *śloks* are not sources of detail concerning his life. As one might reasonably expect, however, it is also true that behind these works and the thought which they express there can be discerned a personality. The quest of the historical Nanak must accordingly be an exercise in discernment supplemented by the glimpses provided in the *janam-sākhīs*.

The second reason for applying the distinction between the figures of faith and history to the case of Guru Nanak is that a failure to do so must inhibit a true understanding and appreciation of the *janam-sākhīs*. If they are read as biographies they will be misunderstood, and by many they will be summarily rejected as a collection of legends. This would be most unfortunate. It is true that the *janam-sākhīs* contain much legendary material, but this should never be regarded as a justification for neglect. The historical importance of legend in traditions concerning the 'founders' of the Buddhist, Christian, and Muslim faiths has been acknowledged and the same acknowledgment should be made in the case of Sikh tradition.

When related to such figures legend can serve two purposes. In the first place it can serve as an expression of the importance of a particular person in the eyes of his later followers. The legends concerning Guru Nanak can legitimately be regarded as expressions of his personality. This impact can be in some measure self-generating, but it must have an origin, and a judicious evaluation of subsequent legend can impart some understanding of the personality which provided the origin. This point should not be too strongly emphasized, but nor should it be wholly overlooked. The magic of Guru Nanak's personality has been, and continues to be, of incalculable importance to the Punjab. The legends which have gathered around him can help us to appreciate something of this magic.

The second function which legend serves is as an expression of a community's understanding, both conscious and implicit, at particular points in that community's history. This is a point of very considerable importance, one which elicits the principal value of the *janam-sākhīs*. The earlier *janam-sākhīs* evidently emerged in their present form during the first half of the seventeenth century and they accordingly serve as expressions of early seventeenth century Sikh belief and of the understanding of the mission of Guru Nanak held by the community during this particular period.[9] *Janam-sākhīs* which were written later reveal the understanding of a later period. The two versions of the *Mahimā Prakāś* serve this purpose for the early eighteenth century, the *Nanak Prakāś* of Santokh Singh serves it for the early nineteenth century, and we should perhaps be justified in taking Bhai Vir Singh's *Gūru Nānak Chamatkār* as the most impressive twentieth-century expression of the same impulse. In some cases, notably the manuscript versions of the *Bālā* tradition, the expression is a sectarian one and can do much to illuminate the tensions which existed at particular times.

This understanding of the nature of the *janam-sākhīs* enables to make certain affirmations relating to the history of Sikhism. It is, for example, evident that within the Sikhism of the early seventeenth century there was strong opposition to Brahmanical pretensions and a vivid awareness of the futility of practices associated with the ritual cleanliness. This is well illustrated by the story of the inordinately scrupulous Brahman who, having insisted upon preparing his own cooking-square of impeccable purity, found bones wherever he dug and finally had to accept food from the Guru.[10] The fact that the *sākhī* cannot be historical does not deprive it of its interest. It retains an interest and a value as an expression of the Sikh understanding of

Guru Nanak's teaching at a particular period. This example is one which, if read as a parable, is in complete accord with the teaching of Guru Nanak. One which is out of accord, but which is likewise of interest as an expression of contemporary belief, is the *Purātan* story of the coal and the thorn.[11] The naive understanding of the doctrine of *karma* which it assumes is one which Guru Nanak could not possibly have held.

Another interesting instance relating to food regulations is the *janam-sākhī* account of how Guru Nanak cooked meat at Kurukshetra.[12] This *sākhī* testifies to an anti-vegetarian view from the *janam-sākhī* period, not to Guru Nanak's own view. The scripture passage which Guru Nanak is said to have uttered on this occasion (*Vār Malār, śloks* 1 and 2 of *paurī* 25[13]) does not necessarily endorse the *eating* of flesh, and if read apart from the *sākhī* can give an entirely different impression.[14] It is quite possible that Guru Nanak may have permitted the eating of meat and certainly there is no evidence that he opposed the practice. We must, however, avoid categorical pronouncements which are based upon the *janam-sākhīs* rather than upon his own works. The testimony which the *janam-sākhīs* give is to their own period and place.

This understanding of the *janam-sākhīs* also enables us to make a positive affirmation concerning the famous utterance 'There is no Hindu; there is no Mussulman'. A measure of doubt must persist in the attributing of these words to Guru Nanak, but there can be no doubt that they represent the early seventeenth-century understanding of a particular aspect of Guru Nanak's teachings. All of the important *janam-sākhīs* agree in this respect and the doctrine which they express through the saying is supported by Bhai Gurdas who also wrote during the early seventeenth century.

The qazis and mullahs gathered and began questioning him on religious matters.
God has unfolded an immense creation; none can comprehend His power!
Opening their books they asked, 'Which is the greater religion—the Hindu or the Muslim?'
Baba (Nanak) answered the pilgrims, 'Without good deeds both lead only to suffering.
Neither Hindu nor Muslim finds refuge in (God's) court.
The safflower's pigment is not fast; it runs when washed in water.
People are jealous of each other, but Ram and Rahim are one.
The world has taken the devil's path.'[15]

The understanding which these accounts represent accords with Guru Nanak's own utterances on the subject as recorded in the *Ādi Granth*.[16] For Guru Nanak's teachings, however, we must rely on the *Ādi Granth*, not on the *janam-sākhī* understanding, however consonant it may be with Guru Nanak's own compositions. The *janam-sākhī* tradition *may* have its origin in an authentic utterance by Guru Nanak, but in view of their general unreliablity in this respect we must insist upon a margin of doubt. What is beyond doubt is that the *janam-sākhīs* testify to a particular doctrinal conviction held by the Sikh community at a remove of almost one hundred years from the death of Guru Nanak.

From this understanding of the importance of the *janam-sākhīs* there follows a third reason for distinguishing between the figures of faith and a history. An appreciation of the *janam-sākhīs* should remind us that every generation engages in processes of selection, emphasis and interpretation, and that the present generation is no exception to this rule. Once again this must not be limited to the Punjab and to Guru Nanak. Church History, records a constant and continuing process of reinterpretations, each new venture being in large measure a response of contemporary or recent circumstances and involving a selection of elements from Christian scripture and tradition. Every culture uses its history in some degree as a vehicle of its own contemporary ideals and values, and this applies with particular force to its religious history.

This can be seen at several levels today. At its crudest it is to be found in press reports of anniversary speeches and in the newspaper supplements which are issues on such occasions. University textbooks provide a slightly more refined version of the same condition, and at its most sophisticated it is to be found in works which have some claim to being regarded as scholarly. A point which receives particularly strong emphasis is the insistence that Guru Nanak respected all religions. There can be no doubt that we find in Guru Nanak an intention to reconcile Hindu and Muslim, and likewise that the current campaign for national integration is a necessary one, deserving all the support which may properly be given to it. The use of one to serve the other can, however, result in some misunderstandings and distortions. It has involved an extremely narrow selection from the total range of Guru Nanak's teachings and it commonly presents the selected aspect in a manner which does not accord with Guru Nanak's own presentation. Guru Nanak's own concept of reconciliation is to be found in a transcending of both Hinduism and Islam, not in an easy acceptance of both. The 'true Hindu' and the 'true Muslim' are to be regarded as one, but their attainment of truth requires an abandoning of conventional Hinduism and conventional Islam.

Sikhism does not face the same historical problem as Christianity and the quest of the historical Nanak is neither as urgent nor as difficult as the quest of the historical Jesus. The need does, however, exist. The Nanak of the *Ādi Granth* has become entwined with the Nanak of hagiographic tradition and this composite figure, the Nanak of faith, has exercised a vast influence upon Punjabi attitudes and accordingly upon the history of the Punjab. Let it be repeated, and with emphasis, that the Nanak of faith is by no means wholly distinct from the Nanak of history—but nor are the two identical. An understanding of both will help us to appreciate much that has happened during the last four centuries and much that we see around us in the Punjab of today.

Notes

1. *Von Reimarus zu Wrede*, Eng. trans., *The Quest of the Historical Jesus*, A Schweitzer, (London: A. & C. Black. 3rd ed., 1963) 1910.

2. *Vie de Jesus*, E. Renan, (Paris: Michel Lévy, 1863).

3. *Leben Jesu*, D.F. Strass, 2 vols, (Tübingen: C.F. Osiander, 1835–6).

4. *Janam-sākhī Srī Gurū Nānak Dev Jī*, eds Kirpal Singh and Shamsher Singh Ashok, pp. 111, 361.

5. These issues are discussed in my *Gurū Nānak and the Sikh Religion*, (Oxford: Clarendon Press, 1968).

6. In the older *janam-sākhīs* of the *Bālā* tradition, the incident is set in Medina, and in the corresponding story in the *Mihārban Janam-sākhī* the setting is a village on the way to Mecca.

7. *Janam-sākhī Sri Gurū Nānak Dev Jī, gost* 135, p. 449. The wording actually suggests that this version is like that given in modern accounts, one from which the miracle of the *miharāb* has been excised.

8. *Purātan Janam-sākhī, sākhī* 11.

9. This also applies to the first *var* of Bhai Gurdas.

10. *Purātan Janam-sākhī, sāk'ī*, 3. Cf. also the tradition concerning investiture of the sacred thread (*Mihārban Janam-sākhī, gost* 7; *Gyanratanavali, saki* 44) and the discourse on ritual bathing in *gost* 112 of the *Mihārban Janam-sakhi*. Other *sākhīs* reveal a similar attitude towards the authority claimed by the *qazis*. Cf. *Purātan Janam-sākhī, sākhīs*, 11, 51, and *Mihārban Janam-sākhī, gost*, 30–32.

11. *Purātan Janam-sākhī, sākhī* 21.

12. *Bālā Janam-sākhī*, Hafaz Kutub-din, (Lahore: Hafaz Kutub-din, 1928), p. 314.

13. *Ādi Granth*, pp. 1289–90.

14. The second line of the first *ślok* has sometimes been interpreted as a direct affirmation of meat-eating (*Srī Gurū Granth Sāhib*, Gopal Singh, [Amritsar: Sikh History Research Department, Khalsa College, 1962], p. 1230). There seems to be no doubt, however, that 'flesh in the mouth' refers to the growth of a tongue in the human foetus. (*Srī Gurū Granth Sāhib Darapaṇ, Cf.* Sahib Singh, [Jalandhar: Raj Publishers, 1964], vol. 9, p. 329). This is made plain by the point at which it occurs in the *ślok*'s description of the development of a human body. The point which Guru Nanak makes in this first *ślok* is that petty quarrels are insignificant in comparison with the paramount necessity of meeting the True Guru. The second *ślok* is a devastating denunciation of hypocrisy.

15. Bhai Gurdas, Var 1.33.

16. *Cf. Mārū Solahā* 2 (6), *Ādi Granth*, p. 1020: 'Neither the *Veda* nor the *Kateb* know the mystery.'

PART II

THE SIKH PANTH

4

THE DEVELOPMENT OF THE SIKH PANTH*

S ant doctrine, with its strong emphasis upon the interior quality of religious devotion, offers no overt encouragement to the emergence of religious institutions or formally organized communities. On the contrary, one learns to expect from its proponents a persistent attack on the futility of institutional loyalties or sectarian allegiance. Truth transcends the various religious groupings which men have contrived. One may be a Hindu or a Muslim, but neither confers any particular insight or virtue, and salvation is certainly not earned by the rituals and conventions which they variously impose. To be a Sant is to be freed from the institutional obligations of organized religion.

For most people, however, actual practice necessarily differs from any theory which seeks to minimize the value of institutional forms. The first gathering of any group of disciples may flourish without acknowledging any formal organization, but if this first generation is followed by continuing family loyalties and widening influence, the pressure to institutionalize becomes irresistible. The Sant tradition has been no exception to this rule. The first acceptance of any Sant as an inspired teacher was inevitably accompanied by the rudimentary organization required by the giving of *darśan* and the assembling of disciples for *kīrtan*. A panth would thus come into

*Originally published in Schomer and McLeod, eds, *The Sants: Studies in a Devotional Tradition in India*, Motilal Banarsidas, Delhi, 1987.

being and if it grew in strength it would also grow in institutional definition.

Within the Sant tradition three panths command a particular importance, and of this select group one has achieved a unique status in terms of its numerical following, range of development, and sustained influence. We may acknowledge the claims to significance which are justly made on behalf of the Kabir-panth and the Dadu-panth. Neither, however, can remotely compare to the Nanak-panth. The purpose of this essay is to sketch the pattern of development which conferred on the Nanak-panth its uniquely important status, a status which entitles it to be known as simply the Panth.

The first emergence of the Nanak-panth is easily identified. This took place in central Punjab, early in the sixteenth century. Well-established tradition records that Nanak (1469–1539), following some years of itinerant preaching, eventually settled in Kartarpur, a village situated on the right bank of the Ravi river opposite the present town of Dera Baba Nanak. This village evidently became the focus of attention and devotion, earned by the appeal of his teachings and by the sanctity of his own life-style. The master thus attracted disciples. Nanak became Baba Nanak and those who were thus attracted to him became his disciples or *sikhs*. The Nanak-panth was born.

In these general terms, the emergence of the Nanak-panth can be viewed as conventional and the same might also be said of one of its major features. The renunciation of caste, or at least the degrading of caste from a religious to a purely social status, has been a characteristic element in the establishing of 'sectarian' movements or panths.[1] The fact that this will normally be a response to ideals rather than to a calculated opportunism should not obscure its practical importance in terms of the founding and growth of a panth. The persistence of an undiluted acceptance of caste distinctions must seriously inhibit panthic recruitment and, unless the leader or leaders of any particular panth are prepared to impose significant limitations on membership, the maintenance of such distinctions must be modified or wholly abandoned. The Sikh Gurus were certainly not prepared to restrict salvation to those with approved caste qualifications. Nanak is outspoken in his denunciation of caste and his successors plainly follow him in his belief. One may well argue that the intention was a renunciation only of those aspects of caste which accord privilege to some and impose discriminatory penalties on others.[2] This claim does not affect the inescapable fact that Gurus were emphatic in their rejection of caste-based religious pretensions and that membership of the Panth was consequently seen to be open to people of all castes or none. In general terms, this insistence may be viewed as a characteristic feature of panthic development in its initial stage.

The first beginnings of the Panth accordingly follow what we may regard as a regular or standard pattern. Even at this initial stage, however, there are distinctive features which deserve to be noted as factors significantly contributing to its strength and longevity. At least three such factors can be identified. One was presumably the immediate impact of Nanak's personality. A second was his *bāṇī*, the hymns which he composed in order to communicate to his disciples the message of salvation through devotion to the divine Name. The third was the nature of his early following.

Although the first of these is an assumption rather than a fact which can be conclusively documented, it is obviously a reasonable assumption. The charismatic appeal of either the initiator or one of his early successors is a feature typical of successful religious movements and there is no reason to suppose that the Nanak-panth was in any sense an exception to this rule.[3] It is an assumption strongly supported by the Panth's later hagiography (the *janam-sākhīs*) and also by the personality indicators which appear in Nanak's own works.

In the characteristic Sant style Nanak gave expression to his convictions in the form of religious songs and these hymns provide a second evident reason for the early strength and subsequent growth of the Nanak-panth. The actual function of Sant *bāṇī* is the provision of appropriate songs, for communal singing (*kīrtan*), a corporate practice which serves to weld a group of disparate devotees into a society with a sense of common identity. This sense of identity will be encouraged or retarded by the nature of the materials which are used in such *kīrtan* sessions. Whereas the most banal of hymns can arouse at least a transient fervour, an inferior composition cannot reasonably expect to survive, and a dependence upon trivial thought or expression is unlikely to provide a secure foundation for any religious society. Nanak's work is at the opposite extreme. Its beauty is a simple beauty and the fact that the early Panth could build on such a foundation must surely be regarded as a major reason for its durable strength. It continues to serve this function even when the hymns are sung for their beauty rather than for their actual import, or when mere presence at *kīrtan* assumes greater importance than any understanding of what is being sung. The reputation of Nanak's *bāṇī* is too firmly established to permit serious questioning of its quality, even by those who might attach little importance to its status as scripture. A like quality is also to be found in the compositions of those of his successors who have left recorded works.

The third factor is perhaps the most important of all, for it helps to explain not merely the strength and longevity of the Panth but also the transformation which it subsequently experienced. This third feature concerns the distinctive response elicited by the early Gurus and the specific constituency thereby conferred on the Panth. Although some uncertainty still obscures the social foundations of the Nanak-panth there are good grounds for supposing that a significant measure of the initial response came from the Jats of rural Punjab. As we shall see, the Jats of central Punjab eventually emerge to a strong numerical predominance within the Panth. The Nanak-panth certainly recruited in rural Punjab from its earliest days and it is therefore reasonable to suppose that the Jat response to the Gurus' teachings should be traced to its first beginnings. It is also reasonable to suppose that the Jat response owed much to the egalitarian emphasis made by Nanak and his successors. During the sixteenth-century period of Guru Nanak and his early successors, the Jats, though evidently growing stronger in terms of actual land control, were still viewed as comparatively humble in terms of ritual status. If this theory is correct, it means that there will have been a widening gap separating their ascending economic status and aspirations from their position within any national hierarchy of Punjab castes. Irfan Habib has suggested that the Jats would be strongly attracted to a panth which rejected caste as a religious institution.[4] This seems to be an eminently plausible conjecture, one which does much to explain both the actual constituency of the Panth and the vitality which it was to sustain.

It appears that even within the lifetime of Guru Nanak, divergent emphases had appeared within the emergent Panth. According to Sikh tradition, one of his sons, Siri Chand, rejected Nanak's insistence upon the futility of asceticism as a necessary means of salvation. The ascetic path of celibacy and austerities was, it seems, the mode of salvation affirmed by Siri Chand, and those of the Nanak-panth who accepted this view eventually took the form of the Udasi-panth without wholly renouncing their connection with the Nanak-panth. This proved, however, to be an early aberration from an established, orthodoxy. The first Guru insisted upon the way of the householder (*grihast*) as the ideal and all-sufficient pattern of life for the seeker of salvation, rejecting in clear and unmistakable terms the ascetic alternative. His successors upheld the same ideal, expressing it in their own lives as well as in their teachings. The doctrine, firmly established in the Panth's earliest days, was subsequently to be challenged but never with real strength and never with success.

The emergence of a separate Udasi-panth is of some interest, but the attention bestowed upon the sons of Guru Nanak in the *janam-sākhī* accounts of his death is appropriately fleeting. There was no necessary reason why either should have possessed particular claims to the succession, at least none which could be derived from their filial connection.[5] Such a relationship could well have strengthened claims which might be advanced on other grounds, but to regard them as sufficient in themselves would clearly have been unacceptable. Spiritual qualities would command much greater importance and the succession was accordingly bestowed upon a disciple who, according to tradition, had earned a reputation for single-minded devotion to his master. This was Bhai Lahina, known in his leadership role as Guru Angad.

Guru Angad succeeded to the *gaddī* following the first Guru's death in 1539. He was already associated with Khadur, a village situated near the right bank of the Beas river approximately thirty kilometres above its confluence with the Satluj. There was evidently no reason why he should remain in Kartarpur and the focus of the Panth's devotion accordingly transferred to a location very close to the point where the Majha, Malwa and Doaba areas converge. His successor, Guru Amar Das, remained within the same vicinity, a choice which presumably helps account for the spread of the Panth's influence in all three regions.

Guru Angad's tenure of the *gaddī* appears, from the limited sources available to us, to have been a period of consolidation.[6] From the small collection of *śloks* by him recorded in the *Ādi Granth*, it is evident that his teachings faithfully reflected those of the first Guru. In them, he stresses the dangers inherent in attitudes which neglect spiritual concerns for worldly pursuits and, in the manner of his own preceptor, he insists that only through regular meditation on the divine Name can one attain purity and salvation. To find and follow this path of salvation one must depend upon the grace of the Guru. For Nanak, the Guru had been the inner voice of God. Angad, however, perceives him as the one who having heard and comprehended that voice subsequently communicated its message in terms of unique clarity. For Angad, the supreme guide is the first Master, Guru Nanak.[7] The reference to Nanak in these terms confirms what we might legitimately have assumed, namely that by the end of the second Guru's lifetime the identity of the Nanak-panth must have been clearly established.

The impression which emerges from our sketchy understanding of the period of Guru Angad is one which implies a panth with a clear identity but an informal organization. Insofar as the Nanak-panth possessed a formal organization at this early stage it related exclusively to the person of the acknowledged Guru. He alone provided a focus for a continuing devotion to the memory and teachings of the Panth's founder. It is under his successor that a more formalized structure begins to appear. Guru Amar Das became the third incumbent in 1552 and directed the affairs of the developing Panth until his death in 1574. In terms of organization and of the increasing clarity of panthic definition, his period is important for at least two major innovations and perhaps a third. As a result, the Panth which he left at the conclusion of his twenty-two years was evidently a more structured and more coherent company than the informal following which he had inherited from his predecessor.

The change introduced by Guru Amar Das included the appointment of territorial deputies or vicars (*mañjī*) and the conferring of a distinctively Sikh status upon a specific place, specific occasions, and specific rituals.[8] These two innovations represent a distinct shift in emphasis, though it is not a development which one finds reflected in the recorded works of the third Guru. Here the emphases are still those of Guru Nanak, with the same insistence upon salvation through inward meditation on the divine Name. The difference is that the growth of the Panth has produced pressures which can only be relieved by institutional means. A first generation of adherents will identify with the fledgling Panth on the strength of a choice dictated by genuine devotion and direct personal contact with the Guru. For subsequent generations, however, more tangible patterns of allegiance will be required and if numbers significantly increase, a greater measure of formal organization will be needed in order to maintain effective contact with the Panth's expanding membership. An extension of the Panth's geographical outreach will emphasize this need still further. This, it seems, was the situation by the time of the third Guru. The measures which he took in order to sustain the Panth's coherence should therefore be viewed as important contributions to its development.

It is possible that Guru Amar Das may have been responsible for a third contribution to the formalizing of the Panth. Another of the many traditions upon which we must necessarily depend concerns the provision of a proto-scripture. According to this particular tradition, Guru Amar Das provided a collection of works subsequently utilized by Guru Arjan as his principal source for the *Ādi Granth*. This collection, the so-called 'Goindval *pothīs*', can be regarded as yet another step towards panthic definition and independence.[9]

Tendencies clearly established in the time of Guru Amar Das were further strengthened during the years of the fourth and fifth Gurus. Once again the actual location of the *gaddī* shifted, this time to the spot where Guru Ram Das established a new village. The village, first known as Guru ka Chak and later as Ramdaspur, was eventually to attain pre-eminence as the city of Amritsar. This status it largely owes to another of the significant steps in panthic development. It was here in 1603–4 that Guru Arjan compiled the sacred scripture variously known as the *Ādi Granth* or *Granth Sāhib* and subsequently as the *Guru Granth Sāhib*.

It would be difficult to exaggerate the importance of the *Ādi Granth* in terms of the Panth's identity and coherence. Compiled under the close supervision of the fifth Guru, it acquired thereby a status which all loyal members of the Panth must necessarily acknowledge as sacrosanct and therefore as the object of profound veneration. It thus served to enhance the clarity of definition which distinguished the Nanak-panthi or Sikh from other men. The Panth now possessed a line of Gurus, a growing number of holy places, distinctive rituals, and its own sacred scripture. There could no longer be any question of vague definition nor of uncertain identity.

Two further developments served to emphasize this coherence still further during the period of Guru Arjan and his successors. The first was the occasional challenge to the *gaddī* offered by rival contestants. One of the most distinguished (or notorious) of these was Guru Arjan's elder brother, Prithi Chand. Another was Dhir Mal, grandson of the sixth Guru. Although it is difficult to evaluate their influence on the Panth, it seems reasonable to assume that the successful resisting of these challenges involved a heightened loyalty on the part of those who adhered to the orthodox line.

The same effect would also have been produced by external attack. Official concern on the part of Mughal administrators first became evident during the period of Guru Arjan and eventually led in 1606 to his death while in custody. Relations between the Panth and the Lahore administration deteriorated further during the time of Guru Hargobind (1606–44), so much so that fighting actually took place on three occasions. Considerable obscurity attends the death of Guru Arjan and neither the cause of the subsequent fighting nor its actual extent is altogether clear. The precise facts, however, are of less importance than the construction subsequently placed upon them. Guru Arjan's death came to be regarded as a martyrdom and tradition proceeds from this interpretation to the belief that it led directly to a deliberate arming of the Panth by his son Hargobind. This in turn heightened Mughal apprehension and the fighting which took place followed as a result of these growing fears.

An interpretation which views death as martyrdom and fighting as heroic struggle against an oppressor must contribute powerfully to a sense of identity. It is difficult to estimate the contemporary strength of this feeling and we must acknowledge that the traditional view of the early seventeenth century owes an indeterminate measure of its appeal to a period of later struggle. At the very least, however, one must acknowledge the development of genuine hostility, and there is no reason to suppose that the later tradition is wholly divorced from the early seventeenth-century Sikh's understanding of what was taking place in his own time. It must assuredly have involved an awareness of external threat, and such an awareness will normally contribute significantly to the cohesion of a society. We may therefore assume that the early decades of the seventeenth century contributed significantly to the growing sense of panthic identity. Sikhs were now united by a common threat as well as by a common devotion.

Precisely what happened to this sense of panthic identity during the quarter-century covered by the period of the seventh and eighth Gurus is impossible to determine. The seventh Guru remained in the Shivalik hills where his grandfather, the sixth Guru, had retired following the outbreak of hostilities with the Lahore administration; and although he occupied the *gaddī* for seventeen years, nothing of any striking importance marks the period. We can do little more than fall back on assumptions, one of which might well be the supposition that a period of prolonged absence from the plains must have produced a measure of weakening in panthic cohesion. This, however, would be an unsubstantiated deduction and even if it could be shown to be true its consequences are unlikely to have been significant. Anything that might have been lost during these years was later restored.

While the Guru remained in the hills relations between the Panth and the Mughal administration were largely uneventful. It was only when the ninth Guru moved to the plains again that serious tension returned. It was only when the ninth Guru, Tegh Bahadur moved to the plains again that serious tension returned. Eventually this was to lead to his execution in Delhi by Emperor Aurangzeb and subsequently to a genuine re-awakening of hostilities during the period of his son, Guru Gobind Singh. Although the circumstances under which Guru Tegh Bahadur met his death have been the subject of some controversy, the question need not detain us. In its impact upon panthic self-awareness, true importance attaches to the construction placed upon his death rather than to the actual facts which led to it. As with the death of Guru Arjan, the execution of the ninth Guru was interpreted as martyrdom and the outcome an ultimate strengthening of panthic cohesion. Understandably, it also involved a considerable strengthening of the enmity which divided the Panth from the imperial administration.

Growing hostility finally led to open war. A struggle between Guru Gobind Singh and other local powers in the Shivaliks assumed a wider importance when a Mughal force from Sirhind entered against the Sikhs. The outcome of this conflict in military terms has plainly been of vastly inferior importance to its psychological impact. To this day the memory of the tenth Guru's struggles remains powerfully present in the Panth, sustaining within it a deep-rooted conviction of military prowess and the fulfilment of duty through the exercise of that calling. Concepts of panthic destiny were thereafter inextricably bound up with traditions of rights attained and protected through the exercise of arms. The ideal becomes the *sant sipāhī*, the servant of the Guru who combines devotion with valour. A history of intermittent warfare extending through the eighteenth century greatly strengthened this self-awareness.

The Panth which emerged from that turbulent century was in consequence one which confidently affirmed its identity as a society built upon the exercise of military power. It would, however, be false to suggest that this alone constituted the Panth's sense of identity. The name of Nanak has never been obscured and loyalty to the sacred scripture has retained its vigour, even if for many that loyalty has been to an external symbol rather than to an actual understanding of content.

But we are leaping ahead. Although warfare has certainly been of major significance in the development of the Panth, warfare alone will not serve to explain the identity which so clearly emerges at the end of the eighteenth century. At least three other issues are of fundamental importance in any attempt to analyse this identity.

The first is the formal pattern of discipline and organization bestowed upon the Panth during the period of Guru Gobind Singh (the Khalsa and its *rahit*). The second is the social constituency of the following which formed the Panth, specifically those members who sustained their loyalty to it through the disturbed years of the eighteenth century. The third is the question of authority raised by the termination in 1708 of the line of personal Gurus.

As with all areas of the Panth's early history, there are aspects of the Khalsa's inauguration which remain obscure. The actual word is itself an example of this obscurity, for its etymology and original purport still remain open to some doubt. Although tradition implies that it was first introduced in 1699 at the actual ceremony of inauguration, it is evident that the term had already been used well before this date as a designation for the Panth.[10] The most attractive theory relates its introduction to the development of the *masand* system, and its apotheosis to the tenth Guru's eventual repudiation of the system. Whereas Sikhs living at a distance from the Guru had been grouped in territorial *sangats* under individual *masands*, those who were under the direct supervision of the Guru himself were his *khālsā* or 'royal domain'. During the latter part of the seventeenth century, many of the *masands* progressively assumed an excessive independence and were finally anathematized by Guru Gobind Singh. Sikhs hitherto under the supervision of *masands* were commanded to renounce their intermediate loyalty and attach themselves directly to *khālsā*.[11]

Theories of this kind are harder to establish when we turn to the actual instituting of the Khalsa as a formal order with a defined code of conduct. Although no grounds exist for doubting that an event of critical significance took place on Baisakhi Day, 1699 (or at least on some specific date late in the seventeenth century), the actual details of the event are less clear. The problem indicated at this point is the conflict between belief in a definitive declaration on the one hand and a theory of extended evolution on the other. In other words, was the form of the Khalsa (and specially its *rahit* or code of discipline) fully defined in 1699? Or did the 1699 event establish a basic pattern which attained its developed and settled form only after a post-1699 period extending well into the eighteenth century? The second of these possibilities raises a further issue. Was 1699 the beginning of the period of evolution? Or should the 1699 event be seen simply as an intermediate stage in a development which was already in progress by that date?

The intended role of the formally-constituted Khalsa is also open to debate. Tradition once again is clear. The Khalsa was established by Guru Gobind Singh in 1699 as a formal and defined order because the Panth in its earlier, looser form was inadequately equipped to resist forces of destruction which loomed threateningly and which were eventually to produce open conflict. The Panth consisted of sparrows which had to be transformed into hawks. The intention may indeed have been as simple as this, but there are other possibilities. A plausible alternative treats the establishment of the Khalsa as a result of militancy within the Panth rather than as its initiator. We have already noted the Panth's seventeenth-century experience of intermittent warfare and persecution, and it could be argued that the role of the Khalsa derived from the attitudes evoked by this experience. This claim would interpret the founding of the Khalsa brotherhood as a means of formalizing and disciplining an increasingly pervasive militancy within the Panth. The same claim could also be extended to cover the theory of a subsequent period of development. Founded as a means of formalizing a growing militancy, the Khalsa assumes its eventual form through the experience of persecution, struggle, and ultimate victory.

This, however, is speculation. It raises questions which we may never be able to answer and, expressed so summarily, it serves only to indicate major limitations on our present understanding of the development of the Panth. Such limitations are certainly important, but let it not be supposed that all is mist and obscurity. We have already stressed the fact that an event of great significance assuredly took place at the end of the seventeenth century and we can add to this the assurance that eventually, if not immediately, the Khalsa order assumed the status of a transformed orthodoxy. The Nanak-panth had produced the Khalsa, complete with a code of discipline which lays down the most explicit of rules concerning the external observances required of its baptized members. Although it would be incorrect to declare the Nanak-panth has, in its entirety, been transformed into the Khalsa, there is no room for doubt concerning the Khalsa predominance within the wider Nanak-panth. It would be very difficult to deny that by the end of the eighteenth century it had become the Sikh orthodoxy.

The emergence of a defined and dominant Khalsa is thus plainly evident, and yet the important questions still remain unanswered. What conditions actually produced the Khalsa, and what process of development did they generate? Militancy, the threat of persecution and the actual experience of warfare have been noted as obvious contributors to its emergence. Alone, however, they are insufficient. For a fuller explanation, we must return to that most fundamental of all issues, the social constituency of the Panth.

All the Gurus were Khatris and the list of leading members of the early Panth provided by Bhai Gurdas in his eleventh *vār* indicated that during the period of early development Khatri prominence extended beyond the Gurus' line. Other names given by Bhai Gurdas cover a sufficient range of castes to suggest that there must have been something resembling a cross-section of Punjab society in the Panth during the period covered by its first five or six Gurus. The lowest ranks in the order of Punjabi caste society are perhaps under-represented, but they are not absent. Moreover, a comparatively light representation in a list of prominent members does not necessarily imply a corresponding proportion of the actual adherents.

Three conclusions are thus indicated with regard to the constituency of the early Panth if we consider the evidence provided by Bhai Gurdas in conjunction with the theory of a Jat presence offered earlier in this essay. The first is the generally representative caste distribution of the Panth's more prominent members. The second is that if any caste group is to be accorded a particular prominence it must obviously be the Khatris. The third is that notwithstanding this Khatri prominence within a representative range, there was probably from the very earliest days of the Nanak-panth a substantial Jat constituency at the less conspicuous levels of membership.

If we are dealing with the early years of the Nanak-panth the third of these conclusions must necessarily be hedged with caution. It is, as we have already observed, a plausible theory, not an established fact. If, however, we traverse three centuries and examine constituency of the late-nineteenth or early-twentieth century, it emerges as a clear certainty and one which no longer concerns merely the less conspicuous orders of Sikh society. The censuses conducted by the British from 1881 onwards were by no means wholly accurate in terms of caste returns, but the general purport of their findings concerning membership of the Panth is beyond question. The first of the effective censuses (1881) clearly established that the Panth of the late-nineteenth century was predominantly Jat in its constituency. An impressive 66% of Sikhs were returned as Jats, the next largest group (the Tarkhans) being a mere 6/5%.[12]

Although the change can be represented as dramatic, it did not cause much surprise. For many it merely confirmed widely-held impressions. Ever since their first arrival in the Punjab, British visitors and administrators had intermittently noted the preponderance of Jats amongst the Sikhs and if the 1881 returns revealed a discrepancy it was that the earlier impressions had been exaggerated. The first clear indication of Jat strength within the Panth actually goes back to the later years of Bhai Gurdas's own lifetime. The author of the *Dabistān-i-mazāhib*, writing during the period of Guru Hargobind, indicates that by the early-seventeenth century Jats comprised a significant section of the Panth,[13] and if it were true of this period it was probably also true of the preceding century.

The sixteenth century, however, does not concern us at this point. It is sufficient for present purposes if we can accept that a substantial proportion of the Panth's seventeenth-century membership was Jat and that a strong numerical presence implies a measure of influence within the Panth. Khatri influence had meanwhile begun to decline, a process which was evidently accelerated by Khatri reluctance to participate in the disturbances of the early-eighteenth century.[14]

Once again the true nature of the argument must be made clear before it is actually offered. The argument is still strictly a hypothesis and there can be no suggestion of definitive proof at this stage. It is, however, a line of reasoning which may prove more persuasive than a simple appeal to military threats and the need to forestall them.

The basis of the argument is the commonplace assumption that if a distinctive social group secures dominant status within a particular society it will inevitably exercise upon that society an influence which reflects its own mores. The Jats are unquestionably a distinctive group, manifesting a correspondingly distinctive range of ideals and conventions. These include strong martial traditions and, as an obvious corollary, the regular use of arms. The direction of the argument will by now be clear. If it be acknowledged that the Khalsa philosophy and code of discipline bear a striking resemblance to Jat ideals and conventions, the conclusion must surely be that an explanation for the rise of the Khalsa should be sought in any analysis of the Panth's dominant constituency.[15]

Does this mean, then, that having acknowledged the strength of Jat attitudes in the historical process which produced the Khalsa we must necessarily regard the Khalsa as an institutionalized conquest of the Panth by its Jat constituency? This, needless to say, would be a naive interpretation. Whereas we can certainly talk in terms of powerful Jat influences moulding the form and philosophy of the developing Panth, we must also retain a clear view of those features which the Panth carries forward from its origins and period of early growth. The reverence which attaches to the memory of the Gurus ought surely to warn us against exaggeration in this respect. Nanak and his teachings are still very much a part of the conscious inheritance of the Panth. The Khalsa may well incorporate powerful Jat influences, but they are certainly not exclusive. If that were true, it would be difficult to understand the survival of a practice such as *nām simaraṇ* or the persistent refusal to abandon the honoured conventions of *saṅgat* and *paṅgat*. Although the *Ardās* belongs to the later period of the evolving Khalsa, it scarcely reads as the petition of a caste-based community, particularly its concluding couplet:

Guru Nanak nām chaṛhadī kalā
tere bhāne sarabat kā bhalā
May Thy Name, taught by Guru Nanak, ever increase;
And by Thy grace may all men prosper.

Such words are manifestly universalist in meaning and as such testify to the enduring strength of the Nanak-panthi ideal. It is an ideal which the Khalsa has retained, notwithstanding the powerful influence of martial affections.

Even those features which plainly derive from the martial experience of the Panth cannot be wholly explained in terms of Jat influence. The prominence given in the early *rahit* to the renunciation of Muslim contacts and example indicates another major element. In this period of strife Muslims come to be identified as the prime enemies of the Khalsa, and injunctions which reflect this hostility find their way into the evolving *rahit*. Some are subsequently shed or modified as changing circumstances affect attitudes towards the *rahit*; others survive to the present day. The clearest of all examples is provided by the ban on *halāl* meat. Another major precept which evidently reflects antagonism towards Muslims is the strict ban on the use of tobacco.

Social constituency and the experience of extended conflict thus combine to produce the all-important *rahit*, mutable with regard to many of its details but thoroughly consistent as an expression of the nature of the later Panth. The outcome is a paradoxical but nevertheless coherent blend of apparent contrasts. The Panth, represented now by the Khalsa, lays strong emphasis upon external forms without abandoning the earlier insistence upon inward devotion. Predominantly unicaste in constituency, it nevertheless preserves the concept of religious equality and freely admits men of other castes to its membership. Nurtured in warfare, it still affirms an eirenic ideal. It has, in other words, absorbed strong influences from its Jat connections and its experience of struggle without renouncing its avowedly religious inheritance from the early Nanak-panth.

An unaffected Nanak-panthi inheritance meanwhile continued to survive, sustained by devotees who perpetuated the old beliefs and practices without accepting the transforming requirements of the Khalsa discipline. Few have questioned their right to be regarded as Sikhs. Ever since the eighteenth-century rise of the Khalsa, however, their numbers appear to have been small and their caste affiliations predominantly non-Jat. The history of this section of the Panth is obscure until some notice is taken of them late in the nineteenth century. This is scarcely surprising for, as we have already noted, the eighteenth-century Khalsa had asserted a claim to orthodoxy which it has never since relinquished.

The final issue to be noted in connection with the eighteenth-century development of the Panth is the question of authority. Until the first decade of the eighteenth century, the nature of authority had presented no problem. Although the exercise of authority had been disputed by rival claimants from time to time, the actual form was acknowledged by all to be the personal leadership and direction of the Guru. Authority resided in the person of the Guru and, for all who acknowledged him as such, the sanctified will of the Guru was beyond challenge. This authority might be delegated to deputies, but never transferred. It was a clearly defined system and in spite of the recurrent disputes caused by rival claimants, it seems to have functioned effectively.

The system was, however, disrupted from 1708 onwards by the death of the tenth Guru without recognized heirs. The office had long since become hereditary and a succession problem now arose because the sons of Guru Gobind Singh had predeceased their father. Tradition records that the tenth Guru himself dictated the solution by declaring that after his death the Guru's authority would pass to the sacred scripture and the corporate Panth. The *Ādi Granth* thus becomes the *Gurū Granth Sāhib*, sharing divine authority with the Guru Panth.

Traditions as deeply rooted as this particular one cannot be lightly dismissed. There is, moreover, evidence which supports it, notably the testimony of the poet Sainapati whose *Srī Gur Sobhā* may date from 1711.[16] As opposed to the received tradition, one must consider the confusion which evidently attended the authority issue during the years following the death of Guru Gobind Singh. It is not possible to elicit from early eighteenth-century sources a clear awareness and consensus acceptance of the concept of dual authority. The impression is rather one of a continuing evolution which eventually issues in clearly defined doctrine. It may well be true that the tenth Guru explicitly conferred his authority on the Khalsa and it is certainly true that the scriptures and already acquired a sanctity which implied divine authority. There remains, however, a strong impression of inchoate rather than clearly defined doctrine. The latter form, implicit in the early eighteenth-century situation emerges to clarity and practical application only after a period of uncertainty.

It is also evident that the theory of dual authority was applied in actual practice for a comparatively brief period. Sir John Malcolm's famous description of the Panth in corporate session vividly depicts a situation of genuine application, even if one which indicates that the greater weight of emphasis was attached to the Guru Panth aspect of the doctrine.[17] Even as Malcolm wrote, however, the balanced doctrine was well on the way to desuetude, sustained in theory but significantly amended in actual practice. Ranjit Singh, having achieved effective political authority in the Punjab by the end of the eighteenth century, was unlikely to look with favour upon a custom which left extensive power in the hands of a Khalsa assembly. Such assemblies were therefore suppressed and with them went the effective application of the Guru Panth doctrine. The ideal has remained a powerful one but in practice it has proved unworkable. The doctrine of the Guru Granth has accordingly advanced and to this day retains an unchallengeable authority if ever an issue is put to its arbitration. Within the Panth the word of the *Gurū Granth Sāhib* cannot be easily transgressed, at least not in an overt sense.

This does not mean, of course, that the question of authority is thereby solved. It is not possible to submit every issue to the arbitrament of scripture if only because many issues will not be covered by it. Even when this is theoretically possible the effect can commonly be negated by differing interpretations of meaning. In actual practice the scripture has been extensively used as a means of securing personal guidance by individuals, but rarely as an agent of corporate decision.

As a result the problem of authority has been a recurrent one. During the eighteenth century, the doctrine of the Guru Panth evidently possessed a measure of genuine if occasional authority, an authority which was consciously exercised in the physical presence of the sacred scripture. This authority was eventually superseded by an assertion of personal power on the part of Maharaja Ranjit Singh and during the first half of the nineteenth century effective authority was political. The destruction of the political base left a serious vacuum and for the next quarter-century the Panth drifted uncertainly amidst frequent prophecies of its impending break up. It was rescued from this fate largely as a result of the Singh Sabha renewal movement with its effective insistence upon a return to traditional panthic loyalties.

The impact of the Singh Sabha movement has been exaggerated by some, ignored by others. Whereas the latter response is indefensible we must nevertheless take care that the emphasis which is properly laid upon this phase in the Panth's development is not excessive. Its ideals were noble, but in terms of objectives, methods and membership it was distinctly elitist. The intention and procedures were very much those of the educated few, the small section of society which had been affected by Western models or by opportunities afforded by the British presence in India. It was no accident that the movement should have emphasised newspaper journalism, literature, educational conferences and modern schools, nor that it should be connected with such enterprises as business and banking. In general terms, the Singh Sabha was replicating a pattern which was emerging in similar circumstances elsewhere. Within the Punjab, some obvious parallels can be seen in the concurrent Arya Samaj development.

This is the first qualification which should be noted, though in itself it is of no great consequence. The importance of such movements must obviously depend upon their influence rather than their antecedents. A second qualification carries rather more weight. It is that the impact of the Singh Sabha can be easily exaggerated as a result of the movement's unquestionable influence in terms of articulate Sikh opinion. Those who depend for their understanding upon the printed word or upon contacts with acknowledged scholars can very easily get the impression that the movement's ideals secured a much greater influence than was actually the case. An understanding derived from such sources would need to be balanced by a representative view of the Singh Sabha influence at the village level. One should, for example, take heed of the significant participation of Khatri reformers, scholars, and entrepreneurs. It would obviously be absurd to brand the Singh Sabha as a Khatri movement, but equally it must be obvious that their prominence within it was substantially in excess of their numerical strength within the

Panth. It was, in other words, a distinctly intellectual movement, one which stressed the importance of consistency in doctrine and in social observance.

A third qualification to be noted is the fact of division within the movement. This feature is perhaps less evident than it ought to be. The discord which separated the Lahore and Amritsar *dīvāns* is well known, but secondary sources offer little information concerning the Panch Khālsā Divan and its somewhat more radical notions.[18]

Having acknowledged these qualifications, we can repeat our insistence that the Singh Sabha was nevertheless a movement of great importance in the history of the Panth. This importance derives directly from the intellectual consistency which provided the true basis of the movement. Because it was consistent it laid rigorous stress upon observance of the *rahit*, affirming thereby precisely those features which provide the Panth with its distinctive identity. The same consistency also produced, by means of scriptural exegesis and other related literature, a revived concern for the patterns of devotion taught by the Gurus. Perhaps most impressive of all (and again a direct product of intellectual honesty and consistency) it campaigned for the full acceptance of men of all ranks and status within the Panth. The result was a significant accession of strength from outcaste sections of Punjab society.

The vigour of the Singh Sabha movement flagged during the early decades of the present century and its surviving descendant, the Chief Khalsa Divan, is now a shadow of its former self. The inheritance in terms of the Panth's self-awareness has, however, been considerable. A continuing insistence on the *rahit*, new or restored Sikh ceremonies, extensive adherence to devotional practices associated with the *Guru Granth Sāhib*, and a genuine communal openness are all features which we properly associate with the twentieth-century Panth. Their continuing strength owes much to the Singh Sabha movement.

Although the influence of the Singh Sabha extended well into the twentieth century, it was not the last of the movements to exercise a perceptible influence on the development of the Panth. At least three others deserve to be noted. The first is the Gurdwara Reform Movement which in a sense grew out of the Singh Sabha concern for purified places of worship, but which moved forward into a pattern of political activity alien to the more restrained and gentlemanly procedures of its predecessor. The political approach stimulated by the Gurdwara Reform Movement carried through to the political activities of the Akali Party (the Shiromani Akali Dal) and to the phase which is still with us today. As a result of this development, the Panth of today is highly politicized and no description of its current condition could possibly ignore this feature. The resources of the Shiromani Gurdwara Prabandhak Committee and the rewards proffered by state politics have served to sustain and encourage political activity.

The second twentieth-century movement is actually an extension of a convention well established during the late-nineteenth century and linked beyond that with the martial traditions of the Jat community. This has been the continued attachment of military service. As one of the so-called 'martial races' of India, the Sikhs (and particularly Jat Sikhs) were encouraged by the British to enlist in the Indian Army and having done so were required to retain their Khalsa insignia. Military service was both a response to traditional values and a strengthening of those values. It was also a comparatively profitable enterprise. Army remittances have contributed to the development of many Punjab villages.

Military service has also contributed to the third feature to be noted as a significant twentieth-century development for the Panth. This has been the Sikh diaspora, the migration overseas of numbers which no one has ever computed but which are obviously substantial. As a result of this movement Sikhs are now to be found in several countries outside India, notably in England, the United States, Canada, East Africa, and Malaysia. The impact upon the Panth of this mobility has yet to be made clear. In terms of economic betterment it has obviously succeeded in a large number of cases, particularly when we bear in mind the straitened circumstances from which so many of the migrants have come. Until recently there were clear indications that overseas conditions acted as an effective solvent on the *rahit* and that the standard symbols of panthic identity could well be under serious threat. Although this still seems to be the case in the smaller expatriate communities, distinct signs are appearing within the larger groups of a reassertion of the traditional forms.

Inevitably we conclude on a note of uncertainty, for the future pattern of a dynamic society must always be uncertain. Four and a half centuries have now passed since the Nanak-panth made its first appearance in central Punjab. During that period it has developed from a loose cluster of disciples through a process of unusually explicit organization to the world-wide community which increasingly we are recognizing as the bearer of a major religion. It is a process which has carried the community a considerable distance from its Sant origins, yet not one which has involved any necessary renunciation of those origins. Sikh loyalty to the memory of the first Guru remains fiercely ardent and respect for his teachings continues undiminished. Although much may have been added during the intervening period, the inheritance which we trace to the Sant tradition still lives and thrives within the contemporary descendant of the Nanak-panth.

Notes

1. Louis Dumont, *Homo Hierarchicus* (Chicago: 1970), p. 190. W.H. McLeod, 'On the word *Panth*,' *Contributions to Indian Sociology*, new series, 12:2 (1978), pp. 287–95. See below pp. 139–48.

2. W.H. McLeod, *The Evolution of the Sikh Community* (Oxford: 1976), pp. 87–91.

3. This point is convincingly made by Terry Thomas in *Sikhism: The Voice of the Guru*, Units 12–13 of the Open University series 'Man's Religious Quest' (Milton Keynes: The Open University Press, 1978), p. 63.

4. Irfan Habib, 'Jatts of Punjab and Sind,' in Harbans Singh and N. Gerald Barrier, eds, *Punjab Past and Present: Essays in Honour of Dr Ganda Singh* (Patiala: 1976), p. 99.

5. Siri Chand presumably disqualified himself as a successor to his father by reason of his ascetic views and his only brother, Lakhmi Das, evidently provided other reasons for suffering a similar rejection. This, at least, is the interpretation suggested by the *janam-sākhīs*. Bhai Gurdas, *Vār* 1:38. See also *Rāmkalī kī Vār, Rāi Balvand tathā Saitā Ḍūm, Ādi Granth*, p. 967 (hereafter *AG*).

6. *Rāmkalī kī Vār, AG*, pp. 966–67. *Mahimā prakāś vārtak* and *Mahimā prakāś kavitā*.

7. *Vār Mājh*, 27:1, *AG*, p. 150. Two *śaloks* which together effectively summarize the message of Guru Angad are *Vār Mājh* 18:1–2, *AG*, p. 146.

8. McLeod, *Evolution*, pp. 7–8, 42.

9. Ibid., pp. 60–61.

10. J.S. Grewal and S.S. Bal, *Guru Gobind Singh* (Chandigarh: Panjab University, 1967), p. 115.

11. Ibid. Also Ganda Singh, ed., *Hukam-nāme* (Patiala: Punjabi University, 1967), pp. 25–26; and J.S. Grewal, *From Guru Nanak to Maharaja Ranjit Singh* (Amritsar: Guru Nanak University, 1972), pp. 60–61.

12. McLeod, *Evolution*, p. 93.

13. Ganda Singh, English translation of relevant portion of the *Dabistān-i-mazāhib* in *The Panjab Past and Present* 1–1:1 (1967), p. 57.

14. Muzaffar Alam, 'Sikh Uprisings under Banda Bahadur, 1708–1715,' *Studies in History* 1:2 (1979), pp. 206–12. Muzaffar Alam also suggests that Khatri support for the Panth may well have been weakened by

the tenth Guru's abolition of the Khatri-dominated *masand* system. He notes a tendency for the Khatris to support Mughals rather than Sikhs as a better means of defending their material interest during the time of turmoil. Ibid., pp. 207, 212.

15. This theory is argued in greater detail in McLeod, *Sikh Community*, especially chapter 3.

16. Sainapati, *Srī Gur Sobhā*, ed., Ganda Singh (Patiala: Punjabi University, 1967), pp. 127–9.

17. John Malcolm, *Sketch of the Sikhs* (London: John Murray, 1812), pp. 120–23, McLeod, *Evolution*, pp. 48–49.

18. An exception to this rule is an article by Harbans Singh, 'The Bakapur Diwan and Babu Teja Singh of Bhasaur,' *The Panjab Past and Present* 9-2:18 (1975), pp. 322–32. See also N. Gerald Barrier, *The Sikhs and Their Literature* (Delhi: Manohar, 1970), introduction, pp. xxxiii–xxxiv.

5

THE SIKH STRUGGLE IN THE EIGHTEENTH CENTURY AND ITS RELEVANCE FOR TODAY*

The Sikhs have been much in the news during recent years and many people have been asking basic questions about them. Who are the Sikhs? Was not Sikhism founded by Guru Nanak who preached a combination of Hinduism and Islam, choosing the best of each and rejecting the remainder? When did they emerge as a people believing a distinctive faith? Are they not really Hindus of a particularly militant variety?

The questions 'Was Guru Nanak the founder of Sikhism?' and 'Is Sikhism a variety of Hinduism?' are misleading because the answers have to be both yes and no. Unquestionably, when Sikhs trace the foundation of Sikhism the line of descent stops at Guru Nanak (1469–1539), yet Nanak's doctrine was the *nām simaraṇ* (meditation on the divine Name) of the Sants. The Sant tradition of northern India developed among people who were predominantly Hindu with the contribution of Islam only marginal in importance. Since then the faith that today is called Sikhism has evolved in response to the pressure of ever-changing historical circumstances. Sikhs of the Khalsa today quite properly regard the dominant version of their faith as distinct from that of every variety of Hindu.

The pressure of historical circumstances began to produce significant changes in the time of the sixth Guru, Hargobind (1595–1644), and these changes became particularly marked under the

*Originally published in *History of Religions*, Vol. 31, No. 4, May 1992.

tenth Guru, Gobind Singh (1666–1708). It was Guru Gobind Singh who established the Khalsa as an order to which all dedicated Sikhs were expected to belong. This order was probably founded in 1699, and all its members were expected to adhere to a formal discipline of belief and behaviour, its prominent features being uncut hair and the carrying of arms. The political threat was now becoming serious. The Sikhs, organized into a tiny state on the edge of the Shivalik Hills, were increasingly threatened by surrounding hill chieftains and by the power of the Mughal empire on the plains. At the beginning of the eighteenth century the battles began that, during the next hundred years, were to transform the Panth (the Sikh community).

It is this century that constitutes the heroic period of Sikh tradition. Gopal Singh, a modern Sikh writer, describes the career and legacy of Guru Gobind Singh in the following terms:

Thus ended, at the young age of 42, an amazing character in the history of the human race. Assuming secular and spiritual responsibilities for not only his immediate followers, but for human freedom in this subcontinent, for man's dignity and his right to his personal beliefs and ways of life, at the tender age of 9, fatherless, surrounded by jealous and intriguing members of his ancestral family, by the hill chiefs around, and above all, the Mughal emperor and his viceroys, he gave a new secular hope and spiritual dynamism to a whole people. He moulded out of sheer clay men and women of steel, sparrows who could pounce upon the hawks and tear them open. Only three years after his death, the Sikhs under Banda were the masters of a large portion of territory in central and south-east Punjab and were threatening Delhi. Thirty years after, they were the masters of the Cis-Satluj states, and a major power in the territories lying between the Ganga and the Yamuna, after a life-and-death struggle which, in its heroism and sacrifice, has few parallels in the history of mankind.

The Guru had made death for a cause so popular that even when [a] price was put on the head of every Sikh, and the whole community was hounded out of its habitations and lived for years in the woods and hideout, not one surrendered or accepted defeat. By the end of the century, they had established their rule over the entire Punjab, and later also in Kashmir, Ladakh and the Pathanland right up to the Khyber Pass. For the first time in a thousand years of India's history, the tide of invasions had turned westwards. This was nothing short of a miracle.[1]

These are enthusiastic words, rather different from the kind of cautious qualified estimate one might expect from an academic historian. This is precisely why they have been chosen. Here our concern is not with the doubting queries and cautious judgements of academic historians. Our subject is history as it is popularly understood, not as it actually happened. To some extent we are indeed the products of the history that actually happened and for this reason we need the kind of research that will uncover that history. At the same time we are also the products of a dominant interpretation of that history, of the received tradition that selects and presents such aspects of the past as match the needs of our present circumstances and nourish the aspirations that we project into the future.

It should require little thought to appreciate the relevance of this issue to present circumstances or those of the recent past. No human situation can be adequately understood without reference to the history that created it, and that same history is commonly invoked as a means of defining a situation or of justifying proposed remedies. But which history do we need to know? Is it the history that actually happened, or should we be concentrating our attention on the history that is popularly believed to have happened? The obvious answer is that we should be concerned with both. The *useful* answer is that for any issue concerning present circumstances or future policies it is the latter that deserves our closer attention.

Because we are talking about two different perceptions of history, confusion can easily arise if we persist in using the same word to cover both varieties. If we reserve 'history' for what actually happened we are left with the need to find a term that will cover what is believed to have happened. There are two words that may appropriately be used to designate the popular version of history as opposed to the strictly academic or scholarly version. For general purposes the word 'tradition' is here preferred and is sometimes used. If, however, we are to engage in a close analysis of popular history there is a better term, and that is the word 'myth.'

There are, of course, some obvious objections that will be raised as soon as the word 'myth' is introduced. Two of these deserve to be noted before we proceed. We should first acknowledge that the word has been variously used by different disciplines and individuals, and that if it is to be effectively deployed a brief definition is necessary. It should also be remembered that in popular parlance 'myth' is typically accepted as a synonym for 'legend.' For this reason its usage can easily suggest that we speak of something that is not true. As the word is used here it is certainly not a synonym for 'legend,' nor does it necessarily imply untruth. A definition is obviously required.

The definition that is here offered is essentially the same as one I stated at greater length when venturing upon a study of the hagiographic narratives of the life of Guru Nanak (the *janam-sākhīs*).[2] We begin by contrasting that which happened (which we shall bravely call 'fact') with that which did not happen (which we shall call 'legend'). The word 'myth' corresponds to neither of these. Typically, it utilizes both fact and legend (or non-fact) in order to construct a particular interpretation of what took place. It may actually use nothing but fact and yet qualify as myth. Similarly its content may consist exclusively of legend. The essential point is that regardless of its sources it produces a coherent statement that amounts to an interpretation of the past. To this we should also add that in order to be effective it must be believable. We should also recognize that there is seldom anything sinister or contrived in the making and subsequent moulding of myths. It is a perfectly natural process, one that all cultures perform.

For present purposes this means that we are not speaking about the 'history' of the Sikh people during the eighteenth century but, rather, about the Sikh 'myth' of the eighteenth century. To be more specific, we can call it the myth of the rise and ultimate destiny of the Khalsa. As we have already noted the Khalsa was the order instituted by Guru Gobind Singh on the threshold of the eighteenth century, complete with ritual initiation (*amrit sanskār*) and a formal code of discipline (*rahit*).[3] The task of unravelling just how the Khalsa did, in fact, develop is an exceedingly complex one, and much remains to be done in this regard. The myth, however, is writ large and clear on each succeeding generation, and emphatically that applies to Sikh society today.

This myth is one that bears a close relationship to recent events and to claims that have been greatly strengthened by those events. For an understanding of the present situation in the Punjab it is not sufficient to focus our attention on such incidents as the Indian Army invasion of the Golden Temple complex in 1984 or the assassination of Mrs. Gandhi later in the same year. We need more than a narrative of these recent events, regardless of how accurate or detailed the account might be. We also require more than the kind of analysis that concentrates exclusively on political developments of the recent past. This too is both essential and insufficient. What we must also understand is the perception of Sikh history (the tradition or the myth) that lies behind current claims to justice and to the due recognition of distinctive Sikh rights.

Like all Sikh tradition the myth of the Khālsā is communicated to succeeding generations of Sikhs in a variety of ways. Those of us who spend much of our lives reading words on paper (or screens) are inclined to assume that the effective means will be literature, ranging from simple stories written for children to mature presentations intended for educated adults. The written word is certainly one of such means and its influence continues to grow. Some of its results are printed in English, many more in Punjabi. For the purposes of this essay we shall necessarily rely on this particular source and specifically on the English variety. In so doing we should remember that the Punjabi material is much more extensive, its idiom much more fluent, and its imagery much more colorful. As such it is vastly more influential.[4]

We should also remember that for all its influence the impact of popular literature is still secondary. The principal mediator of myth or tradition remains oral communication. This includes the telling of stories from Sikh history in Punjabi homes. It also includes the preaching regularly delivered in *gurduārās* (Sikh temples) and at the well-attended gatherings held to mark high points in the Sikh calendar. The stories told in homes and *gurduārās* are repeatedly reinforced by references and allusions occuring in conversation and in public addresses, the latter including the political speeches given with such frequency and vigour in the Punjab. Lest we are tempted to assume that political speeches supply the principal link between the myth and its contemporary application, let it be emphasized that the politicians speak to what is already firmly lodged in the minds and understanding of their listeners. Popular leaders certainly utilize and reinforce the tradition, but they do not create it, nor do they act as primary communicators of it.

The role of the *gurduārā* includes homilies (*kathā*), which repeatedly invoke Sikh tradition. It also includes the regular recitation of *Ardās*, the so-called Sikh Prayer. *Ardās* is recited in unison at the conclusion of most Sikh rituals (including routine services of worship), and for this reason we can assume that its words are firmly implanted in the minds and memories of a substantial proportion of Sikhs. The prayer consists of three parts and of these, the second portion calls to remembrance the past trials and triumphs of the Panth.[5] Its list includes the following: 'Those loyal members of the Khalsa who gave their heads for their faith; who were hacked limb from limb, scalped, broken on the wheel, or sawn asunder; who sacrificed their lives for the protection of hallowed gurdwaras, never forsaking their faith; and who were steadfast in their loyalty to the uncut hair of the true Sikh: reflect on their merits, O Khalsa, and call on God, saying, Vahiguru!'[6]

Popular art also serves to communicate and reinforce the same myth, and one variety has a considerable impact in this regard. This form is not the movie film, regardless of the current popularity of that particular medium in India. There is a traditional embargo on the dramatic representation of the lives of the Gurus, and to a considerable extent this carries over to the postguru traditions. The influential form is the colourful variety of picture variously known as calendar art or as the bazaar poster.

To European tastes these prints, with their uninhibited use of the primary colours, appear garish in the extreme and the evident naïveté of many such pictures can seem positively embarrassing. If we avert our gaze we miss an important point. Bazaar posters are enormously popular and as such they are bound to exercise a notable influence in moulding and sustaining the tradition. Although no one can accurately measure the relative popularity of individual prints the prime contender for the first place is probably a gruesome picture of the decapitated eighteenth-century warrior Baba Dip Singh. We shall return to Dip Singh later.[7]

If we move from bazaar posters to 'respectable' art we shall find the same themes represented with a somewhat greater subtlety of colour and line but little difference in terms of directness. This is particularly true of the influential work of Kirpal Singh, much of which was destroyed during the army assault on the Golden Temple complex. Kirpal Singh has concentrated his efforts on the more stirring episodes from Sikh tradition and several of his canvases were hung in the Sikh Museum attached to the Golden Temple. I well remember watching a group of village people standing spellbound before one of his more gory compositions.

My own awareness of the influence of tradition was also strengthened by student responses during the period I spent teaching Punjab history to Punjabi students. There was never any need for me to complete any of the popular jingles that tradition associates with the eighteenth-century Panth. I merely had to start one, and the students would take it up and carry it through to its conclusion.[8] The problem was that I believed my duty to be the inculcating of history as it actually happened. Against a firmly embedded pattern of traditional understanding the task proved to be a forbidding one. What I soon discovered was that the myth of the Khalsa was an inheritance that all my Sikh students had long since received and interiorized, a condition that ensured that my well-intentioned efforts met with very limited success. It was perhaps fortunate that I failed. Success on my part would presumably have ensured failure in the student's final examination, for the external examiners doubtless shared their perception of eighteenth-century Sikh history.

In case that personal aside should restore the notion that my use of the term 'myth' does, after all, mean something altogether different from historical truth let me repeat that the word is not to be set in opposition to such terms as 'fact' or 'accuracy.' Myth, as I understand and use the word, means interpretation and in order to be credible as an interpretation it must draw extensively from credible sources. In practice this will mean that much of its material is indeed factual. It is to be understood neither as a synonym for fact nor as a denial of that which is factual. What it typically supplies is a combination of fact and traditional belief, selective in terms of specific content and heavily glossed in order to reinforce its distinctive interpretation.

According to this perception of Sikh history the rise of the Khalsa can be conveniently divided into six phases. The first is the period that foreshadows the actual emergence of the Khalsa. This phase begins with the death of the fifth Guru, an event that occurred in 1606. Arjan, the fifth Guru, died while in Mughal custody and his death is traditionally viewed as martyrdom. Prior to his imprisonment he is believed to have commanded his son and successor, Hargobind, to sit fully armed on his throne,[9] and Guru Hargobind is believed to have responded by donning two swords. One sword represented the continuing spiritual authority of the Guru (*pīrī*) while the other signified a newly-assumed temporal role (*mīrī*).[10] The tradition may or may not be accurate. The essential point is that it is firmly believed to be accurate and that it legitimizes developments that were subsequently to occur within the Panth.

The second phase covers the eventful career of Gobind Singh, Guru from 1675 until 1708 and last in the line of personal Gurus. In his case also, accession to the office of Guru followed the execution (and thus the martyrdom) of his father. Threatened by neighbouring states in the Shivalik Hills the young Guru fought a number of battles, and these encounters also occupy an important place in the developing tradition of militancy. The critical event, however, was to be the founding of the Khalsa order in 1699.[11]

This crucial act on the part of the tenth Guru is variously interpreted by Sikh tradition. One view perceives it as a decision designed to turn sparrows into hawks, to convert a meek following into one that would defend itself against the growing threat of attack. Another stresses the need to ensure that Sikhs who shrank from recognition during the execution of the ninth Guru should never again be permitted to conceal their identity, an identity that would thereafter be proclaimed by the highly visible marks of Khalsa membership (notably the uncut hair). A more modern interpretation directs attention to the quest for justice rather than to the need for defence. All three are mutually compatible, and all three agree that 1699 marks the high point of Sikh history. All agree that the Guru's intention was to imbue his followers with the spirit of steel and that if need should thereafter arise the Sikhs must be prepared to fight.[12]

Immediately after the founding of the Khalsa the heroic century began with warfare that conspicuously involved the Mughal authorities of Sirhind. A lengthy siege was followed by the evacuation of the Guru's stronghold of Anandpur in 1704 and by his move to a remote area of southern Punjab. Tradition acknowledges that the Guru suffered considerable losses during the period, but it does not accept any suggestion of defeat. Instead it emphasizes the loyalty, heroism, and endurance of his followers and the supreme example set by the warrior Guru himself. What the rest of the world might well regard as a disaster is transformed into a pattern of strategic withdrawal leading to ultimate victory. The setbacks are, however, acknowledged as such, and in so doing tradition evokes the treachery and cruelty of those who opposed the Guru.

The third phase follows the death of Guru Gobind Singh and concerns the uprising under his military successor Banda, finally ending with Banda's execution by the Mughals in 1716. At this point the tradition falters. Banda is a mighty hero, one who fought bravely in obedience to his deceased master's command and eventually suffered the cruel death of a true martyr. There is, however, a distinct hint of ambivalence as far as Banda is concerned, for there are features of his personal belief and life-style that have not been fully assimilated by the myth. During his brief ascendancy within the Panth there evidently developed disputes concerning the true nature of the Khalsa, with Banda adopting attitudes that conflict with the orthodox view of the Khalsa.[13] Although he retains an honoured place in the role of martyred heroes he remains something of a problem.

With the execution of Banda and the beginning of the fourth phase all trace of ambivalence disappears. This is the period of persecution, the final years of Mughal strength and a time of great hardship and suffering for those who were prepared to stand forth as Sikhs of the Khalsa. Tradition represents it as the period when a determined effort was made to exterminate the Sikhs once and for all. The rapid disintegration of Mughal power did not end this phase, for the Mughals were followed as persecutors by the servants of the Afghan ruler Ahmad Shah Abdali. Ahmad Shah Abdali led a series of invasions beginning in 1747, and the Sikhs were to be numbered among his targets. It was a futile campaign. By the time Abdali died in 1772 the Sikhs were well into the fifth phase, the period that was to witness the triumph of Sikh arms in the Punjab.

Throughout the course of the persecution phase the Sikhs (or such of them as were prepared to display their identity) were subjected to all manner of harassment, torture, and violent death. This treatment they steadfastly endured, spending much of their time in jungles and sandy wastes where pursuit was difficult. There they developed new patterns of war-fare, a guerilla style of fighting that was to serve first as a protection and then as an increasingly successful means of offence. Groups of armed warriors were formed (*jathā*), and these were loosely organized as armies (*dal*). The emphasis, however, was on mobility, and this strategy, combined with the daring bravery of those who adopted it, carried the Khalsa into its period of triumph.

The fifth phase or period of triumph is interpreted as a mixed blessing by the tradition. The scattered *jathās* had meanwhile been consolidated into twelve larger groups called *misals*, and it was a loose alliance of the *misals* that effectively destroyed the enemies of the Panth. Success, however, was soon followed by the problems of success, and *misal* leaders who had combined to overthrow a common enemy were now increasingly inclined to compete with each other. A period of internecine warfare seemed to be developing.

The threat of disruption within the Khalsa was averted by the military and political skills of that great hero of the Panth, Maharaja Ranjit Singh. Emerging as the youthful leader of one of the *misals* (the Shukerchakia *misal*) Ranjit Singh progressively picked off his rivals by negotiation, marriage, or force. In 1799 he secured control of Lahore, and in 1801 he was formally invested with the title of Maharaja of the Punjab. The final phase, the period of unification, had reached its climax. For many this was to be the fulfilment of the ambition so dramatically expressed in the eighteenth-century Khalsa slogan *rāj karegā khālsā*, 'the Khalsa shall rule.' Triumphant over its enemies and united under a single leader, the Khalsa now ruled the Punjab. During the course of a single century it had resisted a powerful foe, suffered a determined persecution, endured unnumbered cruelties, and had yet survived. It had fought bravely and with consummate skill to weaken and eventually destroy those who had once plotted the destruction of the Khalsa. Triumphant it now ruled its homeland, the Punjab, and as long as Ranjit Singh remained its leader, even mighty Britain was constrained to stay its grasping hand.

Such is the myth of the rise of the Khalsa, and let us repeat yet again that it represents neither critical history nor a collection of legends. It is an enormously powerful myth, a version of history that pits truth and justice against treachery and cruel oppression. On one side there are heroes and martyrs, on the other bigots and tyrants. Bravery contends with low cunning, steadfast loyalty with barbarism. Bestriding all is the compelling figure of Guru Gobind Singh, creator of the Khalsa and its supreme exemplar. If anyone should ever doubt the appeal still exercised by this particular man a brief survey of popular Sikh literature and popular Sikh art will soon dispel any such notion.

As noted earlier it is popular literature and art that provide the principal sources for our understanding of the myth, usefully supplemented by listening to sermons or conversation. It is important to realize that much of what claims to be scholarly is in fact popular as far as its treatment of the eighteenth century is concerned. I have already cited a passage from Gopal Singh's *A History of the Sikh People* as an example. To that can be added such works as *A Short History of the Sikhs* by Teja Singh and Ganda Singh and G.S. Chhabra's *Advanced Study in the History of the Punjab*. These we note because they are widely accepted as authoritative. Although far removed from the crude presentations of the truly popular style, they nevertheless project the same interpretation.

Indeed, we can venture even further into the realm of scholarly publication without losing sight of the myth. We can also locate it in the works of British writers whose publications extend from the late eighteenth century to the early twentieth and beyond. Although one will detect in them distinct notes of caution, the earliest generation of British observers were dependent on Sikh informants for much of their information, and with good reason to be impressed by the military skills of the Sikhs, they were strongly inclined to accept the myth in general terms. Joseph Cunningham projects it clearly in *A History of the Sikhs*, thus supplying a major reason for the book's remarkably durable popularity. M.A. Macauliffe does not deal with the greater part of the eighteenth century, but his treatment of Guru Gobind Singh in *The Sikh Religion* is thoroughly in accord with the traditional interpretation.[14]

In these works and their less sophisticated companions certain themes can be easily identified. Some of these themes concern particular qualities of the Sikhs, others the evil nature of their adversaries. Together they combine to produce a cluster of objectives expressing the perceived purpose for which the Khalsa was founded and the glorious climax of its eighteenth-century experience. To these themes we shall now turn, and having listed them I shall briefly note their continuing application to the twentieth-century experience of the Panth. In most instances I shall add an appropriate illustration from one of the books mentioned above or from some other relevant source.

An analysis of the Sikh role delivers at least nine major themes, the first of them being defiance. Here, as everywhere, the supreme example is Guru Gobind Singh himself, and the instance that receives particular attention is the letter entitled *Zafar-nāmā* which he addressed to the Mughal emperor Aurangzeb. 'This letter,' comments Gopal Singh, 'breathes defiance and contempt for an earthly power which is yoked to tyranny and sin, and lays down the eternal rule that he alone wins in the end whose cause is just.'[15]

To defiance is added the sword, leading us to a second theme. Here too the prime example must be Guru Gobind Singh. *Bachitar Nāṭak*, an autobiographical work attributed to the Guru, begins with a salute and an invocation to the sword.

Reverently I salute the Sword with affection and devotion.
Grant, I pray, your divine assistance that this book may be brought to completion.
Thee I invoke, All-conquering Sword, Destroyer of evil, Ornament of the brave.
Powerful your arm and radiant your glory, your splendour as dazzling as the brightness of the sun.
Joy of the devout and Scourge of the wicked, Vanquisher of sin, I seek your protection.
Hail to the world's Creator and Sustainer, my invincible Protector the Sword![16]

This, it will be noted, is no ordinary sword. The sword that Guru Gobind Singh here salutes, the sword that is similarly invoked at the beginning of *Ardās*, is Akal Purakh made manifest. It is the God of justice visibly present as a sword wielded in defence of truth and righteousness. The second theme is not merely armed defiance. It is that the divine purpose is served by physical warfare waged on behalf of truth and justice.

The third theme follows naturally from the first two. The defiant warrior wielding the divine sword in defence of his faith is, predictably, distinguished by his conspicuous bravery. Heroism is the third theme, a quality that informs the entire narrative of the rise of the Khalsa from its first beginnings to its final triumph. A popular example is the story of how the debauched and sacrilegious Massa Ranghar met his death in 1740.

After Abdul Rehman had been killed at Amritsar, one Massa Rangar Mandyalia was appointed as the Kotwal of the city. Massa sat inside the temple, and there, with dancing girls to pacify his passion, and wine to quench his thirst, he defiled the sanctity of the place, where scriptures used to be read and God used to be praised. The blood-curdling details of such deeds reached the Sikhs in their hide-outs, and sent thrills of horror into their nerves. The news of this also reached one Mehtab Singh, who during the days of utter persecutions, having left his village, Miran Kot, near Amritsar, had taken up a service at Bikanir. His spirit revolted within himself, and taking with him Sukha Singh of Kambho Mari, he prepared the steeds and galloped towards Amritsar.

They purchased a few bags, filled them half with stones and half with coins, and dressing as revenue collectors, presented themselves at the gate of the temple, demanding permission to enter and present the revenue to Massa. The permission was forthwith granted, and the Sikhs entering Massa's presence, made their obeisance. As Massah bent to receive the money, down came a falchion, and like a flash of lightning, Mehtab Singh severed Massa's head from his body, and the two Sikhs rode back brandishing their swords, and leaving behind a mass of terror-stricken attendants and people looking aghast.[17]

Mere daring, however, is insufficient. The soldiers of the eighteenth-century Khalsa were certainly brave, but their reputation relied on much more than reckless dash. There was method in their warfare, and the fighting skills of the Khalsa constitute a fourth theme. These skills include their dexterous use of the sword and other weapons, their prowess as horsemen, their bewildering mobility, and their brilliant strategy. In some situations strategy required stratagem and again the Guru set an example for his Sikhs to follow. During the siege of Anandpur in 1704 his enemies promised him safe conduct if he would agree to abandon his fortress. 'The Guru's mother and some Sikhs approached the Guru to accept the offer, but to demonstrate the futility of putting reliance upon the enemy's promises, the Guru sent but some bullocks loaded with rags and stones covered with golden clothes, giving out that it was the Guru's treasure and the Sikhs and he himself were to follow it. As however, the bullocks passed through the enemy lines, they were looted out only to their disappointment.'[18]

Quick of wit and nimble of limb his followers likewise proved to be more than a match for much larger forces. Disaster certainly befell the Khalsa during its long struggle, but invariably it was the product of treachery, overwhelming numbers, or sheer exhaustion. A single soldier of the Khalsa was *savā lakh*, the equivalent of 125,000 opponents. In this celebrated claim we perceive another distinctive feature of the tradition, namely its use of irony and exaggeration in order to make a serious point.

To the fighting skills of the soldier were added the endurance and dogged perseverance of all who accepted the Khalsa identity. This applies to the women as well as to the men. A distinctive feature of the tradition is its frequent reference to the supportive role of Sikh women; if men were distinguished by their resilience, so too were the women. The Sikhs of the eighteenth century never gave up, and their stubborn endurance supplies a fifth theme.

Hearing that the Sikhs had renewed their rebellious activities with redoubled force, [Mir Manu] gave orders to seize them wherever they could be found, and put them to the sword without pity. About 900 of them were killed when the fortress of Ram Rauni was attacked and captured. The countryside was scoured and cartloads of them were brought to Lahore each day and hammered to death. When Sikh homes were divested of men, their women were captured along with their children, and asked to change their faith on pain of extreme torture. Their children were cut up into pieces before their eyes and they were made to wear garlands of their severed heads, but not one of these determined women either abjured her faith ... or showed any dread of a painful and merciless death.

Hundreds were captured under the personal command of Mir Manu and put to death at the *Nakhas* (horse-market) of Lahore, known by the Sikhs as *Shahid Ganj* [the place of martyrdom]. Wells were filled with their heads. But the Khalsa took it all stoically.[19]

For many the price that had to be paid was death. Martyrdom thus emerges as one of the most powerful of the many intertwined themes. Two of the Gurus had met martyrs' deaths during the seventeenth century, and in the eighteenth century many Sikhs were to follow their noble example. The list of names is a lengthy one,[20] with a select group conspicuous for the quality of their devotion and the bravery with which they embraced death. Bhai Mani Singh, brutally butchered limb by limb in 1738, is a famous instance.[21] If the evidence of bazaar posters is any indication, three martyrs command a particular prominence in the modern consciousness. These are the two children of Guru Gobind Singh, bricked up alive by the governor of Sirhind, and the celebrated Dip Singh to whom I alluded earlier.

In spite of the exposure of so many Sikhs to suffering and martyrdom the tradition does not suggest that they retaliated in a similar manner. Vengeance, as well shall see, does indeed emerge as a resultant theme, but at this point it is the theme of compassionate service that I note. Regardless of their identity or allegiance, all who suffered were entitled to humane treatment. For this theme the most popular example is undoubtedly Guru Gobind Singh's servant Bhai Kanihya, a name greatly honored in Sikh tradition. During the siege of Anandpur, 'a Sikh called Bhai Kanihya was reported to the Guru as ministering water to the fallen in battle, irrespective of [whether they were] friend or foe. The Guru called him to his presence and asked him why he was offering water to the enemy's wounded. Kanihya replied, "Since you've taught me to make no distinction between man and man, I do not see amongst the wounded any but you." The Guru was so much pleased with this reply that he blessed him with salvation.'[22]

Gratitude toward all who assisted the Guru or his Sikhs can also be identified as a distinctive theme with a continuing influence. This particularly concerns those who might normally have been expected to support the enemies of the Khalsa, and in eighteenth-century circumstances that usually meant Muslims. A famous example that still evokes a response was the protest lodged by the Nawab of Malerkotla against the decision of the governor of Sirhind to execute the infant sons of Guru Gobind Singh. In 1710 Banda's army razed Sirhind but left Malerkotla unharmed; and during the Partition disturbances of 1947 it was again spared. It remains to this day a tiny Muslim island in Indian Punjab.[23]

Gratitude is a response directed to those who assisted the Sikhs without actually being members of the Panth. It is not for the Sikhs themselves, for they only perform their duty. For them the requirement was unwavering loyalty in all circumstances, and the loyalty that every Sikh was expected to show constitutes yet another of the tradition's major themes. It was a loyalty that every true Sikh gave to the Guru. While Guru Gobind Singh lived it was bestowed on him directly, and after he had died it attached to those features of the Panth that represented his explicit command or that embodied his continuing presence. The command was that Sikhs should observe the discipline of the Khalsa (the *rahit*), and a prime aspect of loyalty was thus construed as the faithful observance of its outward symbols. The continuing presence of the eternal Guru was (and remains) manifest in the sacred scripture (the Guru Granth) and in the gathered community (the Guru Panth). Loyalty to the Guru also meant loyalty to the word of the scripture and to the will of the Panth.

These nine themes concern the duty of the Sikh. We turn now to their enemies and begin by noting that three of the counter themes are actually identical with prominent aspects of the Khalsa role. The Mughal and the Afghan may not be the equal of the Khalsa as soldiers, but they are neither sluggards nor craven cowards. Bravery, fighting skills, and determination are all features of the hostile attacks so persistently mounted against the Sikhs during the course of the eighteenth century. This should come as no surprise. By highlighting the strength of the enemy, the myth simultaneously throws the quality of the Sikh response into sharper relief.

There are, however, other weapons at the disposal of the enemy and an important one is treachery. This we have already illustrated in the spurious promise of safe conduct offered to Guru Gobind Singh at Anandpur. Two other famous examples are provided by the career of Guru Gobind Singh, the first of them being the betrayal of the Guru's children to the governor of Sirhind.

The Guru moved on to Jatpura, from where he was befriended by another Mohammedan, Rai Kalha, who offered his services to him unreservedly. The Guru asked him to send somebody to Sarhind to get information about the fate of his little sons. The messenger sent by Rai Kalha returned in a few days and brought the sad news that the children had been done to death. The bereaved father received the news with perfect composure. Checking his tear and turning his sorrow into strong resolve, he muttered, 'No, no, my sons are not dead. They refused to barter their religion. They live for ever. It is Sarhind that shall die.' Saying this, he knocked out a shrub with his arrow, and added, 'The enemy shall be uprooted like this.'[24]

The second was the treacherous attack, attributed by many to Vazir Khan of Sirhind, that led eventually to the Guru's death.

Soon after, one night, as the Guru was retiring to his bed in his camp, a young Pathan ... entered into his presence. The man had visited the Guru earlier also during the last few days claiming to be his devotee. As this visit was not considered unusual, no one stopped him. The Guru offered him *prasād* (sanctified food) which the rascal devoured at once. Then, as the Guru was bidding him good-bye and in the process of reclining on his bed, he plunged a dagger into the Guru's illustrious body twice. The Guru jumped from his bed with the speed of an angry lion, drew his sword and chopped off the head of the fleeing assassin.[25]

Cruelty, vicious and unsparing, was also a part of the enemy response, a countertheme to the tradition's emphasis on the loyalty and resolute endurance of the true Khalsa Sikh. 'In this campaign [of 1746, the Mughal troops under Lakhpat Rai] must have killed at least seven thousand, besides three thousand brought as prisoners to Lahore. These too were beheaded at the Nakhas, after being subjected to indignities and torture. Their heads were piled up in the form of pyramids, and their mangled bodies were interred under the walls of a mosque.'[26]

The enemies who so brutally strove to subdue the Sikhs during the eighteenth century are variously identified as Mughals and Afghans. To this extent they are perceived as distinct and different opponents. From another perspective, however, they are perceived as a single foe. Both were Muslim peoples and during the eighteenth century Muslims as such came to be regarded as the sworn enemies of the Panth. This is evident both from the eighteenth-century narratives and also from the early *rahit-nāmās* (the recorded versions of the Khalsa code of conduct).[27] The antipathy thus generated supplies another theme, one that has been muted in the twentieth-century presentation but which nevertheless remains a part of the tradition. Muslims are the traditional enemies of the Khalsa. It is also worth nothing that the center of Muslim power was usually perceived to be Delhi and that a suspicion of power emanating from Delhi is arguably another feature of the myth.

The Panth's role is thus defined by a cluster of themes and, likewise, by the role of its enemies. From the conflict between the two there emerge some general themes, aspects of the interpretation that serve to define the nature of the struggle and the objectives to which it leads.

The first of these themes has already been noted. Because it has been unjustly attacked and viciously assaulted, the Khalsa is entitled to take revenge. Vengeance is perceived to be a legitimate response.

As such it is incorporated into the tradition as a part of the justification that it offers for the policies and actions of the eighteenth-century Khalsa. Vazir Khan, the governor of Sirhind, was to be killed and his city laid waste because he had so cruelly executed the innocent sons of the Guru. Massa Ranghar was to be slain because he had willfully defiled the most sacred of all holy places. Jahan Khan was to be challenged by Baba Dip Singh because he had plundered Amritsar, demolished its temple, and filled the sacred pool with rubbish. The theme of vengeance runs through the tradition, demanding a justly punitive retaliation and unflinching sacrifice.

This, however, is only a part of the explanation. The violence required of the Khālsā during its eighteenth-century struggle depends upon much more than mere vengeance for its justification. Violence should never be capricious or unprovoked. The nature of acceptable violence is clearly indicated by two famous extracts from works attributed to Guru Gobind Singh. The first, sometimes called the Prayer of Guru Gobind Singh, occurs in a work entitled *Chaṇḍī charitra*.

Strengthen me, O Lord, that I shrink not from righteous deeds,
That freed from the fear of my enemies I may fight with faith and win.
The wisdom which I crave is the grace to sing your praises.
When this life's allotted course has run may I met my death in battle.[28]

The second is from *Zafar-nāmā*, the letter that the Guru is believed to have addressed to Aurangzeb.

When all other methods have been explored and all other means have been tried,
Then may the sword be drawn from the scabbard, then may the sword be used.[29]

The sword may be drawn only if truth and righteousness are assailed, and only as a last resort. If they are attacked, and if no other defence will serve, the sword must finally be drawn for their protection.

This definition is fundamental, yet it is not the final word as far as the tradition is concerned. From defence the myth proceeds to offense as surely as the scattered *jathās* consolidated to form the victorious *misals*. The theme that this invokes is the triumph of justice. Mere resistance to the tyrant is not enough. Curbing his evil power may be the objective during the early struggle, but eventually his authority must be overthrown.

This in turn leads to the ultimate theme of sovereignty. Who will rule in the tyrant's place? *Rāj karegā khālsā*! 'The Khalsa shall rule!' This is the destiny of the Khalsa, fulfilled in the time of Maharaja Ranjit Singh yet never laid to rest. Whenever tyrants arise, whenever injustice reigns, whenever the Panth is threatened, then must the Khalsa prepare again for struggle. The call to duty may come to any generation. Their destiny is eternal.

It needs little imagination to appreciate how easily this tradition can be applied to the circumstances of the twentieth century. In some respects it has been modified and adapted. 'Democracy' is a word that figures prominently in the twentieth-century version, and so too is 'secular' (by which is meant equal respect for all religions). This distinctively Indian sense of the word 'secular' reflects the greatly diminished emphasis on the role of Muslims as enemies. The overtone is, however, still audible, and it is now accompanied by strong antagonism toward 'Hindu domination.' This latter feature received encouragement a century ago during the period of the Sikh Sabha movement, finding its most famous expression in Kahn Singh Nabha's small book *Ham Hindū Nahīn* (We are not Hindus).[30] Whereas Kahn Singh's approach was avowedly eirenic, the theme has since acquired an increasing sharpness, and for many Sikhs it now amounts to open hostility. Specifically, it is opposition to what is perceived as the Brahman rule of New Delhi or, sometimes, the Brahman-Bania rule.

During the Singh Sabha period (extending from 1873 into the early years of the twentieth century) the myth of the eighteenth century was invoked in order to assert a clear and distinct Sikh identity.[31] In the early 1920s it powerfully supported the Akalis in their efforts to secure control of the principal Sikh *gurduārās*, and since independence in 1947 it has similarly buttressed claims for a distinctively Sikh role in the political fortunes of the Punjab. It significantly aided the drive toward Punjabi Suba (the redrawing of the Punjab boundaries in order to create a Punjabi-speaking state) and from the successful conclusion of that campaign in 1966 it leads on to claims for a larger measure of state autonomy.

During the greater part of the present century the traditional Sikh understanding of Khalsa history has remained a significant feature of the life of the Panth without seriously polarizing Punjabi society or demanding real sacrifice. There are, however, major exceptions to be noted. The Akali campaign that lasted from 1920 until 1925 significantly raised Khalsa consciousness, and Partition in 1947 produced a disaster of unparalleled proportions. Each of these episodes was followed by quieter times and during the early years of Independence the prospect of communal harmony in Indian Punjab seemed reasonably promising. Recent events have seriously eroded that hope. As all the world knows, troubles have returned to the Punjab. Many Sikhs believe that the Panth is under attack and that justice has been denied. In making these claims they inevitably invoke yet again the Khalsa traditions of the eighteenth century.

The attack on the Golden Temple complex in June 1984 has proved to be an event of dire significance. Together with related incidents preceding and following it, the Golden Temple assault has produced a continuing crisis, punctuated by violent acts and recurrent confrontation. Although the Sikh community is by no means united in its demands there is certainly a widespread belief that due rights are being withheld by a government that offers the unity of India as a convenient pretext for justifying its own political interests. For those of moderate inclination the claim remains a demand for a larger state autonomy. For those of radical persuasion it now embraces the ideal of an independent Khalistan.

There are thus significant differences within the community with regard to the precise nature of the objective and the approved means of securing it. This does not mean, however, that the Khalsa tradition has lost its appeal for all but the extremist few. Such a conclusion would be a very dangerous one to draw, for it would lend support to policies that can only prolong the conflict. The tradition teaches Sikhs to be resolute, and resolute they will assuredly remain. That is one of the many reasons why the tradition must be understood if the current crisis is to be comprehended fully and speedily resolved. There are in fact as many reasons as there are themes in the tradition. Loyalty, heroism, and defiance are ideals that still survive and that still command a powerful respect. If we object that the tradition is not always faithful to the actual facts we miss the point. What counts is history as a people actually understand it, and for most Sikhs that history dwells in the present as much as in the past.

Notes

1. Gopal Singh, *A History of the Sikh People, 1469–1978* (New Delhi: World Sikh University Press, 1979), p. 326.
2. W.H. McLeod, *Early Sikh Tradition; A Study of the janam-sākhīs* (Oxford: Clarendon, 1980), chap. 2.
3. W.H. McLeod, *Textual Sources for the Study of Sikhism* (Chicago: University of Chicago Press, 1990), pp. 34–37, 83–86.

4. These range from the numerous works of Satibir Singh on the individual Gurus, through Baba Prem Hoti Mardan's *Khālsā rāj de usaraīe* (Ludhiana: Lahore Book Shop, c. 1942), to all manner of popular presentation.

5. Teja Singh, *Sikhism: Its Ideals and Institutions* (Calcutta: Orient Longman, 1951), pp. 120-33. McLeod, *Textual Sources for the Study of Sikhism*, (Manchester: Manchester University Press, 1984) pp. 103-05.

6. McLeod, *Textual Sources for the Study of Sikhism*, p. 104. *Vāhigurū* literally means 'praise to the guru' but nowadays is usually translated as 'wonderful Lord.' Originally an ascription of praise, *Vāhigurū* is now used as a name for Akal Purakh or God.

7. For a detailed description of the nature and range of bazaar posters, see W.H. McLeod, *Popular Sikh Art* (New Delhi: Oxford University Press, 1991). A reproduction of the Dip Singh print appears in *Popular Sikh Art*, p. 124.

8. A famous example concerns Mir Manu, the hostile governor of the Punjab in the mid-eighteenth century. G.S. Chhabra gives its text in Punjabi in *Advanced History of the Punjab*, rev. ed. (Jullundur City: New Academic Publishing, 1968), 1: 396. For the text in roman, together with translation, see Gopal Singh, *op.cit.*, p. 391.

9. M.A. Macauliffe, *The Sikh Religion*, 6 vols (Oxford: Clarendon, 1909), 3: 99.

10. Teja Singh and Ganda Singh, *A Short History of the Sikhs* (Bombay: Orient Longman, 1950), p. 38; Chhabra, *op.cit.*, p. 200.

11. For a cautiously reliable account of the founding of the Khalsa, see J.S. Grewal and S.S. Bal, *Guru Gobind Singh* (Chandigarh: Punjab University, 1967), chap. 6 and app. C, pp. 103-26, 182-89.

12. This and the succeeding episodes can be found in each of the general histories chosen for examination in this account, namely, Singh and Singh (no. 10 above); Chhabra (no. 8 above); and Gopal Singh (n. 1 above).

13. Gopal Singh acknowledges these attitudes as follows: 'However, it must be conceded that something did happen somewhere which must have irked the devout Sikhs of the Guru like, for instance, his innovation of a new war-slogan, "*Fateh Darshan*."' This, however, is followed by the assurance: 'And yet, when all is said, the same Sikh chroniclers credit him, to the end, with the forbearance, the patience and the religious zeal of a true Sikh even with the miraculous powers bestowed upon him, according to them, by Guru Gobind Singh' (*op.cit.*, pp. 355, 356).

14. Joseph Cunningham, *A History of the Sikhs* (London: John Murray, 1849); Macauliffe, *op.cit.*, vol. 5.

15. Gopal Singh, *op.cit.*, p. 310.

16. *Dasam Granth* (Amritsar: Bhai Javahar Singh Kirpal Singh, 1967), p. 39. Although *Bachitar Nāṭak* is traditionally attributed to Guru Gobind Singh there is a strong case to be made for regarding it as the work of

one of his followers (see Surjit Singh Hans, *A Reconstruction of Sikh History from Sikh Literature* [Jalandhar: ABS Publications, 1988], p. 229).

17. Chhabra, *op.cit.*, pp. 369–70.

18. Ibid., p. 301.

19. Gopal Singh, *op.cit.*, p. 391.

20. Lakshman Singh, *Sikh Martyrs* (Madras: Ganesh, 1923), pp. 57 ff.

21. Singh and Singh, pp. 124–25; Chhabra, *op.cit.*, pp. 361–62. Gopal Singh, *op.cit.*, pp. 368–9.

22. Ibid., p. 304.

23. C.H. Loehlin, *The Sikhs and Their Scriptures* (Lucknow: Lucknow Publishing House, 1958), pp. 18–19. Other examples are provided by the Muslims who are said to have assisted Guru Gobind Singh during his retreat from Chamkaur following the evacuation of Anandpur, especially the two Pathans Nabbi Khan and Ghani Khan (Singh and Singh, *op.cit.*, p. 74).

24. Singh and Singh, *op.cit.*, p. 74.

25. Gopal Singh, *op.cit.*, p. 323.

26. Singh and Singh, *op.cit.*, p. 134.

27. W.H. McLeod, *The Chaupā Singh Rahit-nāmā* (Dunedin: University of Otago Press, 1987), introduction, p. 26.

28. *Chaṇḍī charitra* 231 (*Dasam Granth* [n. 16 above], p. 99); McLeod, *Textual Sources for the Study of Sikhism* (n. 3 above), p. 55.

29. *Dasam Granth*, p. 1390.

30. Kahn Singh Nabha, *Ham Hindū Nahīn* (Amritsar: Khalsa Press, 1899).

31. Strictly speaking this was not the influence of the Singh Sabha so much as of its radical sector, the Tat Khalsa. The Tat Khalsa were concerned with the question of how Sikh identity was to be defined as opposed to Hindu or any other kind of identity. The influential Sanatan Sikhs, who opposed them within the Singh Sabha, were concerned to represent themselves as a special variety of Hindu.

6

THE CONTRIBUTION OF THE
SINGH SABHA MOVEMENT TO
THE INTERPRETATION OF SIKH
HISTORY AND RELIGION*

We begin by stating our thesis. The contribution of the Singh Sabha movement to the dominant interpretation of Sikh history and religion is immense. It would be true to say that the protagonists of the movement created a new mould for our understanding of all things Sikh, and that everyone coming after them (whether Sikhs themselves or others interested in Sikhism) have been affected by their work. For the ordinary Sikh their influence has been substantial. For most Sikh intellectuals and western observers it has been total, virtually every view of Sikh history and religion being seen through Singh Sabha eyes and interpreted in the light of Singh Sabha understanding. The Singh Sabha interpretation has, for almost a century, been orthodox. All other interpretations are wayward, sectarian, or heretical.

Before taking up the question of a definition of the Singh Sabha we should first note that in any question involving the Sikh people history and religion are intimately bound together. It is not possible, except in the very narrowest sense, to answer historical issues without simultaneously handling religious questions and vice versa. In theory it may be possible to consider religious or historical matters in isolation, but in practice the influence of the other must be brought to bear on it almost immediately. One

*Originally published in Andrew, Matheson & Rae, eds, *Religious Studies in Dialogue: Essays in Honour of Albert C. Moore*, University of Otago, Dunedin, 1991.

cannot imagine the Sikhs without their history any more than they can be represented without their religion. The two are inextricably tied one to the other.

The Singh Sabha[1] is a reform movement dating from the early years of British rule of the Punjab. Following the British defeat of the Punjabi armies in the two Anglo-Sikh wars of the 1840s and the final annexation of the Punjab in 1849 the Sikh faith seemed to continue a steady decline. British observers confidently predicted the eventual demise of the Khalsa.[2] This, at least, was the interpretation of events imposed by worried Sikhs and by those westerners with a passing interest in their future.

In fact the decline of the Panth (the Sikh community) was not nearly so pronounced as it seemed,[3] but it was certainly believed by some of its members to be sufficiently serious to give rise to deep anxiety. How were Sikhs to be distinguished from their Hindu neighbours, particularly in the villages of the Punjab? They were (so the interpretation proceeded) abandoning the Rahit (the Sikh code of belief and behaviour) and promiscuously adopting outward forms which made it quite impossible to distinguish them from Hindus. Sikhs were practising caste conventions as routinely as Hindus and their distinctive form of worship was grievously disfigured by manifestly Hindu customs. Even in the precincts of the Golden Temple in Amritsar, the holiest of Sikh holies, idols had been installed and were being freely adored.

This wave rolling across the Panth (so the interpretation proceeded) merely continued what had been practices carried out under the rule of the great Sikh sovereign, Maharaja Ranjit Singh. Before Ranjit Singh died in 1839 costly jewels had been distributed to Brahmans in the hope that this would guarantee him favoured treatment after death; and when he actually did die four of his wives, together with seven concubines, burned themselves on his funeral pyre in the Hindu rite of suttee.

During the lifetime of Maharaja Ranjit Singh people had indeed become concerned about the course which was being adopted and had sought a return to the pristine ways of the Gurus. These were notably the Nirankaris and the Namdharis, both of which laid strong emphasis on the all-important need for Sikhs to return to the way of *nām simaran*, to disciplined remembrance of the divine Name as the only means of liberation for the human soul.[4] Both, however, had departed in other ways from the pure essence of the faith. The real enemy was Hindu tradition and if the wave was not arrested it would end up by submerging all that the Sikh Gurus had preached to their people.

In 1873 four Sikh students attending the Mission School in Amritsar announced their intention of taking baptism and some of their elders, who were already worried, felt that the time had come for action. Not only the Hindus but also the Christians (not to mention the Muslims) taught a different way to their people and the indication that four young Sikhs were going to transfer their allegiance to the Church was cause for serious alarm. A meeting was held in the city by prominent Sikhs and a decision was taken to form a society for the protection of the faith. In this manner the first Singh Sabha (or Singh Society) was born. Conspicuous amongst its early members were titled gentry, affluent landowners, and noted scholars, and this generally upper-class character remained characteristic of the Amritsar group. A programme was planned for the pursuit of its distinctively Sikh objectives and in this programme the distribution of appropriate literature figured prominently.

A second Singh Sabha was formed in Lahore in 1879 and although the two groups were very similar in terms of general ideals the Lahore Singh Sabha proved to be much more aggressive than that of Amritsar in which princely interests and large land ownership played an important part. By contrast the Lahore group attracted more intellectuals, men who could be counted on to pursue a more radical programme as they understood them. As fresh societies were formed in different parts of the Punjab they allied with either the Amritsar group (the more conservative) or, more frequently, with the Lahore group (the more forthright). The two wings of the movement were united as the Chief Khalsa Diwan in 1902, but the two varieties retained their differing emphases and pursued their differing programmes.

Those who represented the conservative branch in Amritsar and elsewhere came to be known as the Sanatan Khalsa (the 'Traditional Khalsa'). Prominent amongst its leaders was the influential Khem Singh Bedi, a direct descendant of Guru Nanak and greatly revered by the Sikh masses for this reason. The radical or reformist section of the Singh Sabha was called the Tat Khalsa (the 'True Khalsa' or the 'Pure Khalsa'), initially led by such men as Gurmukh Singh (a professor from a Lahore college) and Dit Singh (an outcaste Sikh and a vigorous supporter of social reform in the Panth).[5] The British naturally favoured the former group, calling the Tat Khalsa neo-Sikhs and regarding them as a little too inclined to promote disturbance.

There were several causes which accounted for the division between these two factions. The one which concerns us here is the difference separating them over their respective views of Sikh tradition. The Sanatan interpretation was that Sikhs were, after all, one variety of Hindus and although they might have different ways of worship and behaviour they were nevertheless Hindus. Guru Nanak, the first Guru of the Sikhs, had been born a Hindu and he died one as well. His Sikhs (his 'Learners' or 'Disciples') were merely following him in this most important of all respects, Hindus like all others who owned the Sikh identity yet distinctively different in their approach to the way of liberation.

History and religion (so said the Sanatan Sikhs) needed to be interpreted in this light. Sikhs were a part of the wider Hindu world and their traditions should be seen as a distinctive aspect of this larger whole. Guru Gobind Singh had established the Khalsa, a feature of great significance but not one which separated its members from the Hindu society which surrounded them. The Khalsa was a voluntary society within the Sikh Panth and those that joined it did so in order that they might protect other Hindus from Mughal oppression. The Sahaj-dhari Sikhs (those who cut their hair and did not observe the other features of the Rahit) were particularly insistent on this view. Sikhs could choose to join the Khalsa or refrain from doing so. They were not thereby disqualified from revering the Gurus, from attending the gurdwara, or from offering homage to the Adi Granth (the Guru Granth Sahib or sacred scripture of the Sikhs). And they would continue to observe caste, the bonding which cemented all Hindus together in a single whole. Sikh society gave abundant proof of this, with every Sikh born into a particular caste and obeying the laws which were prescribed for that caste.

The followers of the Tat Khalsa view would have none of this and it was the Tat Khalsa interpretation which ultimately came to be identified as that of the Singh Sabha. Men who upheld this view asserted a claim to interpret Sikh tradition and to determine the belief and behaviour of all who regarded themselves as Sikhs. In other words, they laid claim to speak as the voice of orthodoxy and in the years ahead they progressively won a widely-accepted confirmation of their right to do so. Nowdays when we speak of the Singh Sabha we normally mean the Tat Khalsa. When we describe the historiography, doctrinal formulations, and social policy of the Singh Sabha we invariably do so.

As scholars or students of Sikh history and religion we implicitly accept, when referring to these interpretations, that we are accurately describing Sikh history and religion. We believe that we are not relating them from a slanted point of view, but rather that we are seeing them from a perfectly unprejudiced and rational stance. Other interpretations may be biased or mistaken, the voices which utter them being to a greater or lesser extent astray. We, however, speak of Sikh history and religion in eminently reasonable terms and the better books (in English at least and the same applies to many more in Punjabi) reflect the same reasonable attitude.

But we do not. We are not being unbiased. Our understanding has been so moulded by Singh Sabha interpretations that we speak of them in terms entirely congenial to Singh Sabha attitudes without being even remotely aware that our understanding of Sikh history and religion is to some extent missing the mark. We are, if you like, the victims of a sectarian view, a sectarian view which has won complete acceptance by most Sikh scholars and western observers as the most reasonable of orthodoxies. That sectarian view is the Singh Sabha interpretation or (to be more precise) the interpretation of the Tat Khalsa section of the Singh Sabha movement.[6]

Three Tat Khalsa scholars have been particularly prominent in shaping these interpretations and in moulding the attitudes of later authorities, both Sikh and western. The first, and unquestionably the most influential, was the prolific poet, novelist, essay writer, scriptural commentator , traditional biographer of the Gurus, and disputant for the faith, Vir Singh. Bhai Vir Singh (1872–1957) devoted virtually the whole of his life to the concerns of the Panth as he understood them.[7] The second was Kahn Singh of Nabha (1861–1938), particularly prominent as an anthologist and as the writer of an extremely influential encyclopedia entitled *Gurusabad ratanākar mahān koś* (usually known simply as the *Mahān koś* or 'the great dictionary').[8] The third was the Englishman M.A. Macauliffe (1837–1913), author of the work of apparently never-ending popularity *The Sikh Religion* (a work of six volumes published as three by the Clarendon Press in 1909, subsequently reprinted in India).[9]

A prominent example of Tat Khalsa influence is in the account of the life of Guru Nanak. Prior to the time of the Singh Sabha the life of Guru Nanak was drawn from a small range of janam-sakhis (hagiographic collections of anecdotes), particularly from the so-called *Bālā* janam-sakhi tradition. The *Bālā* janam-sakhis consist of many wondrous stories concerning the first Guru and had the

Singh Sabha writers been compelled to use it for their reconstruction of the Guru's life their task would have been a very difficult one. Fortunately the founding of the first Singh Sabha was immediately preceded by the discovery in London of a new janam-sakhi tradition. In 1877 the German missionary Trumpp announced how in 1872 he had come across an old manuscript which had been among those sent to him by the India Office Library and upon inspection of it had discovered that it was a life of Nanak.[10] This was the first janam-sakhi of what later came to be called the *Purātan* (or 'Ancient') tradition, a truly fortunate discovery for the men who were at that time just beginning to get the Singh Sabha movement under way.

There were three reasons why the janam-sakhi seemed so important. The first was Trumpp's belief that it was 'the fountain, from which all the others have been drawn largely'.[11] Secondly, there was the smaller scale of the miracles and marvels which it contained. Miracles and marvels this *Purātan* manuscript certainly had, but their number and scope was appreciably less than those of its *Bālā* rival. Thirdly, the newly-discovered janam-sakhi possessed a certain form and symmetry which *Bālā* lacked. Today this is recognized by janam-sakhi experts as the mark of a later product rather than the loose collection of anecdotes characterizing the earlier model.[12] At the time, however, it seemed to support Trumpp's view of the manuscript being the 'fountain' which had supplied all the remainder of janam-sakhis.

On this basis the authors of the Singh Sabha movement (and this applied particularly to Macauliffe) rewrote the story of Nanak's life. The *Purātan* tradition had sent Nanak out on missionary journeys to the four points of the compass (his *udāsīs*), together with one minor journey within the Punjab. To this date almost every account of the Guru's life accepts this format implicitly, and it likewise accepts the various destinations in the order specified by the *Purātan* account. In vain does one point out that the processes of janam-sakhi growth are very complex and that the *Purātan* version comes at a comparatively late stage within that pattern. The fact is that we know very little concerning the authentic life of Guru Nanak. This, however, counts for very little. In fact it counts for nothing. The Singh Sabha scholars have decreed a pattern for the Guru's life and any attempts to upset that pattern are very vigorously resisted by their later followers. The miracles are ignored or quietly discarded, but the story of Guru Nanak's life is otherwise told on the basis of the *Purātan* sequence. It is one of many marks of the Singh Sabha dominance in Sikh scholarship.

In this particular example, as in the wider field of Singh Sabha scholarship, the motives of the reformers cannot be questioned. The cause was genuinely believed and the methods were honest. Another example, however, brings us rather closer to the margin between truth and falsehood, though it seems only fair to add that the central figure was apparently convinced of the rightness of what he was doing. The central figure was Vir Singh and the issue concerned his re-issuing of that important text in Sikh history, the *Panth Parkas* of Ratan Singh Bhangu.

Early in the nineteenth century Ratan **Singh Bhangu** had been employed by the English enquirer Murray to tell him about the Sikhs and in 1841 he published his account as *Panth Parkāś* (later known as *Prāchīn Panth Parkāś* to distinguish it from a later work of the same name). This portrays the rise of the Khalsa in stirring terms and gives an interpretation which is generally consonant with that later adopted by the Singh Sabha. The Khalsa, he asserts, was created to uphold justice by vigorous means and to combat oppression wherever it might be found.

In some respects, however, there are important details in the work which neither Vir Singh nor any other Tat Khalsa reformer could possibly accept. Ratan Singh Bhangu **must** have been mistaken and the best method of dealing with error was simply to change what he had written in the version of his work published by the Singh Sabha. Vir Singh's own version, published in 1952, has been compared with early manuscripts by Harinder Singh Chopra and Surjit Hans and the results are revealing.[13] Plainly he had altered the text at certain critical points, particularly those which referred to the Sikhs as Hindus.

If Ratan Singh Bhangu were to be confronted with the meaning attached to the words 'Sikh' and 'Hindu' in the early twentieth century (so, we may assume, argued Vir Singh) he would of course use the word 'Sikh'. Some reasoning of this sort evidently went on in Vir Singh's mind and it justified the surreptitious changing of one term for the other. There are other changes also and the authors of the article give a lengthy list of amendments which Vir Singh has made to the 1952 text. Such is the right of the editor, so he evidently believed. As a result almost all readers of the influential *Panth Parkāś* receive a partially false impression of what Ratan Singh Bhangu really said and, in consequence, the interpretation of the Singh Sabha is further strengthened. One must express regret that this information may be used by those concerned to criticise and belabour the Sikhs. It is, however, the verdict to which we are driven.

This verdict is one that we must apply to whole areas of Sikh history and religion. Yet another example is provided by Guru Gobind Singh. The custom of having all Sikhs of the Khalsa observe the celebrated Five Ks may have been introduced by Guru Gobind Singh when he inaugurated the Khalsa in 1699, but if so there is no reference to them until we are well into the nineteenth century. A much more likely origin (or at least a formalization of a recent nineteenth-century convention) lies in the doctrine of the Singh Sabha. Even the year 1699 as the date of Khalsa's foundation is open to question. The case was argued through to the point of Singh Sabha satisfaction, but there still remains some doubt about it.[14]

In summary we restate our thesis. The contribution of the Singh Sabha movement to the dominant interpretation of Sikh history and religion is immense. The influence of the Singh Sabha scholars was indeed determinative. Their concern for a rediscovery of the Gurus' truth has bequeathed a range of understanding to generations within the Panth and beyond. Although by 1920 the political strength of the movement was largely gone their intellectual influence nevertheless lives on. It is in the Singh Sabha period that we still dwell.

Notes

1. The most convenient collection from the Singh Sabha point of view is the issue of *The Panjab Past and Present*, vol. VII, Part I (April 1973), reissued as a book, Ganda Singh (ed.) *The Singh Sabha and Other Socio-Religious Movements in the Panjab*, 1850–1925, Patiala: Punjabi University, 1984.

2. For the order of the Khalsa see John R. Hinnells (ed.), *The Penguin Dictionary of Religions*, Harmondsworth: Penguin, 1984, p. 182.

3. Harjot Singh Oberoi, 'A World Reconstructed: religion, ritual and community among the Sikhs, 1850–1909', unpublished Ph.D. thesis, Australian National University, Canberra: 1987, pp. 146–7.

4. Harbans Singh, *The Heritage of the Sikhs*, New Delhi, Manohar, 1983, chap. xvii. For the Nirankaris and Namdharis see the entry 'Sects (Sikh)', *The Penguin Dictionary of Religions*, Harmondsworth: Penguin, 1984, p. 290. On *nam simaran* and the divine Name see the entry, 'Nam Simaran', pp. 226–7.

5. Dit Singh's only son, Baldev Singh Share, emigrated to New Zealand

in 1920. See W.H. McLeod, *Punjabis in New Zealand*, Amritsar: Guru Nanak Dev University, 1986, pp. 172–81.

6. Tat Khalsa beliefs have been well described and analysed by Harjot Singh Oberoi in 'A World Reconstructed: religion, ritual, and community among the Sikhs, 1850–1909', unpublished Ph.D. thesis, Australian National University, Canberra, 1987, chaps 6–7.

7. There is a substantial literature dealing with Vir Singh, practically all of it written by his admirers. The best short work is Harbans Singh, *Bhai Vir Singh*, New Delhi: Sahitya Akademi, 1972, together with a chapter from Nripinder Singh, *The Sikh Moral Tradition*, Columbia: South Asia Publication, 1990, chapter V. The title 'Bhai' is used for Sikhs of great piety or scholarship.

8. Kahn Singh Nabha has not attracted the same attention as Vir Singh and there is virtually nothing available in English concerning his life and work. A brief account in Punjabi is given in Shamsher Singh Ashok, introduction to *Gurusabad ratanākar mahān koś*, Patiala: Bhasha Vibhag, 2nd edn, 1960, pp. a–j.

9. Macauliffe has likewise been largely neglected. A brief essay in English is Harbans Singh, 'English translation of the Sikh scripture: an arduous mission of a Punjab civilian', in K.S. Bedi and S.S. Bal (eds) *Essays on History, Literature, Art and Culture Presented to Dr M.S. Randhawa*, New Delhi: Atma Ram & Sons, 1970, pp. 139–44.

10. E. Trumpp, *The Adi Granth*, London: Allen & Trubner, 1877, p. ii.

11. Ibid.

12. W.H. McLeod, *Early Sikh Tradition*, Oxford: Clarendon Press, 1980, pp. 178–9.

13. Harinder Singh Chopra and Surjit Hans, 'The editing of *Panth Parkāś* by Bhai Vir Singh', *Punjab Journal of Politics*, XII.1 (Jan-June 1988), pp. 51–2.

14. W.H. McLeod, *The Chaupā Singh Rahit-nāmā*, Dunedin, 1987, pp. 169, 230.

PART III

THE RAHIT AND THE RAHIT-NĀMĀS

7

THE PROBLEM OF THE PANJABI
RAHIT-NĀMĀS*

rahit-nāmā: a work which enunciates conduct and behaviour in accordance
with the principles of the Sikh religion.

Kahn Singh Nabha, Guruśabad Ratanākar Mahān Koś

No occasion is more important in Sikh history than the
Baisakhi festival of A.D. 1699. Sikh tradition relates how
Guru Gobind Singh, the tenth Guru of the Sikhs, had for
long mediated on the parlous circumstances of his time and on the
evident inability of his followers to combat the threat of persecution
and warfare which hung over them. The Guru was at this time residing
in Anandpur, a small town on the southern slopes of the Shivalik
Hills. Surrounded by the jealous rajas of the Shivaliks and confronted
on the Panjab plains by the visibly growing hostility of the Mughal
authorities the Guru could depend on nothing more than a
heterogeneous and ill-organized following of religious devotees. Their
devotion was beyond question, but not their ability to respond
effectively to the assaults which the Guru anticipated. The Guru's
problem was how to strengthen his followers for their imminent trial.

Modern versions of the tradition describe in vivid detail the
solution adopted by Guru Gobind Singh. Word was sent amongst
his followers that the forthcoming Baisakhi festival was to be a

*Originally published in Mukherjee, *India: History and Thought*, Subarnarekha,
Calcutta, 1982.

particularly important one and that all who could attend should do so. A host of Sikhs duly gathered in response to the summons. The Guru, however, remained concealed within a pavilion conspicuously pitched on the fair-ground. Having thus established a sense of mystery and anticipation he eventually emerged with sword in hand to demand the head of any Sikh who was prepared to lay down his life. A loyal disciple was persuaded to volunteer and disappeared into the pavilion. The thud of the Guru's sword signified his despatch and with an impressively blood-stained weapon the Guru returned to demand another victim. This procedure he repeated until a total of five Sikhs had gone to their apparent fate. The Guru then drew back the side of the pavilion to reveal five unharmed Sikhs in the company of five decapitated goats. These loyal disciples were, he declared, to be the nucleus of the new brotherhood known as the Khalsa. To each of them the Guru administered a form of baptism, using sweetened water stirred with a two-edged sword (*khaṇḍe dī pāhul*). He himself then accepted baptism from them and thereafter all who were prepared to accept the discipline of the newly founded khalsa were invited to do likewise.[1]

The essence of the new brotherhood was to be discipline, and following the baptismal ceremony the Guru preached a sermon in which the details of this discipline were spelt out explicitly. Certain groups of people had shown themselves to be inimical to the Guru and were therefore to be spurned by his loyal followers. Those who were prepared to undertake this loyalty were to assume a distinctive uniform consisting of the *pañj kakke* or 'Five Ks'.[2] They were also to regard four specific practices as particularly heinous and, as such, to avoid them at all times. As represented by modern tradition these four cardinal sins are the cutting of one's hair, eating the meat of animals slaughtered in the Muslim fashion, adulterous liaisons, and the use of tobacco.

These instructions, together with others which are believed to have been issued on that celebrated Baisakhi Day, constitute the core of the normative Khalsa discipline. The term which is used for this discipline or distinctive way of life is *rahit* or *rahat*,[3] and it was thus the substance of the Khalsa *rahit* which Guru Gobind Singh is believed to have promulgated at Anandpur in 1699. All who accept membership in the Khalsa must undertake to observe this *rahit* to their lives' end. To violate it in any serious sense incurs the penalty of being adjudged a *patit*, a 'fallen' or apostate Sikh.

Two important supplements are invariably added to this

baptismal core, one a textual contribution and the other a subsequent addition attributed (like the baptismal order) to an oral utterance by Guru Gobind Singh. The textual source is the corpus of Sikh scriptures recorded in the *Ādi Granth* and *Dasam Granth*, together with associated works which are accorded a canonical status. The oral utterance is the pronouncement concerning future succession within the Panth which Guru Gobind Singh is said to have delivered during the days immediately preceding his death in 1708.

The *Ādi Granth* had been recognized as divine scripture since its compilation in AD 1603–04 and it therefore followed that precepts incorporated within its pages should necessarily be regarded as incumbent on all Sikhs. Such precepts as can be extrapolated from the *Ādi Granth* must accordingly be accepted as components of the *rahit*. This, it is claimed, carries the beginnings of the *rahit* right back to Guru Nanak (1469–1539). Indeed, some would maintain that it carries the identifiable origins even further into the past, for the works attributed to major *bhagats* which have been included in the *Ādi Granth* predate the time of Nanak.

The second important supplement brings us back to traditional history. It is believed that prior to his death in 1708 Guru Gobind Singh announced that he would have no personal successor. The authority as Guru which he had inherited from his predecessors would, he declared, pass to the scripture and to the community of his followers. It would be exercised jointly and permanently by the *Granth* (the *Ādi Granth*) and the Panth (the Khalsa brotherhood), which thereby became the Guru Granth and the Guru Panth. This doctrine involved practical consequences for the eighteenth-century Sikhs and these consequences thus became a part of the *rahit*. Prominent amongst them were such features as the proper method to be followed in seeking guidance from the Guru Granth and the procedure to be adopted in eliciting decisions from the Panth.

This combination of scripture and tradition is regarded as the source of the *rahit*, or approved mode of Sikh conduct. In terms of both general principle and specific detail it is traced directly to utterances by the Gurus, particularly to those which are believed to have been delivered by Guru Gobind Singh at the inauguration of the Khalsa in 1699 and during the days immediately preceding his death in 1708. Orthodox Khalsa belief brooks no questioning of this doctrine, nor of the obligations which it involves for all who subscribe to it. The *rahit* derives from the explicit intention of the Gurus and is therefore mandatory for all who owe them allegiance.

It is, in fact, the fundamental doctrine of Sikhism as we know it today. Sikhism without the *rahit* would be unrecognizable.

The object of this essay is not to question this doctrine nor to subject it to speculative criticism. Quite apart from the impertinence of any such enterprise, it is abundantly clear that as a doctrine it properly belongs to the realm of theology. The issues which concern this essay belong to the province of history. They include the complex origins of the doctrine, the manner in which it has developed its orthodox form, and the reciprocal relationship between precept and practice. These issues we shall consider with reference to the basic question which they inevitably raise when set within their historical context. What are the actual sources for our knowledge of the evolving *rahit* and what problems do these sources present? It should be clearly understood that at this stage any such examination can go no further than a preliminary raising of the source-material problems. This is necessarily the case, for the present condition of our understanding permits nothing more. Much research and analysis will be required before a clear understanding of the ultimate origins, growth and delivery of the *rahit* is attained.

In so far as the *rahit* derives from scriptural sources there is no great problem of actual source identification.[4] Within the *Ādi Granth* this problem is raised only by works attributed to predecessors of the Gurus such as Kabir and Namdev (the *bhagat bāṇī*).[5] The contribution of the *bhagat* literature to the *rahit* is, however, slight and consists largely of the citing of proof-texts from the Kabir *bāṇī*. It is to the works of the Gurus that the more important connections are to be traced and here we encounter no serious problems. The *Ādi Granth* attributions are not open to serious question in the case of the Gurus' compositions. There is likewise no apparent reason why the works of Bhai Gurdas should not be accepted as genuine.[6] It is evident that the greater part of the *Dasam Granth* cannot possibly derive directly from Guru Gobind Singh, yet even here there remains a small nucleus of poems which appear to be authentically his, and whenever support for a *rahit* provision is sought from the *Dasam Granth* the appeal is normally made to one of these safe works.

This would appear, at first sight, to be a promising start. In practice, however, the general absence of authentication problems within the Sikh scriptures does little to assist any quest for the origins of the *rahit*. This is because the *Ādi Granth* actually adds relatively little to the emergence of the *rahit* and to the specific injunctions which it has progressively acquired. A comparison of *rahit* material with *Ādi Granth* doctrine leaves little doubt that the link between the two is a slender one. The hymns which have been recorded in the *Ādi Granth* lay their emphasis upon the need for salvation and the means of achieving it by interior devotion rather than on the kind of detailed instructions which find expression in the traditional accounts of the founding of the Khalsa. The one significant exception to this rule is the method prescribed by the Gurus for the attainment of salvation. *Nām simaraṇ* or regular remembrance of the divine Name is a technique which pervades the pages of the *Ādi Granth*.[7] According to Guru Nanak and his successors it is a practice which should ideally be observed during the early hours of the morning. Early-morning *nām simaraṇ* thus takes its place as one of the major precepts of the *rahit* consensus. In other respects, however, the *Ādi Granth* contributes to the *rahit* more in terms of general principles than by way of specific command. Although attempts have sometimes been made to extract specific details of later provenance from the earlier text of the *Ādi Granth* such exegesis is necessarily strained.[8] Apart from the *nām simaraṇ* injunction the connection must be perceived essentially in terms of such general principles as the obligation to deal justly with all men and the promise of the ever-present grace of the Guru. Specific rules of conduct such as one associates with the *rahit* are not characteristic of the Sikh scriptures.

The same qualification applies to other works which are accorded canonical status. The compositions of Bhai Gurdas are extensive and as the 'key to the Guru Granth Sahib' they are treated with a respect exceeded only by the *Ādi Granth* itself and by works attributed to Guru Gobind Singh. As in the case of the *Ādi Granth*, however, the contribution is more in terms of general principle than specific precept. Even the works of Guru Gobind Singh, as recorded in the *Dasam Granth*, lack the variety and range of explicit injunction which is required for a code of discipline. Although their spirit is clearly in accord with the traditional narratives describing the founding of the Khalsa, these works do not possess the precise detail of the latter.

The scriptural stress on general principle rather than specific precept does not mean, however, that direct evidence is completely lacking of the kind of practical instruction imparted by the Gurus to their followers. We may set aside the *janam-sākhīs* as authentic testimony in the case of Guru Nanak,[9] but not the records which derive directly from the sixth Guru and his successors. These are the *hukam-nāmās* or 'letters of command'.[10] From the time of the sixth Guru onwards these documents were used as a means of communicating information and instructions to individuals or groups of followers. Many have presumably been lost, but some survive to provide a source which has yet to be fully exploited. Although the *hukam-nāmās* concentrate on mundane concerns, it was natural that the Gurus should include in them instructions and advice of a recognizably *rahit* nature.

There is no doubt that the *hukam-nāmās* will at best serve as only a supplementary source with regard to the *rahit* and it is quite possible that a careful analysis of their contents will produce a disappointing yield. They nevertheless merit attention. The *hukam-nāmās* have presumably been neglected as *rahit* sources because they seem to do little more than confirm what tradition has already delivered in a more familiar form. We need to remind ourselves that they carry us further back than any of the eighteenth-century narratives and that they should properly be regarded as ultimate sources rather than as confirmatory material. Plainly they will require a more careful scrutiny if ever the task of exploring *rahit* origins is to be adequately performed.

But let us not exaggerate. Though they fulfil the highest of reasonable expectations the *hukam-nāmās* will never provide more than supplementary assistance in the task of identifying and analysing the rules of conduct which constitute the *rahit*. For these specific rules of conduct we must return to the traditions concerning the life of Guru Gobind Singh and in particular to the instructions which he is said to have imparted in recreating the Panth as the Khalsa. A cursory survey of the *rahit* as understood and presented in any accessible period since the tenth Guru's death quickly demonstrates that its substance derives from the traditional understanding of his intention and from the direct personal pronouncements which he is believed to have issued by way of discharging this intention. If, therefore, we are to come to grips with the origins issue we must first grapple with the sources which deal with this critical period of Sikh history. Here we do indeed encounter problems.

For a study of the origins and changing content of the *rahit* two principal varieties of source material can be identified. The first comprises works which narrate the events of the tenth Guru's life. These may be in prose or in poetry, and they may deal with the complete line of Gurus or exclusively with Guru Gobind Singh. The second variety sometimes incorporates narrative sequences, but its primary emphasis lies elsewhere. This is the *rahit-nāmā* or manual of conduct, a style of writing which avowedly sets out to distinguish precepts directly promulgated by the Guru or exemplified by his actions and, having thus identified them, to record them in something resembling a systematic order. In all instances they purport to represent the actual words of the tenth Guru, either verbatim or as reported by a close confident.

Although the narrative works deal with the *rahit* as part of a larger concern their contribution to its understanding is far from negligible. Because the *rahit* has assumed fundamental importance as a means of establishing Sikh identity, any work dealing with Sikh history or tradition must inevitably recognize this importance and refer to the conventions which give it expression. The fact that most of these narratives were written many years after the death of Guru Gobind Singh does nothing to diminish their value in this respect. The *rahit* has not been a static code, immutably established and thereafter immune from all subsequent influence. On the contrary, it has continued to evolve in response to contemporary pressures and it can be easily shown that the process of adaptation is still operating today. Later works can therefore be useful as a means of determining the *rahit* perceptions of their period and the circumstances from which they derive. In this respect they may well be easier to interpret than the *rahit-nāmās* in that it is normally possible to attach a specific date to a particular narrative. The principal difficulty which they raise with regard to the *rahit* concerns neither the period of their composition nor their dubious reliability as chronicles. It concerns rather their status as works representative of their respective periods. Recorded works are not necessarily typical of their period and the larger challenge offered by narrative histories is therefore one of determining the degree to which their notions of Sikh practice correspond to actual realities. This challenge they share with the *rahit-nāmās*.

Narrative histories therefore deserve consideration within the larger range of *rahit* analysis, but it is a consideration which must be deferred. We may note in passing the substantial importance of Sainapati's *Gur Śobhā* (AD 1711) and acknowledge the need to scrutinize the *rahit* treatment of its several successors in the heroic *gur-bilās* and chronicle traditions. Having done so we turn to the *rahit-nāmās* and to the problems, minor and daunting, which they pose.

The first problem happens to be a comparatively simple one. Before beginning the scrutiny it will obviously be necessary to define the nature of the *rahit-nāmā* and determine precisely which works qualify under the definition. One who clearly recognized the importance of the *rahit-nāmās* was the distinguished Sikh encyclopaedist Kahn Singh of Nabha (1861–1938) and here, as in so many other instances, the most succinct of definitions is the one which he provided. A *rahit-nāmā* is, he writes, 'a work which enunciates conduct and behaviour in accordance with the principles of the Sikh religion.'[11]

The definition is clear, but it is immediately clouded by the list of works which Kahn Singh cites as examples of the *rahit-nāmā* form. In his *Guruśabad Ratanākar Mahān Koś* he names eighteen titles as the more important of the *rahit-nāmās*,[12] and in his posthumously published *Gurumat Mārtaṇḍ* the number is raised to twenty-eight.[13] These range from the *Ādi Granth* itself through *janam-sākhī* and *gur-bilās* literature to an anthology of *rahit-nāmās* compiled (and mutilated) by a certain Bhagvan Singh in 1873. Kahn Singh's lists include all but one of the titles which deserve to be treated as *rahit-nāmās*, but obscure their distinctive quality by associating them with works covering a much wider area of interest.

Kahn Singh's inventory must therefore be purged. Before doing so, however, it will be helpful if we briefly distinguish three differing styles within the small corpus of works which may legitimately be regarded as *rahit-nāmās*, two of them simple and the third more complex. All three styles exemplify the essential *rahit-nāmā* concern for compiling and expounding lists of approved precepts, and all can accordingly be regarded primarily as manuals of conduct. The differences which distinguish them relate to style, length, and range of interests. Whereas the two simple varieties do little more than compile and briefly comment, the more complex provides contexts, adds narrative passages, greatly expands the *rahit*, and introduces an apocalyptic element. This latter component possesses a particular significance for the authors who incorporate it in their *rahit-nāmās*, one which to their understanding imparts a special quality and purpose to the *rahit*. The end of the present evil age is near. A joyous reward awaits those who sustain their loyalty to the Khalsa and to the *rahit* which alone can confer salvation.

It should be noted that in thus differentiating three variant styles we do so on the basis of extant texts. As we shall see, the relationship of extant texts to possible originals constitutes one of the major problems to be tackled. Some insist that at least one of the lengthier variety must represent an interpolated version of what was originally a simple text. Although this particular claim may look suspiciously like an attempt to dispense with unwelcome features while retaining the acceptable, the issue which it raises is certainly not one to be summarily dismissed. Given the recent nature of most extant texts the possibility of significant textual corruption must obviously be acknowledged. On this qualified basis the extant versions may be classified in terms of form as follows:

Simple *rahit-nāmās* (verse)

1. The *Tanakẖāh-nāmā*, attributed to Nand Lal
2. The *Praśan-uttar*, attributed to Nand Lal
3. The *rahit-nāmā* attributed to Prahilad Singh (or Prahilad Rai)
4. The *rahit-nāmā* attributed to Desā Singh

Simple *rahit-nāmās* (prose)

5. The prose *rahit-nāmā* attributed to Nand Lal
6. The *rahit-nāmā* attributed to Daya Singh

Extended *rahit-nāmās* (prose)

7. The *rahit-nāmā* attributed to Chaupā Singh
8. The *Prem Sumārg*
9. The *Sau Sākhīān*

These nine works constitute the *rahit-nāmā* literature as it emerges from obscurity during the latter half of the nineteenth century. As we have already noted the texts all purport to record either the actual words of Guru Gobind Singh or at least the authentic sense of his utterances concerning Khalsa conduct and future events. In order to sustain this claim it was obviously desirable to have the authority of one known to be close to the Guru during his lifetime and, as such, in a position to hear and reliably record his pronouncements. It therefore comes as no surprise to find that most *rahit-nāmās* are attributed to various members of his entourage. Nand Lal is intended to be Nand Lal Goya, the celebrated author of Persian works composed during his association with the Guru.[14] The *rahit-nāmā* attributed to Prahilad Singh/Rai claims that its author was with Guru Gobind Singh in the Deccan and implies that he enjoyed a particular intimacy with his Master.[15] Desa Singh, we are told, was a resident of Amritsar who wrote his *rahit-nāmā* on the basis of information received directly from the Guru and Nand Lai.[16] Daya Singh was the first of the five volunteers who responded to the Guru's appeal for severed heads on the Baisakhi Day of 1699,[17] and *Chaupā Singh's Rahit-nāmā* claims that its author was both tutor to the Guru and a favoured disciple.[18] The two remaining works, although anonymous, yield nothing to the others in terms of their claims to authenticity. All declare that the words which they record faithfully represent the actual utterances of the tenth Guru.

The first four *rahit-nāmās* are brief works expressed as simple verse, three of them in a comparatively modern Panjabi and the fourth (the Desa Singh *rahit-nāmā*) in a language which moves strongly towards modern Hindi. Each characteristically begins with a comment on the circumstances in which it was allegedly delivered by Guru Gobind Singh, but wastes little time in setting a scene. Despatching its introduction in a few short words each plunges directly into its catalogue of precepts. The *Tanakhāh-nāmā* typically illustrates this style:

praśan bhāī nand lālji vāk srī gurū gobind siṅgh jī
praśan kīā nand lāl jī guru batāīe mohi
kaun karam in jog hai kaun karam nahin soi
nand lāl tum bachan suṇahu sikh karam hai ehu
nāmu dānu isanān bin kare nā an siun nehu[19]

Questions asked by Bhai Nand Lal and the responses given by Sri Guru Gobind Singh

'Tell me,' Nand Lal asked the Guru,
'What deeds are approved [for a Sikh] and what are to be spurned?'
'Listen to my words, Nand Lal. These are the deeds required of a Sikh:
Let him perform none save those which reflect the threefold rule of the divine Name, charity, and purity.'

Having thus declared the Guru's participation and stated the all-embracing *nām dān iśnān* formula the author moves directly to his specific injunctions.

prātakāl satisang nā jāvai
tanakhāhdār bahu vaḍḍā kahāvai

satisaṇg jāi kar hit ḍulāvai
īhān ūhān ṭhaur nā pāvai[20]

He who does not attend the *satsaṅg* early in the morning.
Let him be treated as a grievous offender.

He who attends but lets his mind wander
Will find no peace in this world or the next.

The *rahit-nāmā* attributed to Prahilad Singh/Rai provides a little more detail in its introduction.

bachan srī mukh vāk pātiśāhī 10 bhāī dariāī udāsī ke parathāi hoiā.
bolanā hoiā sri satīgurū jī kā

abachal nagar baiṭhe gurū man men kīā bichār
bolia sācā satīgurū mūrati srī kartar

hukam hoiā prahilād singh bip jātī hans rāi
nikaṭ bulāiā gurūjī līno kaṇṭh lagāi

panth chalio hai jagat main gur nānak parasādi
rahit batāīai khālse suṇ bhāī prahilād[21]

A statement made by the Tenth Master to Bhai Dariai of the Udāsī order. The Satguru spoke as follows:

While sitting in Abchalnagar the Guru reflected inwardly,
And then he spoke, the Satguru and image of the Creator.

The low-caste Hans Rāi was sent to summon Prahlād Singh.
Calling him near the Guru embraced him.

'By the grace of Guru Nanak I have established the Panth here on earth.
'Now listen, Bhai Prahilad, while I instruct you in the *rahit* to be observed by the Khalsa.'

In this instance an intermediary source is named and a precise setting is provided, one which indicates the intended date of the alleged discourse. It was to Nanded in Marathwada that the Guru came shortly before his death in 1708, and the place on the bank of the Godavari river where he briefly resided and eventually died subsequently came to be known as Abchalnagar. The sense of authenticity is thus strengthened by the implied claim that we are here given the kind of summing up which might be expected of the Guru immediately prior to his death. With authority and context established the author turns to his statement of the *rahit* and to its assurances of dire punishment awaiting transgressors.

hoi sikh sir ṭopī dharai
sāt janam kuśaṭī hoi marai

jo sikh gal mai tāgā melai
cauphaṭ bājī ganakā khelai

janam suān pāvaigā koṭi
bījayo hāth burā is khoṭ[22]

If a Sikh wears a cap [in the Muslim style]
He shall seven times be born a leper.

The Sikh who wears the sacred thread,
Plays at dice or visits a prostitute,

Shall be reborn a dog countless hundreds of times,
For the evil seed which he sows shall bring forth its evil fruit.

The clipped metrical brevity of these simple *rahit-nāmās* is very different from the expansive Panjabi prose of the extended variety. The opening of the *Chaupā Singh Rahit-nāmā* makes this immediately clear:

> 1 *om satigur prasādi*
> *āge rahat satigur kī. sākh granth sāhib jī. rahat*
> *rahati rahi jāi bikārā. jis rahāti kītīa bikāran hovan*
> *so rahit kahie. sākh granth sāhib jī. sācī rahat*
> *sācā man soi. jis rahat vic gurū citāve so aisī*
> *rahat sākh granth sāhib jī. aisī rahat raho hari pāsā*
> *gurū kā sikh havai. so aisī rahat kā khojaṇā karai*
> *jehaṛī rahat gurū khusī āvai. sakh granth sāhib jī ... .*[23]

By the grace of the Eternal One, the True Guru.
   The text which follows is the *rahit* prescribed by the Satguru. As the *Granth Sāhib* affirms:

If one follows the *rahit* the disease [of separation from God] progressively diminishes.
   The prescription which must be followed in order to remedy this disease is called the *rahit*. The *Granth Sāhib* [also] declares:
   The true *rahit* resides in the heart which is true.
   Such is the *rahit* which the Guru prescribes and such the *rahit* to which the *Granth Sāhib* bears witness. He who follows God and observes this *rahit* is a Sikh of the Guru. And so we must examine the *rahit*, this *rahit* which brings joy to the Guru. As the *Granth Sāhib* testifies ... .

The same looseness of style is also evident when the author (or authors) turns to expounding the *rahit*. This is done in vastly greater detail, with frequent repetition and with a commentary ranging from the sensibly helpful to the insufferably gratuitous. The same lack of disciplined order extends to the choice and presentation of the actual material used in the *Chaupā Singh Rahit-nāmā*. Catalogues of *rahit* injunctions turn easily to narratives of events involving Guru Arjan or Guru Gobind Singh, or to an improving story from the *janam-sākhīs*. The *Prem Sumārg* is even more detailed and expansive, though it orders its material into an impressively rigorous pattern of section and sub-section. The *Sau Sākhīān* falls between the two.

Most striking of all are the apocalyptic passages which are to be found in the extant texts of the three extended *rahit-nāmās* and which, as we have noted, add considerably to their distinctive character. Although these passages may well represent later additions to earlier, simpler texts they make the stock *rahit-nāmā* claim concerning their original utterance. Like so much of the *rahit-nāmā* material they purport to represent the actual words of Guru Gobind Singh and thus to have been spoken during the late-seventeenth century or the first eight years of the eighteenth century. The conditions which they describe and the future which they predict accordingly project an early-eighteenth-century context. Invariably, however, the description is vague and whenever precision is introduced it proves to be a spurious precision.

The parlous and rapidly deteriorating circumstances facing the Panth are most vividly described in the apocalyptic portion of the *Chaupā Singh Rahit-nāmā*. Times will be agonizingly bad, the Guru declares, and loyal Sikhs will be subjected to the fearsome consequences of radical disorder. Deceit and licentiousness will abound, men will behave like beasts, castes will be confounded, and all sense of honour will flee. Crafty demons will seduce the unwary and bogus gurus will endeavour to subvert the Panth. Eventually, however, the Guru will reassert his power. A deliverer will be despatched, the enemies of the Panth will be overthrown, and those who have sustained their loyalty to the *rahit* receive their blissful reward.[24]

Whereas the *Chaupā Singh Rahit-nāmā* appends this material as a climax and a conclusion, the *Prem Sumārg* introduces it at the very beginning. Times are already bad, declares its anonymous author, and they will get much worse. Those Sikhs who wish to survive should therefore have a clear understanding of the *rahit* which will provide their only salvation. The details of the chronology predicted by the *Prem Sumārg* differ in some measure from those of the Chaupā Singh version, but the pattern is essentially the same. Suffering will eventually end in the appearance of a divine deliverer. The Panth's enemies will be scattered and the steadfast will inherit the joy which awaits them.[25]

Although it is not possible to analyse this material in any detail at this stage, three features deserve preliminary notice. The first is the generally consistent manner in which the *rahit-nāmā* descriptions of deepening disaster and ultimate triumph accord with the conventional patterns expressed in millenarian literature from other areas and times.[26] The second is the express clarity with which the enemies of the Khalsa are identified as Muslims.[27] The third is the identity of the promised deliverer. Both the *Chaupā Singh Rahit-nāmā* and the *Prem Sumārg* explicitly declare the final deliverer to be the Kalki avatar.[28]

Finally there are the two works which must be placed between the material and the extended *rahit-nāmās*. These are the brief prose works attributed to Nand Lal and Daya Singh. In terms of content and format the first of these is very similar to such portions of the extended *rahit-nāmās* as concentrate on actual *rahit* exposition. It is to be found only in conjunction with the *Chaupā Singh Rahit-nāmā* and its style closely resembles the expository sections of its extended companion. The difference in length is, however, considerable (the *Chaupā Singh Rahit-nāmā* is twelve times longer) and the Nand Lal *rahit-nāmā* lacks the supplementary features which distinguish the extended *rahit-nāmās*. The *rahit-nāmā* attributed to Daya Singh is twice as long as the prose Nand Lal and more orderly as well as more comprehensive in its presentation. Like all *rahit-nāmās* it is invariably recorded in the Gurmukhi script, but its language is a comparatively modern Hindi.

We turn now to the extant manuscript texts and the more important of the printed versions. Although the *rahit-nāmās* all claim to derive from the late-seventeenth or early-eighteenth centuries the texts which we actually possess appear to be nineteenth-century products. One possible exception is a manuscript which records the lengthy *Chaupā Singh Rahit-nāmā* together with its Nand Lal companion. According to its colophon this was written in the town of Jind and completed in S. 1821 (AD 1764).[29] It is, however, by no means certain that the extant manuscript was produced at that time. The numerous errors which disfigure its text are of a kind which plainly indicates that it is a copy of an earlier manuscript, and in the meantime it seems safer to assume that it too probably belongs to the nineteenth century.[30]

A second important manuscript, extant at least until the partition of India in 1947, is a version of the *Prem Sumārg* which was donated to the Lahore Public Library by Sardar Attar Singh of Bhadaur.[31] This manuscript is dated S. 1931 (AD 1874) and owes its importance to the extreme scarcity of *rahit-nāmā* manuscripts rather than to any claims based on age. In view of the acknowledged importance of the *rahit* this scarcity is at once curious and frustrating, a situation further aggravated by the relative modernity of the few manuscripts which do exist. In terms of both numbers and age the corpus of *rahit-nāmā* manuscripts compares very unfavourably with that of the *janam-sākhīs*.[32] The only *rahit-nāmā* collection of any importance appears to be the small group held at the Sikh History Research Department of Khalsa College, Amritsar. In addition to its transcribed copy of the Chaupā Singh/Nand Lal manuscript this collection comprises two copies of the *Tanakhāh-nāmā*, two copies of the *rahit-nāmā* attributed to Prahilād Singh, one *Praśan-uttar*, one *Prem Sumārg*, and two fragments (one from a Prahilad Singh manuscript and one from a *Prem Sumārg*).[33] The Chaupā Singh/Nand Lal copy is a modern transcription and none of the remainder are dated. Shamsher Singh Ashok's catalogue of Panjabi manuscripts notes merely four additional copies, complete or partial, of the *Prem Sumārg*. One of these is dated S. 1931 (AD 1874). The other three are undated.[34]

For most readers access to the *rahit-nāmā* has been through versions produced after the introduction of the printing press to the Panjab. Although the *rahit-nāmās* never acquired a popularity approaching that of the *janam-sākhīs* a number of texts have been published during the past hundred years. Three collections deserve notice. The earliest and most influential is the selection which Kahn Singh included in his *Guramat Sudhākar*, a compendium of works relating to the person and time of Guru Gobind Singh, first issued in 1901.[35] This was followed in 1923 by a small collection with a lengthy introduction by Sant Sampuran Singh, under the title *Rahit-prakāś*.[36] The third and most comprehensive is Piara Singh Padam's recently published *Rahit-nāme* (Patiala, 1974). In addition to these editions of actual texts there has also been a series of works which expound the entire *rahit* or specific doctrines in the light of the *rahit-nāmās* and other records of Sikh tradition. The first important contribution to this genre was Bhai Avtar Singh's *Khālsā Dharam Śastr Sanskār Bhāg* (Lahore, 1894), a work by an individual which foreshadows the committee *rahit-nāmās* of the twentieth century.

Kahn Singh's *Guramat Sudhākar* is a work of some importance in the history of *rahit-nāmā* development in that it serves to bridge the considerable gap separating the earlier *rahit-nāmās* from their twentieth-century successors. To describe the *Gurumat Sudhākar* collection as a series of abridgements would be misleading. It is in fact a collection of expurgated *rahit-nāmās* and the process of expurgating them has plainly been conducted in the light of a perceptible and important range of preconceptions. Kahn Singh was a distinguished representative of the Singh Sabha reform movement and the views which he applied to his editing of the *rahit-nāmās* faithfully reflected the reformist ideals which it had so effectively generated by the end of the nineteenth century.[37] Anything in the *rahit-nāmās* which conflicted with these ideals was accordingly excised on the grounds that *ipso facto* it could not possibly have derived from Guru Gobind Singh and must therefore be an interpolation by a misguided devotee or a non-Sikh.

The mere reproducing of an expurgated selection of the *rahit-nāmās* proved, however, to be an inadequate answer to the demand for consistency and comprehension which grew out of the Singh Sabha movement. It had become increasingly clear that a new *rahit-nāmā* was needed, one which would recover the authentic principles of the Guru's original *rahit* and express them in a systematic and authoritative form. The attempt which was made under the Singh Sabha aegis (through its principal organization, the Chief Khalsa Diwan) was a failure. The manual prepared by a talented committee and published in 1915 as *Gurmat Prakāś Bhāg Sanskār* seems never to have won widespread acceptance. This may have been partly a result of the criticism which it drew from sources hostile to the Chief Khalsa Diwan,[38] but even without such attentions it would almost certainly have proved inadequate. The authors had chosen to concentrate their efforts on producing orders of service for major Sikh ceremonies, incorporating individual *rahit* injunctions at appropriate points within these orders. Although this method achieved the desired consistence its result seems to have been too demanding in length and sophistication for its intended constituency. The committee's efforts retain an importance only in the sense that they provide a useful statement of what the dominant intellectual group within the Singh Sabha perceived to be the nature of the *rahit*. It is, needless to say, very much a product of its period and circumstances.

The failure of the *Guramat Prakāś Bhāg Sanskār* was acknowledged in 1931 by a decision of the Shiromani Gurdwara Prabandhak Committee to commission a new *rahit-nāmā*. After a sub-committee appointed for this purpose had produced a draft within a year a series of delays postponed final approval until 1945. The agreed text was eventually published in 1950 under the title *Sikh Rahit Marayādā*. At some points the organization of this new manual is curiously unsystematic, presumably as a result of committee decisions taken under pressure of contending views. Moreover, the view of the *rahit* which it projects is still essentially the Singh Sabha perception expressed by the *Guramat Prakāś Bhāg Sanskār*. It nevertheless demonstrates convincingly that important lessons had been learnt from its predecessor's failure. An English translation, prompted by the needs of a rapidly growing Sikh population in the United Kingdom, was published from London in 1971 as *Rehat Maryada: A Guide to the Sikh Way of Life.*

This London translation marks the latest stage in the continuing process of *rahit* and *rahit-nāmā* evolution. As circumstances have changed, so inevitably has the response in terms of each generation's understanding of the *rahit*. Although *Rehat Maryada* was evidently intended to be a faithful representation of *Sikh Rahit Maryādā* it contains several interesting variants and these, upon scrutiny, prove to be responses to a distinctively English situation.[39] This, however, is a comparatively small gap. It amounts to very little when contrasted with the differences of content and presentation separating both *Sikh Rahit Marayādā* and *Rehat Maryada* from their earliest extant forbears.

It is to these forbears that we must now return and we do so in order to identify the more serious difficulties which they raise. Two clusters of problems will have to be attacked before the extant versions of the earlier *rahit-nāmās* can be made to yield a useful return as sources of Sikh history. The first of these raises the issue of origins. This does not necessarily require us to identify the actual authors of the earliest texts, interesting though that information would be. What it does require is that we should be able to determine their period and the circumstances under which they were written. The second range of problems concerns the relationship of these supposed originals to the extant versions from which we must work. What pattern of change and development has produced the individual texts as we now know them?

The two clusters are, of course, intimately related and it would be impossible to attempt one without speedily becoming involved in the other. It is, moreover, immediately evident that the metrical *rahit-nāmās* present a radically different prospect from the extended variety. The former are comparatively recent works and it would be very difficult to associate them, even indirectly, with the individuals to whom they are variously attributed. It would be absurd, for example, to suggest that the style of verse and language offered by the *Tanakhāh-nāmā* or *Praśan-uttar* could be traced to the distinguished Nand Lal Goya. In the case of the Prahilad Singh/Rai *rahit-nāmā* the same naiveté extends to the dating offered by its author. The *rahit-nāmā* was, he claims composed in the month of *Māgh* S. 1752 (AD 1695)—three years, prior to the founding of the Khalsa and twelve years before Guru Gobind Singh took up residence in Abchalnagar.[40] The impossibility of connecting these works with contemporaries of the tenth Guru was recognized more than a hundred years ago by Sardar Attar Singh of Bhadaur and no evidence has since been produced to controvert this view.[41]

Kahn Singh acknowledged this impossibility in at least four cases, although he nevertheless published his expurgated versions of these and other *rahit-nāmās* as if they possessed at least a measure of the authority which they claimed.[42] This authority he presumably accepted on the grounds that the modern versions available in the late-nineteenth century must necessarily be the descendants of authentic traditions derived from the period of Guru Gobind Singh. The authorship might be spurious in some instances and subsequent interpolation is rife, but there remained for him a core which represented the Guru's true teachings on the nature and content of the *rahit*.

This, however, is an inference, for Kahn Singh does not declare his position in unambiguous terms. A much clearer view is presented by the only person to devote sustained effort to the origins issue. This was Bhai Randhir Singh. While employed by the Shiromani Gurdwara Prabandhak Committee prior to the partition of India in 1947 Randhir Singh spent several periods of leave copying the *Prem Sumārg* manuscript donated by Attar Singh to the Lahore Public Library. This he subsequently edited and published from Amritsar in 1953 under the title *Prem Sumārg Granth*.[43] In the introduction which prefaces the actual text Randhir Singh comes very close to an explicit rejection of the claims of the simple verse *rahit-nāmās* while insistently affirming those of the *Prem Sumārg* and (rather less emphatically) those of the *Chaupā Singh Rahit-nāmā*.

Guru Gobind Singh, he argues, must certainly have had a *Khalsa-smrti* or *rahit-nāmā* prepared in order to provide a permanent record of the new discipline which he had so recently introduced. This task was entrusted to the Guru's old tutor Chaupā Singh, and his authentic *rahit-nāmā* may still be in existence.[44] The pattern was thus established and although none of the simple *rahit-nāmās* deserve a place within it, the *Prem-Sumārg* assuredly does. Randhir Singh acknowledges that the manuscript evidence is either late or fragmentary, but marshals internal evidence in favour of his claim that the text presented by the Lahore manuscript dated S. 1931 (AD 1874) should be traced to the early-eighteenth century and to an anonymous contemporary of Guru Gobind Singh. This author, he suggests, was probably a scholar attached to the Guru's following and a close associate of the celebrated Mani Singh. The manuscript's claim to represent the actual words of Guru Gobind Singh must be repudiated, but not its close proximity to the Guru.[45]

Although neither the reasoning advanced by Randhir Singh nor his conclusions can be accepted he has at least indicated the only possible way to proceed.[46] In the absence of demonstrably authentic manuscripts from the eighteenth century, and with very few specific or implied references in other early works, it will be necessary to place a major dependence on internal evidence. This method will be required both for the origins issue and also for the questions relating to subsequent development.

The prospects held out by this procedure are, to say the least, unpromising. The Chaupā Singh manuscript may yield useful results and the extant texts of both the *Sau Sākhīān* and the *Prem Sumārg* may respond to determined analysis, but no one who has surveyed this material is likely to be affected by delusions of easy or ultimately convincing results. In the case of the simple *rahit-nāmās* the promise is even dimmer, though not to the extent that these works should be summarily dismissed as nineteenth-century products devoid of eighteenth-century antecedents. Such despair would be premature. Whatever the difficulties the task certainly deserves attention, for if it is not attempted the *rahit-nāmās* can never be utilized as historical sources.[47] The alternative is for historians to set them aside, thereby forfeiting one of their few potential sources for a firmly-based understanding of the *rahit* and its development. This, in turn, will leave us dependent on unconfirmed tradition and speculation in an area of fundamental importance for Sikh history.

The task is thus a forbidding one, and yet one that is by no means devoid of encouragement. One small comfort is the promise of limited assistance from the *hukam-nāmās*, the *gur-bilās* literature, narrative histories, and other related material. A second is the reasonable expectation that although we may find it impossible to extract a significant return in terms of eighteenth-century Panjab history we can at least hope for some light on nineteenth-century attitudes and circumstances. At the very least we can be assured of a clearer understanding of the philosophy associated with the Singh Sabha movement and of the influence which this philosophy has exercised during the past hundred years. This would be acutely disappointing with regard to the eighteenth century, but should nevertheless confer an important gain. No Sikh movement since the time of the Gurus can rival the Singh Sabha as an agent of conscious renewal, articulate scholarship, and deliberate change. An enlarged understanding of its ideals would be a valuable consolation prize.

Notes

1. For a more detailed narrative of the tradition see M.A. Macauliffe, *The Sikh Religion*, vol. 5 (Oxford: Clarendon Press, 1909), pp. 84–97. Also, Khushwant Singh, *A History of the Sikhs*, vol. 1 (Princeton: Princeton University Press, 1963), pp. 96–8.

2. The *pañj kakke* comprise the *keś* (uncut hair), *kirpān* (dagger), *kachh* or *kachhahirā* (breeches which should not come below the knee), *kanghā* (comb), and *kaṛā* (iron wrist ring).

3. From *rahaṇā*, 'to live'. The spelling *rehat* is also used. The word *rahiṇī* sometimes appears as a substitute.

4. For a description of the Sikh scriptures see W.H. McLeod, *The Evolution of the Sikh Community* (Delhi: Oxford University Press, 1975, and Oxford: Clarendon Press, 1976), chap. 4. (Hereafter *ESC*.)

5. There is good reason for believing that the works attributed by the *Ādi Granth* to pre-Sikh *bhagats* should be set at several removes from their putative authors, and that they have been significantly changed and augmented during an intervening period of oral circulation.

6. *ESC*, p. 81.

7. W.H. McLeod, *Gurū Nānak and the Sikh Religion* (Oxford: Clarendon Press, 1968), pp. 214–19.

8. An example is provided by the introductory chapter of the early twentieth-century manual of doctrine and ceremonial entitled *Gurmat Prakāś Bhāg Sanskār* (Amritsar: Chief Khalsa Divan, 1915). This manual is briefly discussed below. There are, of course, *rahit-nāmā* injunctions which affirm the importance of reading the scripture and which specify certain portions as appropriate for daily recitation or for use in particular rituals.

9. *ESC*, ch. 2.

10. Gandā Singh (ed.), *Hukamanāmās* (Patiala: Panjabi Yunivarasiti, 1967); Shamsher Singh Ashok (ed.), *Gurū-khālse de nūśān te hukam-nāme* (Amritsar: Sikh Itihas Risarch Borad, SGPG, 1967). For examples of other preceptive materials from the pre-Khalsa period see Narindar Kaur Bhatia (ed.), *Srī Satgurū jī de muhain dīāṅ sākhīāṅ* (Amritsar: Narindar Kaur Bhatia, 1978).

11. Kahn Singh, *Guruśabad Ratanākar Mahān Koś*, 2nd edn (Patiala:

Languages Department, Punjab Government, 1960), p. 760. (Hereafter *MK*).

12. Ibid.
13. Loc. cit. vol. 2 (Amritsar: Shriomani Gurduara Prabandhak Kameti, 1962), pp. 796–7.
14. *ESC*, p. 81.
15. *Pothī rahit-nāmā te tanakhāh nāmā*, text of the *rahit-nāmā* attributed to Prahilad Singh and the *Tanakhāh-nāmā* attributed to Nand Lāl, published by Lala Maghi Ram Sant Ram (Amritsar, 1922), p. 10. (Hereafter *PRN*).
16. Kahn Singh (ed.), *Guramat Sudhākar* (Amritsar: Vazir Hind Press, 1901), p. 453n. (Hereafter *GS*.)
17. *GS*, p. 503n.
18. *Chaupā Singh rahit-nāmā* manuscript no. 6124 of the Sikh Reference Library, Amritsar, fo. 35a. (Hereafter *CS*.)
19. Gandā Singh (ed.), *Bhāī Nand Lāl Granthāvalī* (Malacca: Sant Sohan Singh, 1968), p. 195; *PRN*, p. 2.
20. Gandā Singh, *op. cit.*; *PRN*, p. 2.
21. *PRN*, p. 10.
22. Ibid.
23. *CS*, folio 1a.
24. *CS*, folios 76b–93a, 96a–b.
25. Randhir Singh (ed.), *Prem Sumārg Granth*, 2nd edn (Jullundur, 1965), pp. 1–5, 59. (Hereafter *PrS*.)
26. For the principal Sikh example of this phenomenon see W.H. McLeod, 'The Kukas: a millenarian sect of the Punjab', in G.A. Wood and P.S. O'Connor (eds), *W.P. Morrell: A Tribute* (Dunedin: University of Otago Press, 1973), pp. 85–104, 272–6. See below pp. 189–215.
27. *CS*, folios 81b, 83a, 85b; *PrS*, p. 4; Attar Singh (tr.), *Sakhee Book* (Benares, 1873), pp. 46, 66–7.
28. *CS*, folios 90b–91a; *PrS*, p. 3. Their source was obviously the *Dasam Granth*.
29. *CS*, folio 104a.
30. A Chaupa Singh/Nand Lal manuscript is, or was, located in Gurdwara Damdama Sahib at Talvandi Sabo in Bhatinda district. Khalsa College in Amritsar possesses a copy which is said to have been transcribed from the Damdama Sāhib manuscript. Kirpal Singh (ed.), *A Catalogue of Punjabi and Urdu Manuscripts in the Sikh History Research Department* (Amritsar: Sikh History Research Department, Khalsa College, 1963), p. 106.
31. *PrS*, Intro. p. 88.
32. Professor Pritam Singh of Guru Nanak Dev University, Amritsar, has suggested that the contrast can be explained by comparing their differing audiences. The *janam-sākhīs* evidently exercised an appeal for

the kind of people (Hindu as well as Sikh) who would have the interest, opportunity, and ability to prepare and preserve manuscripts. The *rahit*, on the other hand, would have been the concern of a much smaller group, one with a weaker literary tradition and with more demanding preoccupations.

33. Kirpal Singh, (Amritsar: Sikh History Research Department, Khalsa College, 1963) *op. cit.*, pp. 106–12.

34. Idem. *Panjabi hāth-likhtān dī sūchī*, vol. 1 (Patiala, 1961), pp. 334–35; vol. 2 (Patiala, 1963), p. 219. In spite of the age coincidence the *Prem Sumārg* manuscript noted by Ashok is not the same as the manuscript donated to the Lahore Public Library by Attar Singh of Bhadaur. A *Prem Sumārg* manuscript which Ashok does not note is to be found in the Mohan Singh Vaid collection at Panjabi University, Patiala.

35. *GS* includes versions of the *Tanakhāh-nāmā, Praśan-uttar*, the *rahit-nāmās* attributed to Desa Singh and Daya Singh, and selections from Chaupa Singh and the *Prem Sumārg*. A fourth edition was published from Patiala in 1970.

36. Recent editions of this work are published under the title *Rahit-nāmā*. The collection includes texts, complete or abridged, of *Praśan-uttar;* the *Tanakhāh-nāmā;* the *rahit-nāmās* attributed to Desa Singh, Prahilād Singh, Chaupa Singh, and Daya Singh; and the nineteenth-century work of Baba Sumer Singh. All editions are published from Amritsar.

37. For a brief account of the Singh Sabha movement see N.G. Barrier, *The Sikh and their Literature* (Delhi: Manohar, 1970), Intro. pp. xvii–xlv.

38. The Panch Khalsa Diwan of Bhasaur, a declared enemy of the Chief Khalsa Diwan, was vigorously outspoken in its criticism of the *Gurmat Prakāś Bhāg Sanskār*. N.G. Barrier, *op. cit.*, pp. xxxiii–xxxiv.

39. One interesting variant concerns the order in which the *chār kurahitān* (the 'four proscribed actions') are listed. In the original version the cutting of hair comes first (*Sikh Rahit Marayādā*, Amritsar: Shiromani Gurduara Prabandhak Kameti, 1958 edition, p. 36). In the version prepared for use in England, however, it has dropped to fourth place (Kanwaljit Kaur and Indarjit Singh (tr.), *Rehat Maryada*, London: Sikh Cultural Society, 1971, p. 15).

40. *PRN*, p. 16.

41. Attar Singh (tr.), *The Rayhit Nama of Pralad Rai or the excellent conversation of the Duswan Padsha and Nand Lal's Rayhit Nāmā or rules for the guidance of the Sikhs in religious matters* (Lahore: Attar Singh, 1876), pp. 6, 11. Attar Singh's English versions of these two metrical *rahit-nāmās* are free paraphrases rather than translations. It is evident that the *rahit-nāmās* exercised a considerable fascination for Attar Singh. Three years earlier he had published an English translation of a version of the *Sau Sākhīān* called *Sakhee Book, or the Description of Gooroo Gobind Singh's Religion and Doctrines* (Benares: Attar Singh, 1973). The unidentified text used by Attar Singh was obviously a very recent one written in the mid-nineteenth

century and adapted to the particular needs of the Namdhari or Kuka sect.

42. Kahn Singh explicitly acknowledged as spurious the two metrical works attributed to Nand Lal and the *rahit-nāmā* attributed to Prahilad Singh. *GS*, p. 453n; *MK*, p. 596. He also claims that the *Prem Sumārg* was written in S. 1880 or 1885 (AD 1823 or 1828), *GS*, p. 476n.

43. This is the work (2nd end 1965) which is cited in this essay as *PrS*.

44. *PrS*, Intro. pp. 73–80. Randhir Singh cites as evidence for the Chaupa Singh tradition the testimony of Kesar Singh Chhibar, author of the *Bansāvali-nāmā dasān pātiśāhīān kā* and believed to be the grandson of an intimate follower of Guru Gobind Singh. In this work, completed in AD 1780, Kesar Singh relates how the Guru's old tutor Chaupa Singh was commanded to prepare a *rahit-nāmā* and how, after modest protestations of ignorance and incapacity, the commission was duly discharged within the space of seven days. Ibid. pp. 76–7. Kirpal Singh, *op. cit.*, pp. 39–9. Kesar Singh is not a reliable source.

45. *PrS*, Intro. pp. 83ff.

46. The argument and its conclusions are vulnerable in several respects. Three important objections are the unconvincing nature of the alleged connection with Mani Singh, the failure to acknowledge the apparently composite nature of the *Prem Sumārg* text, and the extent to which the argument treats unproven assumption as established fact.

47. This point is well made by J.S. Grewal in a perceptive essay on the *Prem Sumārg* entitled 'A theory of Sikh social order.' The essay appears in J.S. Grewal, *From Guru Nanak to Maharaja Ranjit Singh* (Amritsar: Guru Nanak University, 1972), pp. 72–83. I am also indebted to Professor Grewal for comments on the importance of the *gur-bilās* literature as a source for eighteenth-century Sikh perceptions of history and traditional behaviour.

8

THE KHALSA RAHIT:
THE SIKH IDENTITY DEFINED*

Rahit: The Sikh Rahit is the code of discipline which all who enter the Khalsa order must vow to observe ...
Rahit-nāmā: A rahit-nāmā is a manual which records any version of the Rahit.
The Penguin Dictionary of Religions, pp. 265–6.

Sikhs have been much in the news during the past year. Although reports have been dominated by acts of violence, questions of custom, belief, history and aspirations have inevitably been raised. One such issue has been the problem of distinguishing Sikhs from Hindus, an elementary question which many seem able to answer without hesitation. The mobs which assaulted Sikhs and their property in the days following the assassination of Mrs Gandhi evidently had little difficulty with this particular problem, and even the inexperienced foreigner commonly believes that a Sikh can be easily identified. There is a strong likelihood, however, that the points of recognition will be strictly limited. A brief question or two usually reveals that for the foreigner at least it is only the male Sikh who can be recognized, and then only if he presents to outward view the more obvious features of the Khalsa discipline. Most aspects of the discipline remain

*Originally published in Hayes, ed., *Identity Issues and World Religions*, Select Proceedings of the Fifteenth Congress of the International Association for the History of Religions, the Australian Association for the Study of Religions at the South Australian Association College of Advanced Education, 1986.

unrecognized and the poor foreigner will commonly find it quite impossible to distinguish Sikh women from Hindu.

The apparently simple question of a visible Sikh identity quickly becomes an obscure and complex issue when we move beyond the well-known turban and beard. The turban and beard nevertheless serve as an appropriate introduction to the larger issue, for as we have just noted they are prominent features of the Khalsa discipline. We are led directly to the essential nature of Sikh identity and to the substance of this paper. We are led, in a word, to the Rahit.

It is perhaps surprising that the word 'Rahit' should be so little known and so seldom used. A single word which expresses normative Sikh belief and behaviour certainly deserves to be well known and the primary purpose of this paper is to encourage its usage. It shares in the neglect which is typically bestowed on those other key terms 'Gurmat' and 'Panth'. How much closer we should be to understanding the Sikhs and their distinctive beliefs if we possessed even a rudimentary grasp of Gurmat, Panth and Rahit. All three terms are intimately related, each to the other two, and although I shall be concentrating on Rahit I should note in passing that 'Gurmat' may be briefly defined as the corpus of Sikh doctrine and Panth as the Sikh community. I should also mention that the terminology used in this paper is further explained and illustrated in *Textual Sources for the Study of Sikhism*.[1] Chapter 4 of this collection is largely devoted to the Rahit.

What then is the Rahit? The Rahit is the code of discipline which all members of the Khalsa must vow to observe. Sikh tradition binds Khalsa and Rahit inextricably together. According to well-founded tradition the Khalsa order was inaugurated by Guru Gobind Singh on Baisakhi Day 1699. Following the dramatic choosing of the first five members the Guru is said to have initiated them with a form of baptism and then to have promulgated the Rahit or code of discipline which all Sikhs of the Khalsa must thereafter follow.[2] Sikh tradition also affirms that the Guru restated the Rahit in an amplified form immediately prior to his death in 1708. At his death the Rahit was sealed. The Lord of the Khalsa had delivered, once and for all, the pattern of belief and behaviour which his loyal followers must thereafter observe.

The reality of the situation is, needless to say, rather more complicated than the tradition allows. It is slightly complicated by developments which precede the founding of the Khalsa in 1699; and it is vastly complicated by those which follow that crucial event.

Pre–1699 sources indicate that a rudimentary Rahit was evolving prior to the founding of the Khalsa. Contemporary sources fail to deliver an authenticated 1699 version. Post–1699 sources demonstrate that much of the Rahit crystallized during the eighteenth century and the discipline as a whole has ever since continued to mutate. In response to changing circumstances it has predictably introduced items which earlier versions lack, amended some which have come to be unacceptable in their original forms, and discarded others which could no longer be sustained. This should not suggest, however, a process of change so radical that the Rahit of today bears little resemblance to its early eighteenth-century precursor. Plainly this is not the case. The fact that the Rahit testifies to an ongoing evolution quite rightly implies continuity, a continuity which can easily be traced throughout the entire history of the Khalsa.[3]

Pre–1699 sources do little to complicate the issue because there is little in them which one identifies as typical Rahit material. Attention has frequently been drawn to an apparent difference in the spirit and general approach which evidently distinguishes the practices of the tenth Guru from the teachings of the first (the so-called 'transformation of Sikhism'). This particular controversy is essentially irrelevant in that the Rahit is recognizably a product of the later period. The early period, best expressed in the Adi Granth collection, is largely concerned with the interior discipline of mediation on the divine Name. This particular emphasis has ever since remained a conspicuous feature of Sikh belief, and as such it finds a place in the Rahit. Ever since the first versions of the Rahit were formally enunciated Khalsa Sikhs have been enjoined to rise at an early hour and meditate on the divine Name. The injunction has, however, become one amongst many. Although it retains a fundamental importance the Rahit which was to emerge during the eighteenth century includes much more than this Ādi Granth inheritance. A few other items evidently derive from the early practice of the Panth. Most belong to the period of the later Gurus and to the turbulent decades which followed the death of Guru Gobind Singh in 1708.

It was during the fifty years following the death of the tenth Guru that the earliest extant version of the Rahit was committed to writing. This brings us to the rahit-nāmās, the recorded versions of the formalized Rahit.[4] It has been widely assumed that Guru Gobind Singh himself must surely have instructed scribes to prepare copies of the Rahit which he had promulgated at the inauguration of the

Khalsa. Earlier Gurus had already begun the practice of despatching *hukam-nāmās* or 'letters of command' and the tenth Guru had continued the practice. Although a *hukam-nāmā* might well include instructions of a kind which could have been incorporated in a rahit-nāmā these 'letters of command' never supplied the comprehensive list which constitutes the latter form. No extant rahit-nāmā can be safely traced to the life-time of the Guru himself. All belong to the years following his death.

Sikh tradition acknowledges that the earliest rahit-nāmās may have been recorded after the tenth Guru's death, but it does not countenance a significant gap. Several rahit-nāmās claim to derive directly from the words of the Guru himself and if, in fact, the recording took place after he had died, the injunctions which they contain express his actual words and authentic intention. Such is the claim lodged by most of the writers responsible for the earliest versions. One purports to be the work of the Guru's most trusted servant, a faithful retainer who had cared for the Guru during his childhood and who had subsequently remained by his side as a close confidant. Another declares itself to be the record of a conversation held with the Guru shortly before his death in South India. Three different rahit-nāmās are attributed to Nand Lal Goya, a celebrated poet of the Guru's entourage.

The earliest of these claimants apparently dates from the middle of the eighteenth century (between 1740 and 1765). This is the *Chaupa Singh Rahit-nāmā*, attributed to the tenth Guru's tutor and aide Chaupa Singh Chhibbar.[5] In its extant form it presents considerable difficulties from an orthodox Khalsa point of view, difficulties which seem plainly to explain the general neglect which it has suffered. These include the composite nature of the text (it includes narrative anecdotes and apocalyptic prophecy as well as rahit-nāmā material); its insistence upon traditional deference towards Brahmans (Chaupa Singh was himself a Brahman); and its embarrassing involvement in the Devi cult. The neglect is thus understandable, but it is nevertheless unfortunate in that no existing rahit-nāmā carries us nearer to the time of Guru Gobind Singh than this work attributed to Chaupa Singh Chhibbar. It must be added that its value, though considerable, should not raise too many expectations. It emerges almost half a century after the Guru's death and there is insufficient evidence to sustain the claim that its rahit-nāmā portions are the work of the Chaupa Singh who served as an intimate member of the tenth Guru's retinue. What this means is that the *Chaupa Singh Rahit-nāmā* testifies to a later perception of the role of the khalsa and the duty of the individual Sikh. It must also be remembered that it represents the views of a group which had once been influential within the Khalsa but which had since become disaffected.

In spite of these shortcomings the *Chaupa Singh Rahit-nāmā* can at least be dated and located within its appropriate context. Most of the other claimants to an early eighteenth-century provenance are more difficult to fix in terms of time or context. It is obviously safe to assume that like the *Chaupa Singh Rahit-nāmā* they do not derive from the period of Guru Gobind Singh and in the case of the Nand Lal versions their attribution is obviously contrived. If claims to authenticity were to be established it was essential that the relevant text should assert a context involving direct dictation by Guru Gobind Singh. Amongst his retainers none would have better qualifications as an amanuensis than Nand Lal Goya and he thus became a natural candidate for the role of rahit-nāmā author. The actual texts do nothing to sustain these claims, plainly indicating that they belong to a later period. That is the easy part. The difficult bit is to locate them within the decades (or centuries) following the Guru's death, and to identify the groups or individuals who produced them.

One of these later rahit-nāmās which does permit cautious conclusions is the work variously known as the *Prem Sumārg* or the *Param Sumārag*. This particular manual obviously belongs to the middle years of the nineteenth century, a conclusion which follows from its author's obvious knowledge of the rule of Maharaja Ranjit Singh and from his evident nostalgia for that period. The only outstanding question with regard to dating concerns the precise time of its composition, whether shortly before the British annexation of the Punjab or shortly after that event.[6] The *Sau Sākhīān* or 'Hundred Episodes' also belongs to the same period, though in its extant form it probably emerged a decade or two later.[7] Like the *Chaupa Singh Rahit-nāmā* the *Sau Sākhīān* combines Rahit injunctions with apocalyptic prophecy. As such it was to provide comfort and inspiration to the Kukas in their opposition to the alien British.[8]

Much more difficult to place and evaluate are four brief rahit-nāmās written in verse form. Two of these rahit-nāmās are attributed to Nand Lal; one to a disciple variously called Prahilad Rai or Prahilad Singh; and one to Desa Singh, also said to be a contemporary follower of Guru Gobind Singh.[9] This cluster constitutes the principal problem associated with the rahit-nāmās. Their contents are far too important to be ignored and if we are to trace the growth of the khalsa satisfactorily it seems imperative that these verse rahit-nāmās should be firmly fixed in terms of time and context. It is, however, impossible to draw adequate conclusions at this stage. We can certainly detach all four from their purported origins and thereby bring them forward in time. Their language is not that of the period which they claim to represent and the kind of verse which we find in them could scarcely be the work of the highly skilled Nand Lal Goya. But how far forward should they be brought? That precisely is the problem and no sufficient answer has yet been supplied.

The same problem also attaches to one of the two remaining earlier rahit-nāmās. These two are both brief collections of injunctions expressed in prose. One of them (another of the Nand Lal rahit-nāmās) is invariably found in association with the *Chaupa Singh Rahit-nāmā* and like its dominant colleague can probably be placed in the middle years of the eighteenth century. The second is attributed to Daya Singh, one of the first five Sikhs by Guru Gobind Singh at the inauguration of the khalsa in 1699. As with the four verse rahit-nāmās this prose product can safely be detached from its putative author. A nineteenth-century provenance is indicated by the nature of language, but at this stage any such verdict must be a cautious one.

Whatever their dates and origins these were the formal rahit-nāmās which existed when representatives of the Singh Sabha reform movement turned their attention to the Rahit late in the nineteenth century.[10] Given their interest in restoring the purity of Sikh doctrine and practice it was inevitable that the Singh Sabha reformers should have directed a portion of their zeal to the Rahit and its formal enunciation. Their task was not easy. The legacy of the two preceding centuries was a sparse one and much of its content was plainly unacceptable to the educated men who led the movement. The Khalsa allegiance of the various rahit-nāmās may have been obvious, but so too were their many contradictions and the injunctions which no enlightened product of late-nineteenth-century education could possibly accept.

One response was to prepare commentaries on the Rahit or on particular features of it, and several of the works published during the Singh Sabha period belong to this category. A prominent example of this genre was Avtar Singh's *Khālsa Dharam Śāstr Sanskār Bhāg*, first issued from Lahore in 1894.[11] A few years later that most influential of all Singh Sabha intellectuals, Kahn Singh of Nabha, published a different kind of response, one which clearly signalled the true nature of the problem.

Kahn Singh's *Gurmat Sudhakar*, first issued in 1901, was a compendium of works relating to the person and time of Guru Gobind Singh. Such a collection was bound to include material relating to the Rahit, but how could the rahit-nāmā wheat be sifted from the chaff and the weeds? Kahn Singh solved the problem by publishing what appeared to be abridged versions of the principal rahit-nāmās. In reality, however, his selections were expurgated versions rather than abridgements. Portions which were unacceptable were deleted (as well as those which were insignificant) and only those items which matched the reformist philosophy of the Singh Sabha movement were retained. Anything which conflicted with that philosophy must *ipso facto* conflict with the original intention of Guru Gobind Singh. As such it must surely represent interpolation by an enemy, a deviant, or (at best) an ignorant Sikh. Purging these excrescences should produce a version of the Rahit much closer to the original version than that of any extant rahit-nāmā. Although this reasoning was not spelt out it seems clearly implicit in the procedure adopted by Kahn Singh.

Other attempts have subsequently been made to utilise the early rahit-nāmās. It is, however, a method doomed to fail if the objective is to be a comprehensive statement of the Rahit appropriate to contemporary circumstances. This awareness prompted a lengthy quest for the definitive rahit-nāmā, one which would draw into a single agreed manual the various injunctions which together constitute the sum total of approved Khalsa practice. Extant rahit-nāmās could contribute to this process, but alone they must be inadequate. Other sources had to be used for the details which they delivered; and a consensus had to be achieved with regard to inclusion, omission, and the actual form of words. The task was an exceedingly difficult one and the final result bears all the marks of committee procedure. It was nevertheless achieved after several decades of negotiation, a feat of no mean scale.

The attempt made during the Singh Sabha heyday was actually a failure. This was the manual of Sikh rituals published as *Gurmat Prakāś Bhāg Sanskār* in 1915, a work which incorporated Rahit injunctions in proposed orders for various rites and ceremonies. Its failure was implicitly acknowledged in 1931 when the Shiromani Gurdwara Parbhandhak Committee (which by then had become the dominant voice in Sikh affairs) appointed a sub-committee to prepare a new rahit-nāmā. Although a draft was ready within a year the process of discussion was protracted and it was not until 1950 that an agreed version was finally published as *Sikh Rahit Maryada.* The brief introductory portion of *Sikh Rahit Maryada* appropriately offers a definition of a Sikh.

A Sikh is any person who believes in God (*Akal Purakh*); in the ten Gurus (Guru Nanak to Guru Gobind Singh); in Sri Guru Granth Sahib, other writings of the ten Gurus, and their teachings; in the khalsa initiation ceremony instituted by the tenth Guru; and who does not believe in any other system of religious doctrin3.[13]

The remainder of the manual is divided into two sections, a lengthy 'Personal code' and a much shorter 'Panthic code'. The former includes instructions concerning modes of personal devotion; gurdwara worship and administration; approved methods of reading the sacred scripture; practices which are either enjoined or proscribed; and orders to be followed in the conduct of birth and naming-ceremonies, marriage and funerals. The second section consists largely of the order to be observed in conducting the Khalsa initiation ceremony (*amrit sanskār*). Several basic injunctions are incorporated within this rite as portion of the homily delivered to all who receive initiation. The manual concludes with a brief segment on penalties to be imposed for violations of the Rahit.

Sikh Rahit Maryada has stood the test of thirty-five years remarkably well. Having acknowledged this considerable achievement one must added some predictable qualification. For some the problem has been the evident fact that whereas the manual defines *normative* Sikh behaviour, *operative* practice is very different. The answer to this particular objection is, of course, that such manuals are by definition normative statements and that as such they serve to stabilize religious practice in the quicksand world of ignorance and self-interest. A second criticism is that although *Sikh Rahit Maryada* grapples with the problem of the so-called Sahaj-dhari (or non-Khalsa) Sikh, it finally fails to provide a satisfactory place for the latter. To this the answer must be that *Sikh Rahit Maryada* is, after all, a statement of Khalsa practice. It does not pretend to cover the needs of the uninitiated who yet regard themselves as Sikhs.

A final comment is that although *Sikh Rahit Maryada* was meant to be definitive, later editions have introduced surreptitious amendments. It is this comment which brings us to that most basic of all questions associated with the Rahit. Is the Rahit immutable, established once for all by the tenth Guru and subject to no acceptable change thereafter? Or is it to be regarded as firm yet flexible, adapting its forms as the world and its manifold pressures force change on the society of the faithful? The historian and the sociologist may find this an easy question to answer. For the believer it may not be quite so simple.

Notes

1. W.H. McLeod, *Textual Sources for the Study of Sikhism* (Manchester: Manchester University Press, 1984) will hereafter be cited as TSSS. See also W.H. McLeod, *The Evolution of the Sikh Community* (Oxford: The Clarendon Press, 1976), pp. 51–2. Relevant entires in *The Penguin Dictionary of Religions* may also be helpful.
2. *TSSS*, p. 34–7.
3. *TSSS*, pp. 9–10 and chap. 4.
4. W.H. McLeod, 'The problem of the Panjabi *rahit-nāmās*', in S.N. Mukherjee, *India: History and Thought: Essay in honour of A.L. Basham* (Calcutta: Subarnarekha, 1982), pp. 103–26.
5. *TSSS*, pp. 75–5.
6. S.S. Hans, '*Prem Sumārg*—a modern forgery'. *Proceedings of the Punjab History Conference 1982* (Patiala, 1982), pp. 180–8.
7. An early translation of the *Sau Sākhīān* was published by Attar Singh of Bhadaur as *Sakhee Book, or the Description of Gooroo Gobind Singh's Religion and Doctrines* (Benares: Attar Singh, 1873).
8. W.H. McLeod, 'The Kukas: a millenarian sect of the Punjab' in G.A. Wood & P.S. O'Connor (eds), *W.P. Morrell: A Tribute* (Dunedin: University of Otago Press, 1973), pp. 85–103, 272–6.
9. *TSSS*, pp. 75–9.
10. *TSSS*, pp. 14–17. McLeod, 'The problem of the Panjabi *rahit-nāmās*', p. 119.
11. Titles are listed in N. Gerald Barrier, *The Sikhs and Their Literature* (Delhi: Manohar, 1970).
12. One such work was Sant Sampuran Singh's *Rahit-prakāś*, first published in 1923. See also Piara Singh Padam (ed.), *Rahit-nāme* (Patiala: Piara Singh Padam, 1974).
13. *TSSS*, p. 79. *TSSS*, pp. 79–86, supplies a substantial part of the text of *Sikh Rahit Maryada* in English translation.
* Reprinted in W.H. McLeod, *Sikhs and Sikhism* (Delhi: Oxford University Press, 1999).
The Sikhs: History, Religion and Society. (New York: Columbia University Press, 1989)
Who is a Sikh? The Problem of Sikh Identity (Oxford: The Clarendon Press, 1989; Delhi: Oxford University Press, 1989).
Historical Dictionary of Sikhism. (Lanham, Maryland and London: Scarecrow Press, 1995) *Sikhism.* (London: Penguin Books, 1997).

Most of this paper has been incorporated verbatim in the introduction to the author's *The Chaupa Singh Rahit-nāmā: the rahit-nāmā attributed to Chaupā Singh Chhibbar and the associated prose rahit-nāmā attributed to Nand Lal*. Gurmukhi text and English translation with introduction and notes. University of Otago Press, Dunedin, 1986.

PART IV

DEFINITIONS

9

ON THE WORD *PANTH*:
A PROBLEM OF TERMINOLOGY
AND DEFINITION*

I t is our belief that the historical as well as the sociological
understanding of Indian societies and cultures has often been
hampered by the fact that debate and discussion have been
carried on in European languages, most notably English. Many
Indian concepts have been readily and not so readily rendered into
English and have become the standard vocabulary of Indian
sociology. The word 'caste' is of course the best known example.
Recent misgivings about this word, however, suggest that the
problem may be of a more general nature. I would like to argue
here that this problem is faced by students of Sikh society in the
very effort to find an appropriate English word to characterize it.

Early in the nineteenth century Sir John Malcolm referred to the
Sikhs as both a 'sect' and a 'nation' (Malcolm 1810: 198). The two
terms have since recurred in the ongoing attempt to find an English
word which will accurately describe, in a corporate sense, those who
owe allegiance to the teachings of the ten Gurus and call themselves
Sikhs. Other terms have also been introduced and used with varying
degrees of acceptance. One obvious example is 'community', a word
which duly assumed a distinctive and potentially useful meaning
within the Indian context but which unfortunately acquired the fatal
taint of rival enmity. Another is 'church'. Occasional attempts to
revive it quite properly fail because the term so patently distinguishes

*Originally published in *Contributions to Indian Sociology*, Vol. 12, No. 2, 1979.

an institution substantially different from anything offered by Sikh history.

For many, of course, the solution to the problem requires nothing more than a reference to 1699, the year in which Guru Gobind Singh founded the Khalsa and established thereby the orthodox form of corporate Sikh society. But does it really solve our problem? Nobody can possibly deny that the Khalsa code of discipline (the *rahit*) enunciates a clear definition of outward observance and at least a general indication of inward belief. Problems, however, persist if one is seeking an understanding of the actual nature of formalized Sikh society. The word 'Khalsa' is a strictly particular term, one which has served to designate a distinctive religious society but which in itself does not explain the generic nature of that society. There is one Khalsa. Is it a sect, is it a nation, is it both, or is it something different from both?

The term 'Khalsa' raises further problems by reason of its very precision. It is precise in terms of the date of its authoritative introduction. (The word was evidently used prior to 1699, but tradition is firm in the insistence that it received a formalized status and definition in that year.) It is also precise in the clarity with which it distinguishes its members from the rest of mankind. The difficulty raised by this precision is that it leaves uncertain the status of those who would regard themselves as Sikhs but who, for a variety of reasons, cannot be included in the Khalsa. It leaves undefined the Sikhs of the sixteenth and seventeenth centuries, and if rigorously applied it would exclude the so-called Sahaj-dhari Sikhs of the post-1699 period. The problem of incorporating Khalsa and non-Khalsa Sikhs within a single term has persisted ever since 'Khalsa' acquired its clear definition and is currently acquiring a new insistence amongst Sikh migrants in countries where observance of the *rahit* is confined to a dwindling minority.

It would be absurd to deny the normative status of the Khalsa during the period following its foundation and correspondingly absurd to attempt a definition of the nature of Sikh society without repeated reference to it. Plainly it must be fundamental to any enquiry into the nature of that society. In itself, however, it does not serve to define that actual nature. Our purposes may be better served if we use terms and concepts which possess a more general meaning.

At first sight neither of the words used by Malcolm seems to hold out much promise. Although the concept of a Sikh 'nation' has, on occasion, exercised a certain appeal it can, for present purposes, safely be set aside. It belongs to a later period and is, at most, merely implicit in the early beginnings of Sikh society. Some would deny it even this limited application. 'Sect' has attracted even less support as a description of the Sikh movement. In its western usage it assumes the existence of a dominant orthodoxy from which the 'sect' diverges or breaks away as a heterodox offshoot. Commonly it carries connotations of cramping narrowness and an excessive emphasis upon a limited range of doctrine. It is no compliment in the West to be called sectarian or a sectary and no amount of sociological debate seems to have purged the word of its pejorative connotations.[1]

Before summarily discussing both terms, however, let us acknowledge that attempts have been made to detach one of the two terms from its western antecedents and to infuse it with a new, distinctively Indian meaning. Having evaluated a comparatively recent attempt we shall still conclude that the term is too strongly infected with its pejorative western associations to permit a transplant to the Indian environment. Although this is to be expected it should not deter us from examining the actual content of the transposed usage. Such an examination may well assist our understanding of the origins of Sikh society and of the pattern of its subsequent development. Indeed, it may do more. It may point the way to an alternative which is acceptable both in a generic sense and in the specific case of the Sikhs.

The term 'sect' has recurred in western attempts to describe Indian society, commonly in an essentially careless sense but occasionally with a conscious and sophisticated determination to make the word do service in the Indian context. Dumont's is perhaps the most impressive example of the latter kind. In his *Homo Hierarchicus* Dumont is primarily concerned with the analysis of caste, but as a necessary corollary he acknowledges the existence of beliefs and conventions which explicitly reject caste or at least serve to detach some individuals from its controls. Renunciation, he claims, contradicts caste. Because it separates a man from social life proper it enables him to escape the 'network of strict interdependence' which constitutes caste society. Although renunciation is necessarily qualified by the practice of receiving alms and of preaching to those who remain within caste society it nevertheless serves to establish the identity of the 'renouncer' as one who has effectively moved outside that society (Dumont 1970: 184ff, 1966: 234ff).

It also produces, according to Dumont's argument, a social institution which transcends the caste system and it is this institution which he designates the 'sect' (Dumont 1970: 187):

Indian religious groupings which are readily characterized in terms of renunciation are conveniently called 'sects' without prejudging their similarity to what are called by this name in Christianity. The Indian sect is a religious grouping constituted primarily by renouncers, initiates of the same discipline of salvation, and secondarily by their lay sympathizers any of whom may have one of the renouncers as a spiritual master or guru.

The possibility of such a grouping or institutions depends upon three things. It depends first upon the existence of caste as the normative pattern of social organization. Secondly, it requires an explicit rejection of this pattern, and decreed conventions. Thirdly, it assumes the adherence of others who continue to accept the mandate or substantial features of it, but who nevertheless accord respect and allegiance to individuals who have overtly rejected the requirements of caste-related dependence.

The individual who thus rejects the decrees of caste is for Dumont the 'renouncer', one who deliberately abandons the role bestowed on him by society and assumes in its place an independent status. He becomes an 'individual-outside-the-world' as opposed to those who continue to remain 'men-in-the-world'. Some of the latter may, however, attach themselves to the renouncer as lay-sympathizers, superimposing loyalty to their chosen preceptor upon caste observances without obliterating the latter.

The common allegiance of lay sympathizers to a renunciant preceptor constitutes what Dumont calls a 'sect'. Caste conventions have been abandoned by the preceptor and may be directly criticized by him, but caste and sect membership both remain possible because they operate at different levels. Serious conflict arises only if a sect makes exclusive claims not merely as opposed to other sects but also with regard to caste values. This, however, is rare. In place of a total rejection of the actual observance of caste there will emerge one of three possibilities.

The first of these three possibilities is that a particular caste group will bifurcate to produce two sections, one retaining its traditional allegiance and the other attaching itself to the sect. The division is not necessarily complete, for the two sections of any given caste may continue to intermarry. Dumont cites as an example of this particular solution the Hindu/Jain mercantile castes of Gujarat (Dumont 1970:

188). A second possible result occurs in the case of a sect which recruits families and observes sectarian endogamy. When recruitment ceases the sect automatically becomes a genuine caste. The third possibility assumes the recruitment from a representative range of caste, including Brahmans or others who will perform priestly functions. The result in such instances may be 'a whole small localized system of castes in which the sect has replaced Brahmanism' (ibid.). Here Dumont cites the Lingayats as an illustration.

At least some of this analysis will bear a familiar ring to those who are acquainted with the teachings of the Sikh Gurus and the pattern of Sikh society. Is it, however, a sufficient resemblance to encourage a closer comparison between Dumont's model of the Indian sect on the one hand and Sikh society on the other? If we do conclude that a distinct resemblance exists are we thereby committed to the view that the Gurus' following represents what may legitimately be termed a 'sect'?

The obvious rejoinder to the suggestion of a resemblance is to point out that neither Guru Nanak nor any of his successors could be called 'renouncers' in the terms normally implied by such an expression. Guru Nanak was, after all, a family man and the burden of Sikh teaching has emphatically insisted that the pursuit of salvation does not require withdrawal from the world. It is true that one *janam-sākhī* tradition does endeavour to project a conventionally ascetic mode of precept and example.[2] The tradition is, however, demonstrably unrepresentative and we need not pause to question the standard belief that Sikh teachings have in general rejected celibacy as a pre-requisite to salvation or even as an aid. There have undoubtedly been exceptions to this rule, but those who have opposed it represent a heterodox view and receive little support from the Gurus.

Is this, however, the sum total of renunciation? Is the title of 'renouncer' necessarily limited to those who cast aside all human ties and assume the ascetic style? If we focus our attention specifically upon the question of caste we shall very quickly appreciate that here at least there is something which connects the Dumont model to the express teachings of the Gurus. With abundant emphasis Guru Nanak declared that caste is futile and his successors plainly followed him in this insistence (See for example Guru Nanak, *Vār Sirī Rāgu* 3:1 and *Āsā* 3; Guru Ram Das, *Goṇḍ* 4 in the *Ādi Granth*, pp. 83, 349, 861). Their insistence upon this point provides an obvious link with the paradigm sketched by Dumont.

It might therefore be possible to argue that Guru Nanak was a 'renouncer' in the sense that he preached the irrelevance of caste in relation to the pursuit of salvation. Dumont (1970: 190), indeed, seems to accommodate this approach within the terms of his analysis when he writes that:

... it is enough to suppose that the renouncers taught the men-in-the-world their own truth as the absolute truth, without having intended to do away with the other aspects of caste, being content to degrade it in this way from a religious fact to a purely social fact.

There is much to be said for the notion that the Gurus intended to 'degrade' caste rather than to demolish it in its entirety. This, as I have suggested elsewhere, solves the problem of explaining why the manifestly anti-caste Gurus continue to observe customary marital prescriptions (McLeod 1975: 87–8). Dumont, it is true, implies that the renouncers themselves continue to abandon caste in its social as well as its religious aspects, leaving it to their lay followers to retain the former while relinquishing the latter. The outcome, however, amounts to much the same thing. Caste, vigorously denounced as a religious institution, is yet retained as a modified social order.

The connection between Dumont's argument and Sikh society appears to be further strengthened when we follow him onwards from this point to the three possible outcomes which he enumerates. The second of the three can be discarded, but in the case of the first and the third the superficial resemblances are sufficient to warrant a closer investigation. The bifurcating of caste groups into two sections has been an obvious result of adopting the Sikh style and within some of these Sikh/Hindu caste groups intermarriage continues to be practised. The fact that the Jats of the central Punjab swung so strongly to a Sikh allegiance discouraged any such development within the largest of the caste groups with a Sikh constituency. Substantial numbers made cross-confessional Jat marriages unnecessary and geographical considerations made them actually impossible in many areas. Other caste groups, however, have produced their two distinct sections, the most obvious cases being those of the Khatris and Aroras.

There is thus an obvious fulfilment of the first of the three possibilities. It could perhaps be argued that the caste constituency contained within recognizable Sikh bounds is sufficiently varied to amount to a fulfilment of the third type, viz. a 'whole small localized system of castes in which the sect has replaced Brahmanism'. It is true that there is no priestly caste to perform the Brahman's function. Sikh doctrine, however, specifically denies the necessity of sacerdotal castes or functions and accords no special role to the few Brahmans who have become Sikhs. The range of Sikh castes, extending from Khatri and Jat through to Mazhabi and Ramdasia, provides a spectrum which some might regard as sufficient to qualify as a 'localized system'.[3]

It can therefore be argued that Sikh society manifests those features which Dumont identifies as the components of a 'sect' and in terms of the actual content of his theory the argument is a convincing one. Acknowledging this to be the case, should we proceed to adopt the terminology which he proposes? There are, I suggest, good reasons for rejecting the term 'sect' both as a generic term and as an appropriate designation in the specific case of Sikh society.

The fundamental reason is that the word has been too deeply dyed with western connotations to let us transpose it to an Indian context. Merely to give notice that these connotations should be discarded is insufficient, for it is illusory to suppose that words can easily be stripped of associations sanctified by long usage. The hope that a portion of an original meaning can be retained and invested with a fresh range of associations is at best a faint one. It involves a difficult process and one which we should surely avoid if an alternative is available.

In the case of Sikh society this general objection is strengthened by the clear impression that 'sect' must assuredly fail to do justice to the uniqueness of that particular society. If we wish to be trite we can, of course, insist that every 'sect' must possess distinctive features and that all must accordingly be unique. There are significant differences of degree, however, and the society which was to produce the Khalsa is assuredly entitled to a designation which stresses its particularity. Even if 'sect' were not to be construed as insulting it would still prove to be inappropriate as a means of characterizing Sikh society. The term is misleading in its generic sense and inadequate in the specifically Sikh context. We need an alternative.

The proper way to find an alternative is, I suggest, to ask once again whether any European term is available for either the generalized concept or for the specific Sikh example. The answer is indicated by the persistent uneasiness which has attended efforts to make 'sect' serve the purpose. There is no such term available and it therefore follows that the solution must surely lie in adopting an appropriate word from an Indian source into regular English and French usage. This need has been recognized (reluctantly but compellingly) in the acceptance of such untranslatable terms as *karma* and *dharma*. It is true that the entire problem is not thereby solved, for the actual meanings of such words can continue to provide grounds for doubt, disagreement, and perverse or ignorant misconstruction. At the very least, however, we displace the burden of historical usage and connotation borne by European terminology. Provided that one's readers or hearers are not tempted to assume instant 'translations' for such terms we achieve significant progress.

Needless to say, this has all been said many times before and the real test is whether or not an actual word can be found which will pass with relative ease into regular currency. What terms are therefore available for the particular purpose which we have in mind. At least three have claims to consideration by reason of their usage in the context indicated by Dumont's discussion. They are *sampradāya, qaum,* and *panth.*

There are, I suggest, two strong objections to *sampradāya.* The first is that its appearance and pronunciation will assuredly cause many minds to boggle. Citizens of India or foreigners who have achieved fluency in a north Indian language may use it with ready ease, but we should remember that the problem of communication is by no means limited to such people. There is a much wider audience to be reached.

A second and stronger objection is that *sampradāya* does not really serve the intended purpose. Its definition is too vague, its bounds too uncertain. Whereas one may properly speak of the Sant *sampradāya* it would be misleading to apply it to bounded societies of the kind which we are seeking to designate. This is indicated by the mere fact that one so seldom hears the term Sikh *sampradāya* in Punjabi or Hindi usage, and that its occasional appearance usually implies a meaning much closer to philosophical content than to social structure. Its usual translation as 'tradition' actually provides a reasonably accurate rendering precisely because the English term is as vague and ill-defined as *sampradāya* itself.

Neither of these objections applies to *qaum,* the second of the possibilities. It is simple in form and clearer in terms of the boundaries which it implies. Although the word is a foreign import it has been sufficiently naturalized (in north India at least) to be acceptable if there are no other objections to be brought against it. The term Sikh *qaum* is sometimes used and a well-known Sikh newspaper bears the name *Qaumī Ektā.*

There are, however, at least two other objections which would have to be brought against *qaum.* The first is that it possesses and ethnic dimension which extends its range beyond the area we seek to cover. The second is that even when it lacks this dimension it commonly retains the kind of overtones which have done so much to debase the English words 'community' and 'communal' in their distinctively Indian usage.

This leaves us with *panth* and I suggest that this word provides the answer. Etymologically it derives directly from the notion of a 'path' or 'way' and it can still assume this literal meaning. Its dominant application, however, is in precisely the area which concerns us. In its actual usage the word covers the kind of group or community which Dumont characterizes as a 'sect' and does so without invoking the problems associated with the European term. It is true that the word can be used in a wider, looser sense and insofar as this is possible it falls short of the ideal. The connotations which it bears are nevertheless those which we seek and if carefully used *panth* should do good service as a substitute for 'sect'. It should, I suggest, be inducted into such languages as are used for Indian studies, preferably without italics.

This could answer the general objection to 'sect'. The specific objection to its Sikh application can be settled by adapting our use of the same word. Sikhs themselves have a strong affection for the term and use it with considerable frequency. If we acknowledge the usefulness of 'panth' as a generic term we can give it particularity by adopting the convention of a capital letter when using the Roman script. The sense of the Sikh usage is well expressed by the form 'Panth' and the actual form is commonly used by Sikhs in English-language publications. I see no reason why others should not accept the same convention.

If this argument is acceptable it must surely follow that the claims here advanced on behalf of 'panth' and 'Panth' should properly be extended to other key terms in Indian sociology which present problems of translation. Terminology which derives its substance from one culture may transplant easily—or it may not. If it does not transfer easily it will normally be advisable to utilize an indigenous term, and if an indigenous term is not available the failure to find one will alert us to the possibility that we are endeavouring to give expression to something which does not exist. Very occasionally the exotic term proves useful, as in the case of 'caste'. More commonly it proves to be a misconceived quest for clarity which may do more to obscure than enlighten. If substituting 'panth' for 'sect' makes sense we can safely assume that there are other key terms awaiting a closer linguistic scrutiny.

Notes

1. We should however acknowledge the extent of the debate from Weber onwards, and also the enlarged understanding which it has generated.
2. This is the *Narrative II* tradition. See McLeod, *Early Sikh Tradition: a study of the jānam sākhīs* (Oxford: Clarendon Press, 1980) chap. 10.2, pp. 197–210. Reprinted in W.H. McLeod, *Sikhs and Sikhism* (Delhi: Oxford University Press, 1999).
3. For a note on the range of Sikh castes, see McLeod (1975: 93–103). The existence of this range of castes within Sikh society does not necessarily negate the interesting application of structural method presented by Uberoi (1969). This essay does, however, involve a transposition of the discussion from Sikh society to Sikhism as a theory of religious belief and as a rationale for a particular pattern of ritual behaviour. The only possible justification for claiming that Sikh society has not returned to the 'citadel of caste' must surely be that it never moved out. If, however, the claim concerns the belief system as an ideal it might be possible to maintain that Sikhism embodies a theory of caste renunciation in that it 'set out to annihilate the categorical partitions, intellectual and social, of the medieval world' (ibid.: 135). I am not myself convinced that this is true, nor that the social function of the Sikh initiation rite is necessarily to be seen as an expression of this intention. It is, however, a suggestive argument and we must hope that its author will one day pursue it at much greater length.

References

Dumont, Louis. 1966. *Homo Hierarchicus: Essai Sur la Systeme des Castes*. Paris: Editions Gallimard.

———. 1970. *Homo Hierarchicus: The Caste System and Its Implications*. London: Weidenfeld and Nicholson.

Malcolm, John. 1810. 'Sketch of the Sikhs'. *Asiatick Researches* (Calcutta) Vol. 11.

McLeod, W.H. 1975. *The Evolution of the Sikh Community*. Delhi: Oxford University Press.

———. 1980. *Early Sikh Tradition*. Oxford: Clarendon Press.

Uberoi, J.P.S. 1969. 'The Five Symbols of Sikhism' in Fauja Singh *et al.*, eds, *Sikhism*. Patiala: Punjabi University Press, pp. 123–38.

10

THE MEANING OF 'SANT' IN SIKH USAGE*

The Sant whom we were seeking proved rather hard to find. Normally Sant Hazara Singh remains in the village of Ghumani, ten kilometres from Batala. The day we had chosen for our visit happened, however, to be one of the rare occasions when importunity had triumphed and he had agreed to visit another village. There were already seven people in the Ambassador car and the addition of two guides from Ghumani slowed our progress still further. Eventually we located our quarry beyond Dhariwal in the village of Sujanpur and there had our brief *darśan* of the Sant. The inevitable *satsang* had gathered and Sant Hazara Singh was all but invisible in the midst of the crowd assembled in the large courtyard. On such occasions there is advantage in being a foreigner, as Punjabi courtesy ensures that the stranger will receive special consideration. We soon found ourselves sitting in front of the Sant.

Although Punjabi courtesy confers special favours on the foreigner, such discrimination is not part of Hazara Singh's custom. All men are equal in his view including himself. He is renowned (so we were assured) for the vigour and the colour of the language which he uses whenever anyone tries to touch his feet. Anyone who offers him money will find it rejected with scant ceremony and the earnest seeker after enlightenment will be greeted either with the

*Originally published in Schomer and McLeod, *The Sants: Studies in a Devotional Tradition in India*, Motilal Banarsidas, Delhi, 1987.

terse suggestion that he look elsewhere or (more commonly) by total silence. A request from one of our company for permission to take his photo produced an immediate refusal. The one gesture which he seems willing to accept is a gift of food, all of which will be distributed amongst those who happen to be present at the time.

The impression which Hazara Singh communicated was that of a decent and genuinely humble man who regards adulation as a sacrilegious bore. In this, of course, lies much of his appeal. The more offerings he rejects the wider spreads the fame of the (almost) silent Sant of Ghumani. We soon discovered that the local folklore concerning Hazara Singh laid heavy emphasis upon his reputation for curt, unpretentious common sense. Once, a couple came to him with the request that he should marry them. 'Go,' he said, 'you are married.' They protested that a marriage normally involved reciting of *Anand Sāhib* and circumambulating the *Guru Granth Sāhib*. 'Sit on your cycle,' he replied, 'that is enough—you are married.' Such, at least, is the local tradition. Hazara Singh is something of a rarity in terms of his approach to 'santhood', but there is nothing untraditional in the response which he evokes.

We were not in the business of collecting Sants that day and so we resisted any temptation to linger as we entered the village of Naushehra Majha Singh on our way back to Batala. Naushehra Majha Singh is the abode of an even more famous Sant, Harnam Singh, and passing through the village one observes the distinctive blue turbans and sashes worn by his followers and the curious long-handled trowels which they carry.[1] We were, however, unable to resist another Sant whom we happened to spot. Our attention was actually caught by his garish minibus, bedecked with Khalsa flags and appropriate slogans. *Deg, teg, fateh,* proclaimed the front of the wagon. *Rāj karegā khālsā,* declared its rear,[2] and if one were to spend a few minutes on the task one could learn many things about the owner by reading the extensive inscriptions on either side of the vehicle. That, however, came later. The owner, sitting nearby on a charpoy, proved to be every bit as impressive as his chariot and the welcome which we received from this jovial soldiers of the Khalsa was in the best traditions of rural Punjab. This time, there was no hesitation when the camera appeared, merely some small delay as a handsome sword was set at the best possible angle. Our new friend was Sant Jogindar Singh of Gurdwara Tahali Sahib in Bhangali Kalan, a village near the town of Jaintipur. He is, it seems, known far beyond the bounds of Bhangali Kalan, for he has paid a visit to England in his role as Sant. We departed amidst warmly insistent invitations to visit his *ḍerā*,[3] coupled with promises to drive us around the surrounding villages in the splendid minibus.

Within the space of a single morning we had encountered two extremes of the modern Sant movement in the Punjab. As we shall see, there are other varieties to be found within the range marked by these two extremes, and the extensive influence wielded by many of these men makes it a very important movement indeed. At first sight, the modern Sants of the Punjab may seem to represent a complete break with the earlier tradition which we associate with Sant literature and devotion, particularly if we focus our attention on political activity or emblazoned minibuses. A connection nevertheless exists and one of the two purposes of this essay is to trace the lineage linking the two. The second purpose is to extend the description, already initiated, of the Sant phenomenon in modern Punjab.

An examination of the early Punjabi usage of the term *'sant'* will inevitably carry us back to the works of Guru Nanak. This is the obvious place to begin, for Nanak is conventionally ranked as a distinguished representative of the *sant paramparā* of northern India.[4] In so doing, we immediately encounter the first hint that Punjabi usage of the term *'sant'* may perhaps bear connotations distinguishing it from the meaning attached to it elsewhere in North India. Although Nanak may be acknowledged as a representative of the *sant paramparā*, he will *never* be called 'Sant Nanak'. Sikhs and scholars join in agreeing that the title is inappropriate in his case. Whereas the latter presumably refrain from doing so in response to the dictates of convention,[5] the former would certainly regard it as altogether demeaning. Any reference to 'Sant Nanak' would be treated as an insult. The Sants of today may be accorded reverence in modern Punjab, but assuredly theirs is not the highest order in the conventional hierarchy of religious authority and piety. The proper title is *'Guru'*, and if one seeks a variant it will have to be the *'Bābā'* of the *janam-sākhīs* or the highly exalted title *'Satgurū'*.[6]

This, however, concerns a later perception of the figure of the Sikh Guru and does not necessarily imply that the word *'sant'* possesses a derogatory connotation if applied to individuals other than the actual Master. For Nanak himself, the word certainly possessed no derogatory overtones. When he uses it (and he does so with considerable frequency) he employs it in a sense corresponding precisely with the usage and understanding of the wider *paramparā*.

bhāī re santajanā kī renu
santasabhā guru pāīai mukti padārathu dheṇu

Be as dust beneath the feet of Sants, brother.
It is in an assembly of Sants that one finds the Guru; like the *kāmadhenu*, [a gathering of Sants] confers the blessing of salvation.[7]

The Sant is thus identified as the pious devotee, he who in consort with others of like mind and commitment gathers in a *satsang* to sing the praises of God and seek the guidance of the eternal Guru within. Join them, Nanak repeatedly insists, for in their company salvation is attained. The same understanding is sustained by Nanak's successors and is most strongly asserted by the fifth Guru, Arjan.

jinā sāsi girāsi na visarai harināmāh mani mantu
dhanu si seī nānakā pūranu soī santu

They who treasure the mantra of God's Name in their hearts and minds, remembering it with every breath and with every morsel,
Blessed are they, Nanak, for they are the true Sants.[8]

For the Gurus, the term 'sant' thus designates any seeker after truth and salvation who pursues his objective by means of a particular range of activities. These include association with other devotees, regular participation in the singing of *kirtan*, the individual practice of *nām simraṇ*, and pure living. Although the word recurs frequently in the *Ādi Granth*,[9] it is by no means the only term used to describe the Guru's followers, nor has it proved to be the most durable. In Sikh usage, the most popular of the several synonyms has been the word which tends to be overlooked by reason of its subsequent dominance—the word 'sikh'. In the works of the Gurus 'sikh' and 'sant' are normally interchangeable, and the meaning which they express is also covered by several other terms. One which seems to have been particularly favoured is 'gurmukh', he who is 'turned towards the Guru' as opposed to the reprobate 'manmukh'. Others which serve essentially the same purpose in the *Ādi Granth* are 'sādh', 'sādhū', 'bhagat' (Hindi *bhakta*), 'sevak' and (occasionally) 'gursikh'. In this assembly 'sant' takes its place as an important word, but certainly not one possessing a unique meaning or importance.

The usage, with the some variety of synonyms, is continued in the Sikh devotional literature of the seventeenth, eighteenth, and nineteenth centuries. The differences which one encounters are shifts in preference, with 'sikh' surging strongly forward (accompanied by '*gursikh*') and '*sant*' dropping well behind it. The declining popularity of '*sant*' is emphasized by a shift in the meaning attached to '*bhagat*'. A particular distinction was conferred on '*bhagat*' by Guru Arjan who, when he compiled the *Ādi Granth* in 1603–04, chose it as the term to be used when designating works which were not by one of the Gurus. These were hymns attributed to people whom most would probably call Sants, notably Kabir, Namdev, and Ravidas (Raidas). In the *Ādi Granth*, however, they are distinguished as '*bhagats*' and, since the compiling of the *Ādi Granth*, it is by this title that they have characteristically been known in Sikh parlance. This usage the *janam-sākhīs* naturally reflect on the rare occasions when reference is made to Kabir or to the *bhagat bani*. No such distinction is bestowed upon '*sant*'. For most of the *janam-sākhī* narrators it commands no great popularity and, if it finds a place in their anecdotes concerning Guru Nanak, the reason is normally because it has been prompted by a quotation from the Guru's *bāṇī*. This is particularly marked in the case of those *janam-sākhīs* which concentrate on narrative rather than on scriptural exposition or exegesis. The B40 *janam-sākhī*, for example, has little use for the word.[10]

The same preferences are sustained by the authors of *rahit-nāmās*, the Khalsa 'codes of discipline' which first appear during the eighteenth century.[11] A partial exception to this rule is the *rahit-nāmā* attributed to Chaupa Singh, a work which employs the formula '*sant sakh*' when introducing an *Ādi Granth* quotation from the works of Kabir or Namdev. In other respects, however, the *rahit-nāmā* uses '*sant*' in the *janam-sākhī* sense, introducing it only occasionally[12] and demonstrating a much stronger preference for '*sikh*', '*gursikh*', and '*gurū kā sikh*'. The *rahit-nāmā* known as the *Prem Sumārg* offers the same pattern of preference, adding only an adjectival use which continues to the present day. In the *Prem sumarg*, descriptions of the Khalsa sometimes refer to it as the '*sant khalsa*'.[13]

By the time we reach the nineteenth century the trend seems to be clearly set. Although the term '*sant*' survives, it does so principally in the context of *Ādi Granth* usage and exposition. In the specifically *Ādi Granth* sense it continues, to the present day, to retain an intimate association with scriptural commentary and exegesis. Meanwhile, however, it has assumed its new connotation. This new usage is a twentieth-century development and its period of growth is not yet over. We return now to the Sants of the modern Panth, to the variety of precept which they communicate and to the nature of the response which they attract.

Although the title is a twentieth-century style, the kind of person to whom it is applied has been a part of Punjabi society for much longer. Indeed, one might well argue that the antecedents of the modern Sants are as ancient as India's reverence for individuals distinguished by their piety, asceticism or supernatural powers. In general terms, this traditional reverence for gurus, *pīrs* and *mahants* is indeed a part of the modern Sant development. More specifically, the Sants of today represent a distinctive range of piety, one which can be clearly traced to earlier developments within the Sikh Panth. These earlier developments and the general change which they produce, explain the shift in meaning from the *'sant'* of Guru Nanak's hymns to Sant Jogindar Singh and his minibus.

An earlier essay in this collection describes the substantial changes which overtook the Sikh Panth as a result of its increasingly dominant Jat constituency and the disturbed conditions which it encountered during the eighteenth century.[14] A significant aspect of this transformation was a considerable shift in the popular understanding of piety, a shift which substituted strongly extrovert forms for the earlier insistence on interior devotion. Changes in notions of piety are naturally accompanied by corresponding changes in the meanings of associated terminology and the term *'sant'* seems plainly to provide a clear, if belated, example of this process. Whereas the extrovert forms are firmly established during the course of the eighteenth century, the actual application of the title *'sant'* to one such form does not achieve widespread popularity until the twentieth century.

The fact that such men existed within the Panth well before the twentieth century can be vividly illustrated by the career of Bhai Maharaj Singh during the period immediately following the British annexation of the Punjab in March, 1849. Maharaj Singh lived in a *ḍerā* and imparted religious instruction to his followers. As the British were to discover, however, his interests and ideals were certainly not those of a quietist ascetic. They incorporated, explicitly and actively, a determination to defend the honour of the Khalsa as perceived by a man of militant understanding. As such, Maharaj Singh embodied a concept of religious duty corresponding closely to attitudes expressed by some of the modern Sants and a twentieth-century writer can refer to him as a Sant without any evident sense of incongruity.[15] Only the title *'bhāī'* is different.[16]

Maharaj Singh demonstrates that a pattern of militant religious leadership was current in the Punjab by the middle of the nineteenth century. In fact, it had been current within the Panth for generations

earlier, as Maharaj Singh's own background shows. Prior to assuming
a position of personal authority, Maharaj Singh has been the follower
of another activist leader, Bhai Bir Singh of Naurangabad (1768–
1844).[17] Bir Singh in turn had been the disciple of Baba Sahib Singh
of Una (1756–1834), heir to a succession within the family of Guru
Nanak's descendants.[18] Individuals in direct male descent from any
of the Gurus had always been accorded reverence, and the lineage
represented by Sahib Singh evidently received veneration from the
time of the first Guru onwards.

The tradition of a subsidiary master–disciple relationship thus
has a lengthy history within the Panth. Reverence for the Guru
himself (or his subsequent embodiment in the scripture and the
community[19]) remained the primary loyalty, but plainly it did not
permanently displace the tradition of loyalty to a present and visible
master. During the time of the later Gurus the role of immediate
master was evidently discharged by the Guru's appointed surrogates,
the *masands*. The fact that these representatives were expressly
disowned by Guru Gobind Singh did not destroy the pattern of
allegiance to a present and visible master, as the lineage of Sahib
Singh demonstrates. Although the *masands* were excommunicated
and eventually destroyed, the tradition of fealty upon which they
had depended was far too deeply rooted to disappear with them.
Others attracted it, and thus sustained the convention to which the
twentieth-century Sants are the present heirs.

In this manner, individuals continued to attract permanent
followings. With his group of disciples each master lived in a *ḍerā*,
almost always in a rural location. The following might be large or it
might comprise a mere handful. Other adherents would visit the
ḍerā from time to time, and individuals with no specific loyalty
would come for *darśan*. Normally the benevolence of adherents,
visitors, and neighbouring villages would provide for the sustenance
of a *ḍerā*, though some (such as the Una establishment) attracted
official support in the form of land grants. Instruction in the
principles of Sikh belief and practice was understood to be a function
of the *ḍerā*, and for this reason its residents commonly included
children.

This convention is as old as the Panth itself and, as we have
observed, represents a tradition of much greater antiquity. What
changes is not the essential form of the convention but the notion
of piety which it communicates and the consequent behaviour
patterns which these ideals encourage. The fact that the *ḍerā* was a

rural institution is important in this respect, for it was within the rural constituency of the Panth that the tradition of militant piety ascended to dominance during the eighteenth century. This ascendancy was faithfully reflected by many of the *ḍerās*, and found expression in the teachings and example which they offered.

Today the tradition is continued by the modern Sants and as the ideal has changed, so too has the connotation of the term which has been appropriated to express it. The word *'sant'* seems to have found currency because each of its several competitors had meanwhile acquired a distinctive usage of its own. Its most intimate associate, *'sikh'*, had long since assumed its present meaning as the general term applied to all members of the Panth, and *'gursikh'* is used to designate one who is strictly loyal to the *'rahit'*. The less common *'gurmukh'* applies to ordinary Sikhs of acknowledged piety and, as we have noted, *'bhagat'* has been firmly attached to poets such as Kabir whose works have been included in the *Ādi Granth*. Most people now regard a *'sādhū'* as an itinerant Hindu ascetic (commonly as a spurious pretender) and *'sevak'* implies *sevā* or 'service' in a *gurduārā*. This leaves *Baba*, *bhāī*, and *sant*. *'Bābā'* can still be used as a an appropriate title, but only for the few who possess distinctly impressive credentials. It is too exalted to serve a generic purpose. *'Bhāī'* meanwhile has acquired a diversity of usage ranging from the highly respectful to the openly condescending. Scholars of traditional Sikh learning are still accorded the title of *'bhāī'* and when used in this context it expresses genuine respect. This is the upper end of the scale. At the lower end is the *gurduārā* musician (*rāgī*). He too may be addressed as *'bhāī'* in some instances the title retains its deferential connotation. Commonly, however, it expresses a sense akin to 'hired servant'.

The process of elimination leaves us with *'sant'*. For whatever reason this is now the dominant title, though obviously not one with an agreed or static connotation. The response which the modern Sants elicit ranges from fervent devotion through indifference to outright condemnation. Some place total faith in their guidance; others regard them as ignorant exploiters of the credulous. There is, however, little doubt that the former greatly outnumber the latter and there is no visible indication that the popularity or authority of the Sants is waning.

The spectrum of response is well illustrated by the establishment developed during recent decades in the name of a famous Sant, Baba Nand Singh of Kaleran on the western edge of Ludhiana District. Nand Singh, originally from Sherpur village near Jagraon, earned a reputation as a devout ascetic by meditating for lengthy periods in holes dug underground. One of his caverns was located at Kaleran, five kilometres west of Jagraon, and it was here that he died. His successor, Sant Ishar Singh, commenced an ambitious *gurduārā* project at Kaleran in 1950, a plan which achieved a speedy and splendid success thanks to the reputation of the original Sant and the skill of his successor. Gurdwara Nanaksar is an expensive multistoried marble structure with gold-covered cupola and marble-paved tank. In the cellar marking Nand Singh's cavern, a portrait of the deceased Sant rests on a costly dais and elsewhere in the *gurduārā* his summer and winter clothes are preserved in a glass case as relics. Approximately one hundred attendants (*sevādār*) are permanently attached to the establishment and many thousands of devotees throng the *gurduārā* precincts during the annual celebrations of the Sant's birth.[20] There can be no ambiguity as far as these pilgrims are concerned. They come for a view of the great Sant's relics and thus combine in a conventional manner the benefits of *darśan* with the pleasures of a Punjabi outing. Others, however, are scornful and some plainly dismayed. Devotion of this order is due to the Guru alone, never to one of his disciples.

In another respect, of course, this particular example is far from typical. Most *ḍerās* are comparatively humble establishments. Sant Hazara Singh's abode in Ghumani is nothing more than a tiny mud hut attached to a mud-walled courtyard. The difference between multi-lakh grandeur and a mud hut illustrates the range of life-styles one encounters amongst the Sants, and one will also observe substantial differences in terms of their varying presentation of the Khalsa faith which all affirm. Four general categories can be recognized. First there are those like Hazara Singh who say little, but attract followings through a reputation for self-denying piety. Secondly, there are men with traditional *gurduārā* or *ḍerā* educations who emphasize the teaching of doctrine and kirtan. Thirdly, there are those whose message is more concerned with the heroic traditions of the Panth. This third variety is, in a sense, the latter-day descendant of the *ḍhāḍhī*, the itinerant preacher who earned a meagre living by entertaining village audiences with stirring stories from the traditional history of the Panth. Sant Jogindar Singh, with his minibus, presumably belongs to this category, though he would probably regard the *ḍhāḍhī* tag as an insult. Finally, there are the muscular Sants who stress deeds rather than teaching and who today express their beliefs in political action.

The second of these groups attracts the most widespread sympathy, though it may be a sympathy without a notable fervour. One *silsilā* with a substantial and continuing reputation is the line of Sants who have successively occupied the *gaddī* in Bagrian village.[21] Even the skeptical pay a certain deference to the Bagrian reputation for panthic service, and likewise to a few individual Sants noted for what all recognize to be a genuine piety. A distinguished example from the early twentieth century was Sant Attar Singh of Mastuana (1886–1926), renowned as a teacher of the scriptures and of kirtan.[22]

In a few instances Sants of this second category have been associated with the institution known as *taksāl*. The *taksāl* (literally 'mint') is a school or group of students attracted to a Sant of particular eminence. Anyone seeking an eduction in traditional Sikh learning may join a *taksāl* and there receive instruction from its Sant without charge. A famous example is the Bhindranwala *taksāl*, so named in 1906 after Sant Sundar Singh of Bhindran village. Although the *taksāl* has a permanent base in Mehta Sahib village (Mehta Chowk) it spends much of its time on the move. The Sant, together with his students, settles for a few weeks in a *gurduārā*, thus enabling local Sikhs to hear the regular discourses in return for the hospitality which they provide. Having spent a period in one particular *gurduārā* the Bhindranwala *taksāl* then moves on to another. A recent incumbent of the Bhindranwala *gaddī* was Jarnail Singh. Sant Jarnail Singh Bhindranwale achieved considerable prominence during the years following 1978 as a result of his involvement in Punjab politics and his eventual death during he Indian Army's assault on the Golden Temple complex in June 1984.[23]

Jarnail Singh's political involvement effectively translated him from the second to the fourth category, achieving for him a fame (or notoriety) equalled by no other Sant. As such, Jarnail Singh came to be regarded as an 'extremist', contending for panthic authority with the so-called 'moderate' leaders of the Akali Party. The most prominent of the 'moderates', Harchand Singh of Longowal, was another Sant who had moved from traditional religious leadership to highly conspicuous political activity.[24] Although his political style differed markedly from that of Jarnail Singh the two Sants shared a common conviction that political action is inseparable from panthic loyalty. An earlier example, one who achieved renown in the struggle for Punjabi Suba, was Sant Fateh Singh.

The term *sant* has thus travelled a considerable distance since the days of Guru Nanak, though the connection between the early usage and its modern descendant is plainly visible. The path which it has followed is the path which the Panth itself has followed. As ideals have developed so too have important elements in the traditional terminology, and of these *sant* provides a prominent example. The process is by no means over. The Sants of today are a dynamic group and it would be naive to suggest that their days of influence are numbered.

Notes

1. Sant Harnam Singh and his following have been described by Gurdeep Singh Bajwa, 'The New Namdhari Sect at Naushehra Majha Singh,' in John C.B. Webster, ed., *Popular Religion in the Punjab Today* (Delhi: S.P.C.K., 1974), pp. 36–9. The long-handled trowel (rather like a blunt spear in appearance) has been prescribed in order that the disciple's daily excrement can be buried. The burying of excrement is a part of the rule prescribed by Sant Harnam Singh.

2. The two inscriptions are the most famous of Khalsa slogans, both dating from the eighteenth century. The first, 'Cauldron-sword-victory!', combines the ideal of charity with the promise of success in battle. The second declares the ultimate result: 'The Khalsa shall rule!'.

3. *ḍerā, ḍerāh*: 'camp', dwelling-place of a Sant and his followers. The term was also used for Kanphata yogi establishments.

4. Parashuram Chaturvedi, *Kabīr-sāhitya kī parakh* (Allahabad: Bharati Bhandar, 1955), p. 15, and *Uttarī Bhārat kī sant-paramparā*, 2nd edn (Allahabad: Bharati Bhandar, 1965), p. 421. Ramkumar Varma, *Hindī sāhityā kā ālochanātmak itihās*, 4th edn (Allahabad: Ramnarayan Benimadhav, 1958), p. 57.

5. The distinction implied by the title is particularly striking in Parashuram Chaturvedi's edited selection of Sant works entitled *Sant-kavya*, 3rd edn (Allahabad: Kitab Mahal, 1967). A succession of thirteen poets, all bearing the title *'sant'*, is eventually broken by *'Gurū'* Nanak Dev. Hazariprasad Dvivedi uses the same honourific form. See also Varma, *Hindī-sāhitya*, p. 270.

6. This distinction in modern Punjab between *'sant'* and *'guru'* is not confined to the Sikh Panth. Mark Juergensmeyer encountered the same feeling in the course of his work on the Ad Dharam movement. Some years ago, the Indian government issued a commemorative stamp honouring Sant Ravidas. This produced an objection in the Ad Dharam journal *Ravidās patrikā*, protesting the use of *'sant'* instead of *'gurū'*. Mark Juergensmeyer, 'Political Hope: The Quest for Political Identity and Strategy in the Social Movement of North India's Untouchables, 1900–1970,' (Ph.D. dissertation, University of California, Berkeley, 1974), p. 403.

7. *Siri Rag* 12, *Ādi Granth*, p. 18 (hereafter *AG*); see also *Prabhātī* 17 (1),

AG p. 1332. The *guru* to whom Nanak refers is the mystical presence of God. W.H. McLeod, *Gurū Nānak and the Sikh Religion* (Oxford: Clarendon Press, 1968), p. 199. The *kāmadhenu* is the 'wish-cow' which miraculously produced anything desired by her master, the rishi Vasistha.

8. *Gauṛī kī Vār* 8:1, *AG* p. 319. For another arresting definition see Guru Arjan's *Āsā* 88, *AG* p. 392. This latter *sabad* expounds the *sant rahit*, or 'way of life of a Sant'.

9. All examples of the *Ādi Granth* usage of the term are listed by Gurcharan Singh, ed., *Ādi Granth śabad-anukramaṇikā* (Patiala: Punjabi University, 1971), Vol. 1, pp. 250–3. A comprehensive collection of *Ādi Granth* examples, giving the actual text in each case, is provided in Piara Singh Padam, ed., *Guru Granth vichar-kos* (Patiala: Punjabi University, 1969), pp. 123–30. Kahn Singh Nabha, ed., *Gurumat martaṇḍ*, Vol. 1 (Amritsar: Shiromani Gurduārā Parbandahak Kamiti, 1962), pp. 196–204, provides a shorter collection, but adds to it examples from Bhai Gurdas, Nand Lal, and Mani Singh.

10. For the *janam-sākhīs*, see W.H. McLeod, *The Evolution of the Sikh Community* (Oxford: Clarendon Press, 1976), chap. 2, and idem, *Early Sikh Tradition* (Oxford: Clarendon Press, 1980). See also Narinder Kaur Bhatia, ed., *Srī Satgurū jī de muhain dīān sākhīān* (Amritsar: by the Editor, 1978), pp. 41, 53, 59, for examples of seventeenth-century usage from works other than the *janam-sākhīs*. The last of these is particularly interesting as it sets *'sant'*, *'bhagat'*, and *'gurumukh'* in joint contrast to the supremely exalted *'maha-purakh'*. The *janam-sākhīs* also use *'maha-purakh'* as a means of distinguishing the Guru from ordinary people (*purakh*) or disciples (*sikh, sant*, etc.)

11. McLeod, *Evolution*, pp. 51–2.

12. Sikh Reference Library, Amritsar, manuscript no. 6124, ff. 45a, 49b, 89a.

13. Randhir Singh, ed., *Prem sumārg granth*, 2nd edn (Jalandhar: New Book Company, 1965), pp. 3, 4, 8.

14. See W.H. McLeod, 'The Development of the Sikh Panth,' above, pp. 49–69.

15. M.L. Ahluwalia, *Bhāī Mahārāj Singh* (Patiala: Punjabi University, 1972), p. xiii. For Maharaj Singh's conflict with the British, see, in addition to Ahluwalia, Nahar Singh, ed., *Documents Relating to Bhāī Maharaj Singh* (Gurdwara Karamsar, Punjab: Sikh History Source Material Search Association, 1968).

16. Maharaj Singh actually bore two titles. Originally his name had been Nihal Singh, a name which was subsequently abandoned as devotees insisted on addressing him as *'maharāj'*. To the new name of Maharaj Singh the honorific *'bhāī'* was subsequently added. Ahluwalia, *Bhai Maharaj Singh*, p. 8.

17. Kahn Singh Nabha, *Guruśabad ratanākar mahān koś*, 2nd edn (Patiala:

Languages Department, Punjab Government, 1960), p. 658.
Naurangabad is in the southern portion of Amritsar District.

18. Ibid., pp. 133, 658. Una is in the southern corner of Kangra District, near the Bhakra Dam.

19. See above pp. 63–5.

20. *Punjab District Gazetteers: Ludhiana* (Chandigarh: Punjab State Government, 1970), pp. 660–1.

21. Bagrian is in Ludhiana District, seven and one half miles north-west of Nabha. Kahn Singh Nabha, *Mahān koś*, pp. 636, 783.

22. Ibid., p. 39. Like most of the famous Sants of his period, Attar Singh was a Malwai. Most Sants are Jats by caste, a feature which is scarcely surprising in view of the essentially rural nature of the modern Sant phenomenon. There are, however, some very important exceptions. Nand Singh of Kaleran was a Ramgarhia, and likewise the representatives of the Bagrian line. The Una line (descendants of Guru Nanak) are Khatris and so too is Sant Harnam Singh of Naushehra Majha Singh.

23. Narendra Aggarwal, 'Portrait of a Religious Leader,' *The Overseas Hindustan Times* 16:27 (3 July 1980), p. 11. The influence of the Bhindranwala *ṭaksāl* is attested by the fact that its alumni include a recent chief *granthī* at the Golden Temple and *jathedārs* of all the *takhats*. Ibid.

24. For an interesting if adulatory account of the life of Sant Harchand Singh, see Surjit Singh Gandhi, 'Sant Harchand Singh Longowal' in *The Spokesman Weekly* 27:49 (31 July 1978), pp. 7–8. For a perceptive comment on the current political role of the Sants see Bhagawan Singh Josh, 'New Dimensions in Sikh Politics' in the *Economic and Political Weekly* 13:4 (7 October 1978), p. 1697.

11

SIKH FUNDAMENTALISM*

An effort is here made to ascertain whether or in what way the epithet 'fundamentalist' is applicable to the Sikh religion. In the course of the essay, several valences of the word current in popular or academic discourse are examined; most are found irrelevant or misleading when applied to the Sikhs, being founded on Western, secularized understandings of the word or, at worst, loose journalistic usage.

I s there such a thing as Sikh fundamentalism? Sikh theologians deny that such a concept can be applied to their faith and would presumably explain the recent situation in the following terms. Most Sikhs to not ever hear or read the term (or its translation) and few of those who do encounter it ever understand it. Of the tiny minority who do both hear and understand it, practically all dismiss it as a term which could be applied to Sikh belief.[1] It is a Western term, foisted on the Sikhs by the loose usage of journalists. The term is certainly used in recent publications with marked frequency. It is, however, one which has been transferred from its Western context to the Islamic movements associated in particular with Iran, and from there was conveniently appropriated to describe the Sikh movement for Khalistan. The Khalistan movement was regarded as extreme and therefore it was fundamentalist.

Is this a fair assessment? It is true that many of the participants in

*Originally published in *Journal of the American Oriental Society*, Vol. 118, No. 1, 1998.

the campaign for an independent Sikh state ('Khalistan') were correctly described as activists or militants, and many of them adopted a traditional view of their inherited faith. It is tradition in the sense that they revere their Gurus and the sacred scripture. It is also traditional in that those who upheld it adhered to a view of history which sanctifies the use of the sword when the need is compelling and when all other means have failed. Many of them could be described as fanatical in maintaining this particular faith. But this is not fundamentalism. The term 'fundamentalist' does not mean 'traditional,' on the one hand, nor 'fanatical,' on the other. It came to be increasingly used because journalists and other people in search of meaningful equivalents adopted this particular word as a loose equivalent of 'fanatical.' Jarnail Singh Bhindranwale was a fanatical exponent of Sikh separatism. Therefore Jarnail Singh Bhindranwal was a Sikh fundamentalist.

This view of fundamentalism as an equivalent of 'traditional' or 'fanatical' seems, on the face of it, to be a wrong use of the term. Fundamentalism, surely, concerns a belief in the inerrancy of holy scripture. Before accepting that this view is mistaken, however, there are at least six questions which deserve to be considered.

1. Is our understanding of the term 'fundamentalism' in the Sikh context astray?
2. Are there really any groups within the Khalsa which can legitimately be described as fundamentalist?
3. What should we make of the views of some Sikh writers, mainly in English-language journals (particularly those which circulate amongst overseas Sikhs), who sound suspiciously like true fundamentalists?[2] Are there some Sikhs who, under the influence of Western models, do adopt fundamentalism after all?
4. What are we to make of the usage by journalists and other commentators who appropriated the term to refer to militant Sikhs? Their introduction of the term may not correspond to its original meaning, but introduce it they assuredly have.
5. What should we make of the argument offered by T.N. Madan in the first volume of Marty and Appleby's *The Fundamentalism Project*?[3] Madan evidently believes the use of 'fundamentalism' to be an appropriate term for the Akali Dal (he is quite explicit about this) and for the Khalistan movement associated with Sant Jarnail Singh Bhindranwale.[4]
6. The strong defence of the term 'fundamentalism' as applied to Khalistani Sikhs made by Harjot Singh Oberoi in the third volume of the series also needs to be considered.[5]

Consideration of these six objections may perhaps lead us to modify the claim that fundamentalism is absent from the Sikh faith.

My own definition of fundamentalism is as follows. Fundamentalism, in its original and Christian sense, holds a central doctrine, together with a number of subordinate doctrines which flow from it. The central doctrine is the inerrancy of the Bible, and all the other issues which we associate with the fundamentalist faith are consequences of this one affirmation—such things as belief in the virgin birth or, at a vastly greater distance, hostility to abortion.

This definition has subsequently been applied to Islam, where it seems to fit satisfactorily. Many Muslims also attribute verbal inerrancy to the Qur'an, just as fundamentalist Christians do to the Bible. The transference to the Sikh community (the Panth) raises some doubts, but at least the Sikhs have a sacred scripture and it is possible to argue that some of them attach a fundamentalist meaning to it. In theory at least it is possible to envisage fundamentalism within the Sikh Panth.

With this definition in mind we can now proceed to consider each of the six objections which can be made to the original statement that there is no such thing as fundamentalism in the Sikh Panth.

Is 'Sikh fundamentalism' correctly understood?

This question can be briefly considered and then set aside. Some Sikhs may be fundamentalists, but we must be careful not to align them with the more extreme forms of Western fundamentalism. Sikh fundamentalists (if the term is permissible) do not seek to build walls around themselves and to live lives separated from the remainder of their community or other communities. There is no thought of a border which should be sealed, nor of modernist ideas which must be shut out. Whatever else may be said of this category of Sikhs, they are definitely prepared to face the world. If we are to declare some Sikhs fundamentalist, their fundamentalism must be understood in a modified form. At the same time the beliefs of certain groups within the Sikh Panth are indeed close enough to the definition offered above to warrant a closer examination.

Two modern Sikh sects

Let us therefore consider the possibility that there may indeed the fundamentalists within the Panth, those who correspond to my own strict definition of the term. There are certain groups within the Panth which take a rigorous view of their Sikh duty and of the Sikh scriptures, particularly the Adi Granth (the 'Guru Granth Sahib'). Do any of these groups qualify as fundamentalists? Do the Namdharis, for example, adopt a position which entitles them to be called fundamentalists?[6]

1. *The Namdharis (Kukas)*

The Namdharis (or the Kukas, as the are commonly known) emerged in northwestern Punjab during the later years of Maharaja Ranjit Singh, who died in 1839. During these years some Sikhs believed that the Panth was being led astray by the pride which accompanied Ranjit Singh's military triumphs, and one of these Sikhs, Balak Singh by name, gathered around him a group of followers dedicated to meditation on the divine Name. The Namdharis differed from orthodox Sikhs because they came to believe that Guru Gobind Singh did not die in 1708 but lived on in secret until the age of 137, eventually conferring the succession on Balak Singh. In 1841 Ram Singh arrived as a soldier in Hazro up in northwest Punjab where Balak Singh delivered his teachings and, according to the Namdhari tradition, was instantly recognized by Balak Singh as his successor.

In 1862 Balak Singh died and under Ram Singh, twelfth Guru by Namdhari reckoning, the centre of the group moved down to his home village of Bhaini Raian in Ludhiana District. There the sect briefly blossomed, ran foul of the British administration of the Punjab in 1871–2, and were treated with considerable severity. Ram Singh was exiled to Rangoon and the sect declined into obscurity. It still continues today, but only as a tiny group. The fact that the Namdharis maintain a continuing line of personal Gurus means that on this particular point they are distinctly unorthodox to the great majority of other Sikhs. Their numbers are, however, insufficient to cause any trouble. Moreover, the Namdharis, by their generally strict observance of other Khalsa conventions, are commonly regarded with admiration, rather than as heretics.

The Namdharis or Kukas are easily recognized by their practice of wearing white homespun clothing and (in the case of men at least) by tying their turbans horizontally across the forehead. Around their necks they wear a white woollen cord, woven as a series of 108 knots and serving as a rosary. They are strict vegetarians, and it was partly their vigorous concern for cow protection which led to the encounters with the British administration in 1871–2. Their most distinctive ritual is fire-ceremony, another point of disagreement with orthodox Sikhs.

During the performance of this ceremony several of the worshippers would attain a condition of ecstasy and in this condition would shriek. The Punjabi for 'shriek' is *kūk*, from which the alternative name 'Kuka' originated.

In one respect the Kukas are better suited than their orthodox brethren to be taken as fundamentalists. In addition to the Adi Granth and the Dasam Granth (they do not share the orthodox Sikhs' misgivings about the latter) they possess the Namdhari *Rahit-nāmā*,[7] the author of which was undoubtedly Ram Singh. To the Kukas it is Gurbani, an 'utterance of the Guru', and it must therefore be wholly accepted and obeyed. The overwhelming bulk of the Adi Granth concentrates its practical instruction in the repeated obligation to practice *nām simaraṇ* or *nām japaṇ* ('remembering, chanting the divine Name'). The Kukas extend this same obligation to the Namdhari *Rahit-nāmā* and it conveys to them very explicit commandments, indeed.

Rise during the last watch of the night and taking a pot of water [for cleansing] go out into the fields to relieve nature. When you return scour the pot twice, remove the clothes which you were wearing while in the fields, clean your teeth, and recite [the prescribed portions of] sacred scripture.[8]

This is very different from the sacred scripture (the Adi Granth, or Guru Granth Sahib) which all Sikhs accept. The Namdhari *Rahit-nāmā* continues in a thoroughly practical vein, communicating some very explicit instructions from Ram Singh to his followers:

Always wear the approved breeches (*kachh*). When taking off a *kachh* withdraw one leg and put it in the leghole of another pair before withdrawing the second leg.[9] Never conceal an evil deed committed by another person. Do not sell or barter a daughter or a sister. Constantly repeat the Guru's name. Never eat meat or drink alcoholic liquor. Continue always in the fear of God.[10]

Loyal Kukas obey these commandments, as indeed they obey all the words of scripture (both the Adi Granth and the Dasam Granth) that are amenable to belief or behaviour. These they obey literally. Others may disagree with some of their interpretations, but nobody seems inclined to question their sincerity. The Kukas are accordingly literal believers in the words of their Guru and as such they are plainly fundamentalists.

But, say devout Sikhs of the orthodox Khalsa, we too are literal believers in the words of the Gurus, and we too uphold the Rahit of the Khalsa (the code of belief and conduct). The wording of the orthodox Rahit may differ substantially from that of the Namdhari *Rahit-nāmā*, but the Rahit it remains and the devout accept it absolutely. Are we not fundamentalists also? As an example of strict and devout Sikhs let us next consider the followers of Bhai Randhir Singh.[11]

2. The followers of Bhai Randhir Singh

Bhai Randhir Singh, a Jat from the large village of Narangwal in Ludhiana District, was distinguished by two things in particular. First, he was strongly opposed to the British presence in India and spent lengthy periods in gaol. His life of protest and lengthy imprisonment is told in his *Jehl Chiṭṭhīān*, translated as *Autobiography of Bhai Sahib Randhir Singh*.[12] Secondly, he was singularly rigorous in his observance of the Khalsa discipline, creating all manner of difficulty for his jailers while he was imprisoned. He was, of course, a strict vegetarian, but this created no problems. The problems with his food arose because of his insistence upon *sarab loh*, 'all iron.' The words *sarab loh* are closely associated with the way of life imparted by Guru Gobind Singh and with instructions given by him to his Sikhs. Randhir Singh took these instructions to an extreme length and refused, for example, to eat anything which had not been cooked in an iron vessel. Moreover he insisted on food which had been brought or prepared by a strictly orthodox Sikh.[13]

For some time he was closely associated with Babu Teja Singh of Bhasaur and the Panch Khalsa Divan, but parted company with them when Teja Singh was excommunicated from the Panth.[14] His career, in many ways, runs parallel with that of Bhai Vir Singh, with the significant exception that whereas Vir Singh is well known to the English-speaking world Randhir Singh is almost completely unknown. It is a measure of the Singh Sabha success. Whereas their representative (and also their version of Sikhism) is abundantly known to those who read only English, as well as those who know Punjabi, other representatives and other versions are largely hidden, at least from the former group. Only when they present a conspicuous presence (like the Nihang Sikhs) are they noted and even then there is very little that can be discovered about them.[15]

Around Randhir Singh there gathered a group of followers (the *Bhai Randhīr Siṅgh dā Jathā*) who, although they are certainly members of the Khalsa, can perhaps be described as a sect. To these people Randhir Singh is known simply as Bhai, never as Sant. Their way of life, following that of their master, is extremely strict. Particular emphasis is laid on the practice of *kīrtan* (singing of the scriptures) and his followers frequently devote the whole night to *raiṇ sabāī* ('all night') performance of it. *Nām simaraṇ* is also practiced in a distinctive way which includes an hour of reciting the word *vāhigurū* every morning.[16] There is also a special ritual at *amrit sanskār* (Khalsa initiation) in which the five Gursikhs administering initiation each places a hand on the initiate's head after the actual ceremony. They then rapidly repeat the sacred word *vāhigurū*, turn about for as much as five minutes, the five Gursikhs together alternating with the single Sikh whom they have just initiated. This is known as *guramantar driṛ karaūṇa*, 'rendering the Guru-mantra firm'.

When they charge a new initiate not to commit the four *kurahat* (breaches of the Rahit, or 'sins') the second one is the commandment not to eat any meat, instead of the normal version which enjoins the Sikh not to eat meat which has been slaughtered according to the Muslim rite.[17] The Five Ks as observed by his followers do not include the *kes* (the uncut hair), for members of the sect say that whereas the Five Ks are all outward *symbols* the *kes* is something with which a person is born. In its place they list the *keski* or small under-turban as one of the Ks, and women members also wear one.

In many other ways the followers of Bhai Randhir Singh are also noted for their strict observance of their own distinctive Khalsa discipline. They issue their own *Rahit Maryādā* and from the Bhai Randhir Singh Publishing House in Ludhiana many other works are also distributed. Members almost invariably marry within the sect; and *got* (sub-caste) names are never used. Although Randhir Singh was a Jat, the leadership of the sect is now largely concentrated in the hands of urban castes (Khatri and Arora, particularly the former). The sect has little time for scholars, preferring always the words and example of Bhai Randhir Singh as adequate for all their needs. Dr. Trilochan Singh was their only member with claims to scholarship. And he was recognized not as a scholar, but as an ordinary member of the sect.

In the recent Punjab disturbances they played an important part, but eventually they felt that matters had gone altogether too far. When the protest was mounted against the meeting of the Sant Nirankaris in Amritsar on Baisakhi Day 1978 (the occasion which thrust Jarnail Singh Bhindranwale before the public gaze), ten out of the thirteen Sikhs who were killed were members of the sect.[18] Later, when the leader of the Sant Nirankaris, Baba Gurbachan Singh, was assassinated, it was another member who allegedly did the deed. In June 1990 this member, Ranjit Singh, currently in jail awaiting trial, was elected absentee Jathedar of Akal Takhat, perhaps the highest honour that the Khalsa can bestow.[19] The sect was, however, strongly opposed to the Damdami Taksal and regarded their activities with considerable distaste.[20] Many of its members are government servants and there were indications that in the latter years of the agitation they were anxious to distance themselves from it.[21]

As one would expect, the scripture is, for the followers of Randhir Singh, absolutely inviolate. The scripture has been definitively given and no tampering with the text is even remotely tolerable. The meaning imparted by the sacred text is also perfectly clear. It requires no explanation and as a result there is no place in their services for any *kathā* or exposition of the text. This also sounds like fundamentalism. Ordinary members of the Khalsa might have their doubts and hesitations, but fervent members (such as the followers of Bhai Randhir Singh) can surely earn the title of fundamentalist.

The definitions offered by other Sikh writers

What, then, of our third objection, the claim that certain Sikh writers have expressed theories which sound rather like fundamentalism. Here it must be clearly understood that we are not talking about Sikhs of a sectarian persuasion, but those of an orthodox Singh Sabha point of view. More precisely they were members of the Tat Khalsa wing of the Singh Sabha, the radical group within the Singh Sabha that won a total victory over the conservative Sanatan Sikhs. There are two varieties of opinion available in this respect. One is the small group of later Tat Khalsa writers (of whom the most notable was Bhai Jodh Singh), whose concern was with the recensions of the Adi Granth. The second is a cluster of doctors of medicine, civil servants, and academics writing at the present time whose main objective is to protect the Sikh faith against what they feel are the hostile attacks of certain people who, they allege, are enemies of the Panth.

The first of these groups can be summarily exonerated. Jodh Singh was certainly a loyal Sikh and he was most anxious to establish the claims of the Kartarpur recension (*bīr*) to be the full and final text of most of the Adi Granth.[22] The Kartarpur *bīr* was believed to be the manuscript which Bhai Gurdas had inscribed at the dictation of Guru Arjan when the scripture was definitively recorded in 1603–4. To it were later added the works of the ninth Guru and tradition holds that one couplet was the work of Guru Gobind Singh, but these were the only supplements. The final version which contained these supplements was the Damdama *bīṛ* which (it is believed) was lost to the Sikhs during the disturbances with the Afghans later in the eighteenth century. The loss was not critical, however, in that the Kartarpur *bīṛ* still existed and Jodh Singh conducted careful research on it with the intention of showing that modern versions of the Adi Granth were faithful replicas of it. One problem was the existence of the Banno *bīṛ*, which contained some additional material. Jodh Singh was concerned to show that the material was not in the Kartarpur *bīṛ* and was accordingly unacceptable.

This approach did not make a fundamentalist of Jodh Singh, however, nor did the work of other people associated with the Tat Khalsa (such as Professor Teja Singh and Professor Sahib Singh). They were strongly traditionalist in their approach to the text, but their concern was the actual text of the scripture rather than the meaning of every word, and it is difficult to envisage them being totally immune to the textual work which is being done today or to the discoveries which are being made. They were, after all, committed to the belief that the Adi Granth was the work of Guru Arjan, a belief which no one has ever tried to upset because the evidence for maintaining it is strong. But what did Guru Arjan actually dictate and what was the process by means of which he finally produced the text? However conservative Jodh Singh may have been it is difficult to picture him being adamantly opposed to any careful research or resolutely refusing to accept its results.

The second group is much more varied in content, and certainly some of its statements would seem to tend strongly towards the fundamentalist position. In his essay written for the third volume of *The Fundamentalism Project*, Oberoi draws attention to one of the clearest of these statements, in the work of Daljeet Singh, who upholds the view that only devout Sikhs should study Sikhism.[23] Another Sikh who, in recent times, has expressed views similar to Daljeet Singh is the orthopedic surgeon, Dr. Jasbir Singh Mann of California. In a letter to *World Sikh News* he has expressed disappointment that the University of British Columbia retains complete control over the recently instituted chair of Sikh Studies, arguing vigorously that the 'community who pays the donation for the chair' must have a significant measure of authority over it. This is necessary, he maintains so that a Sikh may be chosen.

Credentials of the person in selection must be verified and whether the person concerned is a believer or not.[24]

Dr. Mann's concern is that the holder of the chair should not simply be a believer, but that he or she should be a *reliable* believer, one who 'presents an authentic image of the Sikh religion.' This is the conclusion which must be drawn, as the present incumbent of the chair, Professor Harjot Oberoi, is a Sikh who 'has used the art of suppression, distortion, misrepresentation and in academic conduct (*sic*) while representing the Sikh position.'[25]

These are the sort of statements which one might well expect from a fundamentalist believer. Oberoi is a fine scholar, yet because he is critical in the academic sense of the word he draws fire from some sensitive members of the Panth. Even in the loose sense of the term, however, neither Daljeet Singh nor Jasbir Singh Mann strictly qualifies as a fundamentalist. Their position has not been thought through to the point where one can precisely and definitively say just where they stand in such matters. It is rather that they conceive of the academic field as the arena for conducting the skirmishes which are so much a part of the Sikh way of life.

Are militant Khalistanis or other political radicals fundamentalists?

We come to the fourth objection. To detect true fundamentalism in the Panth might require careful analysis, but ordinary journalists are not particularly noted for activities so detailed or so time-consuming. They are much more interested in finding a word which will serve their immediate purpose and for this purpose the word 'fundamentalism' has done the job. It worked for Beirut and the Ayatollah, and so it was made to work for the Khalistanis also. Journalists and others with an interest in quick returns have used the term freely because for their purposes it serves the need.

Their usage has, in turn, been taken over by scholars who have reinterpreted 'fundamentalist' and 'fundamentalism' in terms which are congenial to this originally popular usage. Emphatically, this does not mean that the scholars who have appropriated this contemporary usage have also taken over the superficial understanding of many of the journalists. To argue this on the basis of the two excellent articles by Madan and Oberoi would be misguided in the extreme. Those who do assume this meaning are, however, distinguished by the contemporary meaning they impart to the term, and to this extent journalists and these scholars operate on the same wave-length.[26]

The person who rigorously adopts the meaning favoured by this essay must learn anew the lesson that the distinction between his usage and that of the journalists normally favours the latter. Words have a habit of changing their meaning if they are used with sufficient frequency by sufficient people over a sufficiently lengthy period. 'Fundamentalism' shows every sign of being a word of this kind. If, in popular usage, the word is insistently applied in the meaning of the journalists, the journalist's meaning will come to be firmly accepted. There is every indication that this has indeed happened and that the popular meaning is, in fact, popularly accepted. The supporters of Khalistan were repeatedly branded as fundamentalist Sikhs. Strictly speaking, the usage may be inaccurate and commonly it is very loosely used by scholars as well as popular writers, but it will remain inaccurate only for as long as it remains unabsobed into the language of regular discourse. The signs are clearly that it has been progressively absorbed, and the protest of some scholars that it is an inaccurate usage have been increasingly disregarded.

Madan's definition

The point made in the preceding section is well illustrated by T.N. Madan in his article published in the first volume of *The Fundamentalism Project* series.[27] We shall briefly consider the meaning which he attaches to the terms 'fundamentalist' and 'fundamentalism,' noting in particular on which side of the fence he stands.

Early in the essay Madan offers the following definitions:

> In contemporary political discourse in India, a 'fundamentalist' is a person who resorts to selective retrieval, picking out from his religious tradition certain elements of high symbolic significance with a view to mobilizing his coreligionists for action. The goals of such action are usually a mixture of religious objectives . . . and the politico-economic interests of one's own community as against those of similarly defined other communities. The government, too, is opposed if it comes in the way. Fundamentalists are seen by their critics as closely associated with, or as being themselves, political

'extremists' . . . and, in certain situations with 'terrorists.' . . .
The fundamentalist is very much a creature of his situation rather than a
pure traditionalist, and fundamentalism is not pristine orthodoxy.
Orthodoxy would in fact discourage fundamentalism: if the teachings of
the gurus are our guide, they advocate catholicity and not narrowness of
the mind.[28]

This, clearly, is not the understanding of the terms with which
this essay began. Madan imparts to both terms a much wider meaning.
It does not follow, however, that he is necessarily wrong in his
definition. It will be noted that he precedes his definition with the
words, 'In contemporary political discourse,' and the sentence that
precedes this quotation makes it abundantly clear that it is a
contemporary political understanding which he has in mind.

In the judgement of the government, largely shared by the public (including
many Sikhs), Bhindranwale was a fundamentalist.[29]

Later in the article he states:

During the two decades between the passing of the Gurdwara Reform Act
in 1925 and the independence of the subcontinent in 1947, Sikh public
life became polarized between fundamentalists (Akali Dal), who retained
control of the SGPC, and secularists (Congress and the Communist Party),
who dominated politics.[30]

Sikh fundamentalism is orthoprax rather than orthodox and this
Madan declares to be generally true of the teachings of Bhindranwale.

It will be worthwhile at this point to clarify briefly the nature of the Sikh
canon or scripture (as a source of basic teachings) and of the codes of conduct
which define the outward signs of Sikh identity. In his speeches Bhindranwale
laid more stress on the latter than on the former, talking little of theological
or cosmological ideas as such and more about behavioural matters and
politico-economic issues.[31]

The sanctity of the scripture was certainly not eliminated in
Bhindranwale's call to the faithful,[32] but the emphasis was on
behavioural matters.[33] It will become clear, as we proceed with the
argument, that the whole subject of fundamentalism is burdened
with at least two differing definitions; and where I may be correct in
maintaining mine Madan may be equally right in maintaining his.
Or perhaps we are both right, fundamentalism having acquired in
modern usage two very different meanings.

Oberoi's definition

The same difference essentially applies to the article by Harjot Oberoi, though his definition leans much more strongly on the importance of the Sikh scripture. Oberoi affirms the existence of Sikh fundamentalism for three reasons. First, there exists in modern Punjabi a term corresponding exactly to fundamentalism, the word *mūlvād*. In this Punjabi word,

Sikhs possess a term that exactly corresponds to fundamentalism and stands in stark opposition to *adharma*, a Punjabi word for secularism. Although the term mulvad is of recent coinage, resulting from the need to have a Punjabi counterpart to fundamentalism, Sikh journalists, essayists and politicians, in discussing contemporary religious and political movements, now constantly use the term mūlvād, connoting a polity and society organized on the basis of religious (particularly scriptural) authority.[34]

Secondly, Sikhs of this authoritarian persuasion, much like Christian fundamentalists at the turn of this century, 'have no patience for hermeneutic or critical readings of Sikh scriptures.'[35] In this respect he draws attention to a recent book which questions the use of Western historiography and textual analysis for the study of Sikh history and sacred texts, and firmly upholds that Sikhism should be studied only by those scholars who can strengthen the faith and espouse its 'fundamentals.'[36] Jarnail Singh Bhindranwale allowed no form of insult to be paid to that Sikh scriptures and, should need arise, 'Sikhs were morally obliged to kill an individual who dared to show disrespect towards the holy book.'[37]

Thirdly, the current Sikh movement 'amply manifests many tendencies like millenarianism, a prophetic vision, puritanism, and antipluralism.'[38] These, he indicates, are trends which have commonly been associated with fundamentalism. He points out that the debate is being conducted in terms which are strongly reminiscent of the debates concerning the introduction of other Western terms into non-Western societies—terms such as feudalism, millenarianism, religion, class, and so on.[39] He concludes his preliminary statement:

For these three reasons—linguistic, cultural and associative—I think we are justified in speaking and thinking in terms of Sikh fundamentalism.[40]

In the argument which follows he then assumes and develops this definition, applying it to the supporters of the Khalistan movement.

Of these three reasons it is the second one which matters. The first one merely reflects the loose usage of Western journalists, a term having been recently coined (as Oberoi admits) to accommodate a word which is currently popular in the English-speaking world. Journalists have been using 'fundamentalism' to describe radical or extremist movements; a term was not available in the Punjabi language; and so one was invented from the word *mūl* meaning 'root' or 'source'.[41] As a very recent addition to the Punjabi language it merely replicates the wider meaning of 'fundamentalism' in Western usage.

The third reason can also be discounted. Millenarianism and puritanism may certainly figure as features of some forms of Christian fundamentalism, but they existed long before fundamentalism and it is quite possible to envisage fundamentalism without either of them. Moreover, the debate which employs the terms 'fundamentalist' or 'fundamentalism' as part of its equipment is essentially a debate amongst scholars and many scholars, in fact, do not admit *any* of the terms which Oberoi has put forward. 'Feudalism' and 'peasant' are, in the opinion of such scholars, strictly limited to their Western context; and 'religion' creates difficulties in India because there is no native word for it. Even 'class' is relevant only in so far as the Asian or African economies have assumed Western features. I am not taking sides in this debate, merely pointing out that it is conducted primarily in academic circles.

The second reason is, however, rather weightier. Throughout the Sikh Panth there is a very pronounced insistence upon the Adi Granth being regarded as the Guru Granth Sahib. It is, in other words, the living Guru, and disrespect towards it is regarded as a particularly grievous act. Anyone who doubts this need only attend the Golden Temple or some other Sikh gurdwara and watch the Guru Granth Sahib being installed or put to bed. Even witnessing the manner in which a Sikh enters the presence of the Guru Granth Sahib in a gurdwara is sufficient for this purpose, observing how homage is paid to it by bowing down and touching the floor with the forehead. Devotion is indeed profound, and always the sacred volume is handled with the greatest of care. The pious Sikh's touching and handling of his sacred scripture is certainly noteworthy, in comparison to the pious Christian's treatment of the Bible. For the Christian the Bible *contains* the word of God. For the Sikh the Adi Granth *is* literally the Guru. The Adi Granth is the actual embodiment of the eternal Guru and for this reason it is known as the Guru Granth Sahib.

If this attitude were to lead us to label all who upheld it as fundamentalists it would, though, include the vast majority of Sikhs within the definition. With relatively few exceptions, all Sikhs would be fundamentalists, for all pay respect to their scripture in this way. This clearly is not the meaning intended by the use of 'fundamentalist,' neither in the loose usage of journalists nor the careful application by Madan or Oberoi. It is not the sacred scripture as a Book which serves to differentiate 'conservative' and 'liberal' Sikhs, but rather the meaning of the scripture. Is the meaning of the text to be wholly accepted by all Sikhs or can it speak to different people in different ways and with different meanings?

It is at this point that the question becomes very difficult indeed to answer. Many Sikhs are quite adamant about the meaning of the Guru Granth Sahib. The sacred scripture is indeed the Guru, but it conveys its message in different ways to different people, communicating with some on one level of perception and with others on a different level. It is foolish to imagine that the scripture will speak at the same level and degree of understanding to the ordinary villager as opposed to the person who has devoted many years to meditation. Clearly it will speak in different ways, the one to a person requiring a simple meaning and the other to someone of deep perception. All people will derive a message from the Guru Granth Sahib, but not all receive the same one. The range is indeed infinite as people differ in their perception and their diversity. Non-Sikhs are certainly encouraged to consult the scripture, but the Guru's message for a person of Western background will be distinctively different from that of a Punjabi Sikh.

This liberal point of view seems quite clear. The meaning is distinctly more obscure when we move to that of the Sikhs who could be regarded as fundamentalists. Here, it must be emphasized, I am seeking to understand the kind of person whom Oberoi and Madan call a fundamentalist and trying to establish a bridge between their definition and my own. Is this differential interpretation the meaning which these 'fundamentalists' attach to their scripture? Does the Guru speak to different people in different ways; or does the Guru come across with exactly the same message for all people, regardless of their experience, their level of understanding, or their culture? Or (to put the question rather differently) does the Guru express a variety of solutions to the problems of daily living for people of different backgrounds; or does the Guru communicate a single set of answers which must order human society for all people at all times?

The answers to these questions are extremely difficult to obtain, if not impossible. It may be because the answers are thought to be so obvious that they do not need to be expressed. The so-called fundamentalists have been too busy with the business of fighting for Khalistan to be bothered with such questions, just as they were fully occupied during most of the eighteenth century. Alternatively, it may be because we are putting an essentially Western question to people who do not perceive what it is that is bothering us.

The truth, as we have already acknowledged, is that it is almost impossible to get a clear answer to this question, at least from those orthodox Sikhs whom we might regard as being true fundamentalists. Many Sikhs will certainly answer the question in a sense which forbids their being so labelled, but from those whom we might regard as conservative or traditionalist the answer is not forthcoming. In the narrowly Western sense of the word the response, when we are compelled to communicate, is that we do not really know. The question is one which assumes a Western attitude and understanding, a question which we are not really entitled to put because it involves the transference of a Western mode of thinking to people who think in ways which are distinctively different. Why should a Sikh be required to answer the question of whether or not his scripture is verbally inerrant? The question carries him away into a world which attributes literal meanings to all words, a world which he has never entered.

This, however, is fastening a narrow Western orientation on the word 'fundamentalism.' If the word is shaken loose from its original Western sense and given a broader definition which enables it to cross cultural boundaries, a rather different impression emerges. In this looser sense the Sikh who solemnly reveres the scripture as Guru and who adopts a traditional view of Sikh practice can surely be regarded as fundamentalist. The traditional view of Sikh practice will presumably mean a firm acceptance of the Khalsa Rahit (the code of belief and conduct). Surely the Sikh who upholds belief in the Gurus, the sacred nature of Guru Granth Sahib, and rigorous maintenance of the Rahit can be regarded, loosely defined, as a fundamentalist. This brings us close to Madan's argument.

Here, however, two further problems arise, the second of which is the more serious. The first problem concerns the nature of the Rahit. We may agree that for all such Sikhs the Rahit was given by Guru Gobind Singh (the scholarly debate need not concern them), but what does it actually contain for them? Here there is considerable disagreement (in practice if not in theory) and there are some features of the Rahit (such as vegetarianism) which are strongly disputed.[42] There is, however, an accepted minimum and all Sikhs would agree (all Khalsa Sikhs, at least) that a Sikh of the Khalsa will be recognized by his wearing of the Five Ks (even if their precise meaning is disputed). This also involves (in the case of men at least) the wearing of a turban. The first problem is amenable to a solution.

The second problem is, however, more difficult. Should all Sikhs be truly Sikhs of the Khalsa, true Gursikhs? In other words, should they all accept initiation into the Khalsa, become Amrit-dharis and promise to obey the Rahit?[43] Alternatively, is it enough to forego *amrit sanskār* (the Khalsa initiation) and merely remain a Kes-dhari Sikh, observing the Five Ks but not strictly bound by the terms of the Rahit?[44] Or should we consider the Sahaj-dhari Sikhs? It is true that the term Sahaj-dhari (signifying a Sikh who cuts his or her hair) is not often heard these days. This is perhaps understandable as the term 'Sahaj-dhari' was normally applied to a Sikh of the Khatri or Arora caste, and the clarifying of the Sikh identity which has followed the assault on the Golden Temple has, on the whole, led to most of the Sahaj-dharis being regarded as Hindus. But what of the Jat Sikhs who have cut their hair, particularly those residing abroad, or indeed any from Khalsa backgrounds who no longer observe the Khalsa traditions?[45]

It has proven quite impossible to get any clear indication of whether these people are all to be regarded as proper Sikhs or, alternatively, whether some of them are (in the eyes of the strict Gursikh) to be deregistered or regarded as less than adequate Sikhs. Probably it would be safe to say that there exists a small number of Amrit-dhari Sikhs who insist that only a person who reveres the scripture, who accepts the Guru's initiation into the Khalsa, and who thereafter observes what is generally understood to be the Rahit can be understood to be a Sikh. All others are not Sikhs.

These people might perhaps come within this looser definition 'fundamentalist,' but it is a singularly fragile application of the term. How many of this indefinite number, for example, would be thoroughly firm and precise in so defining all who are or are not Sikhs? Those who are loyal Amrit-dhari Sikhs are in; all others are out. In practice the definition is rarely as clear as this. These people would certainly be prepared to classify Amrit-dhari Sikhs as within the bounds of the Panth (other than proclaimed offenders against the Rahit), but they rarely go on to add that all others are outside it.

As a result, in so far as we are seeking to define one group of Sikhs as fundamentalists we are left with a distinctly imprecise group. Not all the radical Sikhs agitating for Khalistan by any means answered to this definition.[46] The greater number of these Sikhs were young men, the *nau-juān* or *muṇḍe* (the 'boys') who were so prominent in the movement. Youths are not necessarily the most discriminating when it comes to deciding, on the grounds of doctrine, who are the truly upright and who are lax. For the most part their reasons were essentially economic and were aimed at the Brahmans whom they believed to control the Indian government. The definition was just as likely to apply to older men and women who, while sharing their view of the Indian government, were by no means certain that the answer to the Sikhs' problem lay in the creation of Khalistan.

It is nevertheless a definition with which we have to live. In fact, we have to live with both of these definitions, one strictly applied and the other much looser. The possibility of a bridge between the two is indicated by the career of Jarnail Singh Bhindranwale. Both definitions seem to take account of this man and to some extent also of the Damdami Taksal of which he was the head. When his influence was at its height baptismal *jathās* regularly toured the villages of the Punjab, exhorting all who called themselves Sikhs to take *amrit* (initiation as an Amrit-dhari) and administering it to those who responded; and to these Sikhs he preached absolute loyalty to the holy scripture. Perhaps in this sense Jarnail Singh Bhindranwale was a fundamentalist of both types. Perhaps also the Damdami Taksal should be regarded as fundamentalist according to both definitions. While the guerrilla war was still continuing in the Punjab, the acting head of the Taksal declared the need for all Sikhs 'to place complete faith in the Guru Granth Sahib.'[47] Care must be taken, however, to distinguish members of the Damdami Taksal from the much broader group of those who were fighting for Khalistan. To the latter variety of Sikhs only the second definition of fundamentalism applies.

The two definitions of Sikh fundamentalism

Where does this leave us as regards the existence of fundamentalism within the Sikh Panth? It leaves us with two general conclusions.

The first conclusion is that fundamentalism is indeed present amongst the Sikhs, but that in the strict sense of the word adopted in this essay it is confined to those members of the Panth who adopt a particularly fervent belief with regard to the scriptures and the tradition. Their presence is, by and large, hidden from us for two reasons. One is that they have among them very few people who could be described as genuine scholars. Their publications are, as a result, almost all in Punjabi and almost all concerned with the narrow needs of their sectarian interest. The other is that the scholars and commentators of the Panth have almost all belonged to the Singh Sabha (or, more correctly, to the Tat Khalsa group within the Singh Sabha). The inevitable result of their frequent writings (in English as well as in Punjabi) has been to establish the Singh Sabha version of Sikhism as the only orthodox and acceptable one. All other groups (the Nirankaris, the Namdharis, the Nihangs, the followers of Bhai Randhir Singh, and all the rest) are relegated to the status of sects.

This relegation is perhaps unfair, at least as far as some of these 'sects' are concerned. Many of them would argue that the Singh Sabha, for all its claims to orthodoxy, is itself a sect (a large one admittedly). The Panth, they would insist, consists of no definite orthodoxy and the situation is not accurately depicted if it leaves the others mildly or seriously heretical in the light of the pretended orthodoxy of the Singh Sabha. This claim may or may not be true. What is true is that some of these groups or sects are truly fundamentalist, the followers of Bhai Randhir Singh amongst them.

The second conclusion is that the term 'fundamentalists' has been applied by journalists to the Khalistani militants of the Panth and that the word (with the associated term 'fundamentalism) has been increasingly employed in popular usage. Harjot Oberoi has argued that these terms were correctly applied to the militants. Without fully agreeing with him as to the correctness of the terms in the case of the militants, we should nevertheless recognize that the usage is probably here to stay. Whatever uneasiness we may feel when confronted by these terms we should try to get used to the fact that they have been joined to the Khalistan cause and that this popular usage will remain.

'Fundamentalist' and 'fundamentalism' are accordingly terms that are acquiring two different meanings in their application to the Sikh Panth. They may be used in their precise, original meaning (the meaning which assumes the absolute inerrancy of scripture) when applied to certain groups or sects within the Panth. Alternatively, they may be used in a general sense when applied to political militants who embraced the cause of Khalistan, or any similar radical group. One is a religious usage. The other is political. And they are very different.

The origins of Sikh fundamentalism

How then do we explain the origins of these two distinctive meanings? What gives rise to the belief and behavior which, in these varying senses, we describe as fundamentalist?

The first usage is both very easy and very embarrassing to answer. It is embarrassing to answer because it means implicitly holding up these groups or sects to ridicule. Why are they fundamentalist? Why do they adhere so rigorously to a particular doctrine of the inspiration of holy scripture? The answer is that they have a singularly narrow view of life, one which enables them to shut out a vast range of belief and experience which inevitably presents a considerable degree of uncertainty. Or (to put the situation in rather different terms) they do not listen to other people with other experiences. There are, in their midst, very few individuals who could be described as genuine thinkers or as authentic scholars. Indeed, one is constrained to say that they do not have a single person who could be so named.

This makes the explanation acutely embarrassing to offer, yet there seems to be no alternative. After all, it is the explanation which is characteristically offered for Western fundamentalism, with or without apology. The same explanation applies exactly to the Sikh case. The belief and behaviour of strict Sikh fundamentalists certainly differs from that of their Western counterparts because the scripture and the tradition which they embrace are different. They are, however, truly fundamentalists, believing in the verbal inerrancy of their scripture.

All castes are affected by it and many different classes, ranging from the simple faith of many of the Kukas through to the high-tech professional activities of many followers of Bhai Randhir Singh. There is actually a very general classification available at this point. The Kukas and the Nihangs generally belong to the simpler orders of society, and one usually expects the poorer Jats or the Ramgarhias to be their members. The Nirankaris and the followers of Bhai Randhir Singh (at least the leaders) are, by contrast, generally drawn from the Bhapa castes (the Khatris and the Aroras, with a few Ahluwalias also drawn in).

Most such fundamentalists usually live very quiet lives and only occasionally (as for example the Baisakhi Day march on the Amritsar meeting of the Sant Nirankaris in 1978) participate in the agitations which have been such a regular feature of the Panth's politics. Political activity, with all the agitations and disturbances associated with it, is particularly the province of the Jats (and especially the wealthier variety). Needless to say, the wealthier ones require a large army of volunteers to conduct agitations and hold large processions, but for these they depend largely on their following in the villages. The Jats of the villages, whatever their level of prosperity, are the most likely to respond vigorously to the call of the Panth in danger, particularly if they are not engaged in harvesting at the time.

This is not to deny the participation of other castes in politics. Master Tara Singh was, after all, a Khatri. Their involvement is, however, much less than that of the Jats. Even in the case of the Khatris it is less than their prominence in other areas of the Panth's activities would suggest. The vast majority of those who participate in political activity are either Sikhs who adhere to Tat Khalsa views or are people without any great concern for doctrine. One does not expect to find many strict fundamentalists amongst them. The fundamentalists may well have a considerable sympathy for their co-religionists and likewise a rooted dislike of the Indian Government, but as actual activists they will not be very prominent.

The case was, however, very different for the militant supporters of the Khalistan cause. Here we are dealing with the second meaning of the word 'fundamentalist,' the meaning which has been attached to it by journalists and adopted by some scholars. What persuaded these people to conduct campaigns and to wage guerrilla war against the Government of India? They were certainly Sikhs and their objective was an independent Sikh state of Khalistan. The cause is now lost, but we should presumably expect that some new issue will eventually arise. The twentieth century has, after all, produced two earlier campaigns, in the Gurdwara Reform Movement and Punjabi Suba. In the strict sense of the word the proponents of Khalistan are not normally fundamentalists. It is only the transposition of the term on political grounds which justifies its application to them. They may be called fundamentalists and we may have to become used to hearing the term applied to them, but strict fundamentalists they certainly are not.

It appears, however, that those of us who stubbornly insist on the correct usage of the term have been fighting a losing battle. We may maintain that there are indeed fundamentalists among the Sikhs, but they do not include most Khalistanis or other political radicals. Rather, they are inconspicuous members of the Panth and are very rarely brought before the public gaze. The reason for their fundamentalism is normally the influence of nurture or marriage, with relatively few joining such groups by direct conversion.

But the term has been widely applied to the Khalistan militants and it will doubtless be applied to those of radical persuasion who may take their place. In vain will we protest that the word 'fundamentalism' is not properly used when it is applied to the supporters of Khalistan, or to other radicals, and that the older, and more authentic meaning of the term has been compromised by such usage. A second meaning has been conferred on the term and it seems safe to conclude that this dual usage will probably continue. For my part, though, the words 'fundamentalist' and 'fundamentalism' will retain a sole and exclusive meaning. The Khalistanis or other political radicals will seldom be true fundamentalists and should never be understood as authentic examples of Sikh fundamentalism.

Notes

1. 'When we talk . . . of Sikh fundamentalism, we do a great disservice to this great catholic, all inclusive faith.' Gopal Singh, *The Religion of the Sikhs* (Bombay: Asia Publishing House, 1971), p. 191.

2. This was particularly the case in *World Sikh News*, published from Stockton, California. At the end of 1996 *World Sikh News* ceased publication.

3. T.N. Madan, 'The Double-edged Sword: Fundamentalism and the Sikh Religious Tradition,' in *Fundamentalisms Observed*, eds Martin E. Marty and R. Scott Appleby, Vol. 1 (Chicago: University of Chicago Press, 1991), pp. 594–627.

4. Ibid., 569f., 609. The Akali Dal is the Akali Party, first formed in 1920 with the intention of taking over the principal Sikh gurdwaras from their hereditary owners.

5. Harjot Singh Oberoi, 'Sikh Fundamentalism: Translating History into Theory,' in *Fundamentalisms and the State*, eds Martin E. Marty and R. Scott Appleby, Vol. 3 (Chicago: University of Chicago Press, 1993), pp. 256–85.

6. For the Namdharis, see Fauja Singh Bajwa, *Kuka Movement* (Delhi: Motilal Banarsidass, 1965); and W.H. McLeod, 'The Kukas: A Millenarian Sect of the Punjab,' in *W.P. Morrell: A Tribute*, eds G.A. Wood and P.S. O'Connor (Dunedin: University of Otago Press, 1973), pp. 85–103; repr. in *The Panjab Past and Present*, 13.1 (April 1979): pp. 164–79. See below pp. 189–215.

7. Strictly speaking it is a *hukam-nama* (letter of command). It does, however, contain items which can properly be regarded as the Rahit as observed by Kukas and as such is correctly regarded as the Namdhari

Rahit-nāmā. For a complete translation see W.H. McLeod, tr., ed., *Textual Sources for the Study of Sikhism* (Chicago: University of Chicago Press, 1990), pp. 129–30.

8. Ibid., p. 129.
9. In other words, always wear a *kachh* (one of the Five Ks) in the literal sense.
10. Ibid., p. 130.
11. Much of the information concerning Bhai Randhir Singh I owe to my former student Dr. Pashaura Singh.
12. Randhir Singh *Jehl chiṭṭhīān,* 1st edn (in three parts) (Ludhiana: Bhai Sahib Randhir Singh Publishing House, 1936–8; 6th edn 1978). English translation with introduction by Trilochan Singh, *Autobiography of Bhai Sahib Randhir Singh* (Ludhiana: Bhai Sahib Randhir Singh Publishing House, 1971).
13. *Autobiography of Bhai Sahib Randhir Singh,* chap. 11.
14. Ibid., p. 82. Teja Singh was a radically eccentric figure who diverged from both the Amritsar and Lahore singh Sabhas early this century and established his own group, the Panch Khalsa Divan. In 1893 a branch of the Singh Sabha had been founded in Teja Singh's village of Bhasaur in Patiala district with Teja Singh as secretary; and in 1905 this was converted into the Panch Khalsa Divan, with Teja Singh as the leader. Several features were introduced into the Khalsa code of belief and conduct (the Rahit) by the Panch Khalsa Divan, including an obligation for all women to wear the turban. The most serious of these innovations concerned the text of the Adi Granth. Eventually Teja Singh was excommunicated; he died in 1933. Kahn Singh Nabha, *Guruśabad ratanākar mahān koś,* 2nd edn rev. (Patiala: Bhasha Vibhag, Panjab 1960), p. 591; app., p. 73.
15. Nihang Sikhs are still conspicuous in the Punjab today for their distinctive blue garments, their array of steel weapons (swords, daggers, quoits, etc.), and commonly for their high turbans. Very little has been recorded in English concerning their particular beliefs. See R. Leech, 'The rites and ceremonies of the Sikhs and Sikh sects,' written in 1844; *Gurduārā Gazaṭ* (August 1969): pp. 54–7; *Textual Sources for the Study of Sikhism,* p. 132.
16. Randhir Singh testified to the paramount importance of the 'mystic Word' *vāhigurū* in his own life. *Autobiography of Bhai Sahib Randhir Singh,* chap. 5.
17. *Textual Sources for the Study of Sikhism,* p. 85. Randhir Singh may possibly have derived this emphasis on vegetarianism from the example of the Namdharis. The Namdharis were active in the area around his village while he was growing up.
18. Harminder Kaur, *Blue Star over Amritsar* (Delhi: Ajanta, 1990), p. 55.
19. *The Statesman,* June 9, 1990.
20. *Blue Star over Amritsar,* 55. Kuldip Nayar and Khushwant Singh, *Tragedy*

of Punjab (New Delhi: Vision Books, 1984), p. 32n. For the Damdami Taksal, see Oberoi, 'Sikh Fundamentalism,' pp. 266–70. The Damdami Taksal is an organization within the Khalsa which is strictly defined in terms of doctrine and practice. Jarnail Singh Bhindranwale was its leader until his death in the army assault on the Golden Temple in June 1984. Arguably it too deserves to be regarded as fundamentalist according to the narrower definition here being applied. In this connection the Damdami Taksal is briefly alluded to above. See p. 79.

21. The organization which gives expression to the attitudes of the followers of Bhai Randhir Singh is known as the Akhand Kirtani Jatha, founded by Amarjit Kaur, who was the widow of Fauja Singh, one of the victims of the shooting on Baisakhi Day, 1978. *Blue Star*, p. 55. See also Chand Joshi, *Bhindranwale: Myth and Reality* (New Delhi: Vikas, 1984), pp. 36–8; and Gopal Singh, 'Communal Organisations in Punjab 1978–1984,' in *Punjab Today*, ed. Gopal Singh (New Delhi: Intellectual Publishing House, 1987), p. 216. The magazine of the Bhai Randhir Singh dā jathā (*Sura* of Amritsar) bears on the title page the inscription: 'The monthly magazine of pure Gurmat [the teachings of the Guru] from the Akhand Kirtani Jathā.'

22. Jodh Singh, *Sri Kartarpuri bīṛ de darasan* (Patiala: Punjabi University, 1968).

23. Oberoi, 'Sikh Fundamentalism,' pp. 257–8, citing Daljeet Singh, 'Issues of Sikh Studies,' in *Advanced Studies in Sikhism*, eds Jasbir Singh Mann and Harbans Singh Saraon (Irvine, Calif.: Sikh Community of North America, 1989), p. 21.

24. *World Sikh News*, July 13, 1990.

25. Ibid.

26. One writer who does not adopt this contemporary meaning of fundamentalism is Pritam Singh, 'Two Facets of Revivalism: A Defence,' in *Punjab Today*, ed. Gopal Singh (New Delhi: Intellectual), p. 177, n. 1. Pritam Singh prefers the term 'religious revivalism' as a description of the attitude of militants in the Punjab today.

27. T.N. Madan, 'The Double-Edged Sword: Fundamentalism and the Sikh Religious Tradition,' in Marty and Appleby, 1: pp. 594–627.

28. Ibid., p. 596.

29. Ibid.

30. Ibid., p. 609. SGPC, the Shiromani Gurdwara Parbandhak Committee, is the elected body of Sikhs set up by the 1925 Sikh Gurdwaras Act which controls the historic gurdwaras in the Punjab. N.b., 'Sikh Gurdwaras Act' is the correct title, not 'Gurdwara Reform Act.'

31. Ibid., p. 598.

32. 'The priority of the canon is, however, unquestionable in principle.' Ibid., p. 599.

33. Ibid., pp. 599–602.

34. Harjot Oberoi, 'Sikh Fundamentalism,' p. 257.

35. Ibid.
36. Gurdev Singh, ed., *Perspectives on the Sikh Tradition* (Chandigarh: Siddharth Publications for Academy of Sikh Religion and Culture, Patiala, 1986); Oberoi, 'Sikh Fundamentalism,' p. 257.
37. Oberoi, 'Sikh Fundamentalism,' p. 258.
38. Ibid.
39. Ibid., p. 257.
40. Ibid., p. 258.
41. As in the *Mūl Mantra*, the basic credal statement with which the Adi Granth begins.
42. 'Up to now, in spite of several attempts by Sikh intellectuals, the SGPC has not been able to issue a certified code of Sikh conduct, as there was great difference of opinion among the participants themselves,' Gopal Singh, *The Religion of the Sikhs* (Bombay: Asia Publishing House, 1971), p. 191. This Gopal Singh is not the same person as the editor of *Punjab Today*.
43. An Amrit-dhari Sikh is one who has been initiated into the Khalsa, promising to live in accordance with the Sikh code of belief and behaviour. W. Owen Cole and Piara Singh Sambhi, *A Popular Dictionary of Sikhism* (London: Curzon Press, 1990), pp. 38, 131.
44. Ibid., p. 95.
45. Sikhs of these various kinds are defined and discussed in W.H. McLeod, *Who is a Sikh?* (Oxford: Clarendon Press, 1989), pp. 112–14. See also idem, *Sikhism* (Harmondsworth: Penguin Books, 1997), chap. 11, 'Defining a Sikh.'
46. 'That most terrorists have little interest in religion or piety seems to have dawned on many Sikhs, particularly after the indisputable desecration of the Golden Temple in May 1988, when a group of terrorists occupied it for several days during which they performed polluting bodily functions of evacuation within it.' T.N. Madan, 'The Double-edged Sword,' p. 620.
47. *Indo-Canadian Times*, September 28, 1990. I owe this reference to Harjot Oberoi.

PART V

CASTES AND SECTS OF THE SIKHS

12

THE KUKAS:
A MILLENARIAN SECT OF THE
PANJAB*

S ikh fortunes prospered during the first four decades of the
nineteenth century. The anarchy which had afflicted the
Panjab during most of the preceding century had given way
to the strong centralized dominion of Maharaja Ranjit Singh. Ruling
in the name of the Sikh community and ostensibly as its servant
Ranjit Singh had extended the boundaries of his Panjab kingdom
as far as Kashmir, the Khyber Pass, and Multan. These conquests
were completed by 1824 and for the remaining years of Ranjit Singh's
reign the Panjab enjoyed an unaccustomed peace. Throughout the
turbulent years of the eighteenth century the Sikh community (the
Khalsa) had been sustained by the confident assurance that 'the
Khalsa shall reign' (rāj karegā khālsā). To many it seemed that this
prophecy had come true.

Others, however, were troubled. The ascent to military and
political power seemed to them to have been accompanied by a
corresponding decline from the true glory of the Sikh faith. The Sikh
Gurus had insisted on the absolute primacy of devotion to God.
Where now was the fervent, regular remembrance of the divine Name
upon which they had laid such unyielding stress, and where the
disciplined purity of life which must inescapably characterize the
true believer? These questions became increasingly acute as the Sikh

*Originally published in P.S. O'Connor & G.A. Wood, eds, *W.P. Morrell: A Tribute*,
University of Otago Press, Dunedin, 1973.

kingdom slipped into confusion and defeat during the decade following the death of Ranjit Singh in 1839.

One of the troubled was Balak Singh, a resident of Hazro in the north-western corner of Ranjit Singh's domain. Balak Singh had been influenced by another teacher, Jawahar Mal. Like his master, Balak Singh exhorted his followers to return to the simple religious message of the Gurus and in accordance with this message he taught a strict doctrine of salvation through meditation on the *nām* (the divine Name). The sect which was established in this manner has been known by a variety of names. Whereas Balak Singh evidently referred to his followers as Jagiasis,[1] their modern descendants prefer the title Namdhari, 'Adherents of the Divine Name'. Between the earlier and later periods, and particularly during the sect's brief years of prominence, the term most commonly used (at least by outsiders) was Kuka, or 'Crier'. The impact of Balak Singh's personality was evidently considerable, for by the time he died in 1862 he had been recognized by his followers as the eleventh Guru.[2] At his death he was succeeded as leader of the sect by Ram Singh, a disciple who had fallen under his spell while serving as a soldier in the army of Ranjit Singh's successors.

Ram Singh transferred the Kuka centre from Hazro to his own village of Bhaini in Ludhiana District and at once the sect began to grow rapidly, both in numbers and in prominence. Barely six months after Balak Singh's death the Assistant District Superintendent of Police at Attock drew attention to the sudden change.

Though the sect seems to have failed in the neighbourhood of Hazru since Balak Singh's death it has thriven in the most remarkable manner in the district adjoining the home of his more energetic successor.[3]

In his comments on this and other police reports Mr T.D. Forsyth, officiating secretary to the Panjab Government, mentioned that Ram Singh's activities had first been detected in April 1863.[4] Eight years later Mr Forsyth was to play a leading role in the episode which so abruptly arrested the sect's rapid rise to prominence. In this, the first of his recorded comments, he noted that Ram Singh's numerous converts were 'confined chiefly to the lower classes'.[5] This vague remark was clarified four years later by Major Perkins, District Superintendent of Police at Ludhiana, who observed in a report on the Kukas that 'converts are chiefly made from Juts, Tirkhans, Chumars, and Muzbees' (i.e. Jat agriculturists, carpenters, and outcastes).[6] He added that very few Khatris, Brahmans, or Banyas had been attracted to the sect.[7]

This caste-occupational constituency is of fundamental importance for any understanding of the sudden acceleration in the sect's popularity, and it deserves careful analysis. It was not, however, the aspect which primarily interested the Panjab Government. Sedition was the danger which it perceived and which prompted its investigations. In 1863, memories of 1857 were still vivid and any movement which combined rapid growth with a promise of militancy could scarcely escape official attention. This attention it received in abundance. Police officers were instructed to observe members of the sect carefully, informers were employed to report on its activities from within, and narrative accounts of its beliefs and customs were prepared for the guidance of administrators. As early as June 1863, Ram Singh's movements were restricted to Bhaini,[8] a decision which was reversed only when it was realized that this endued him with martyr qualifications and thereby increased his popularity.[9]

Police reports and the narrative accounts based upon them provide much detailed information concerning the sect. The reports are, to some extent, vitiated by the fears and suspicions which prompted them, but the damage is slight and due allowance can be made for it. It is the contemporary analysis which is so commonly awry, not the actual details collected by police officers and their informants in villages with Kuka concentrations. The description of the sect which emerges from their efforts is one which in its essentials is confirmed by later materials produced within the Kuka community,[10] and by recent works dealing with the remnant which survives today.[11]

All agree that the Kuka sect had begun as a religious reform movement within the Sikh community and that in spite of its suspected inclination towards sedition it still preserved this emphasis. Ram Singh, following his master, looked for a return to the pristine purity of the doctrines taught by the Sikh Gurus. In its negative aspect this took the form of a vigorous polemic directed against the corruptions of the contemporary Sikh community. Positively it found expression in a rigorous insistence upon the devotional practice of *nām simraṇ* (meditation on the divine Name) and upon a strict puritan ethic. Kukas were to rise between 3 and 6 a.m. and having bathed they were to repeat passages from the Sikh scriptures. Virtue and continence were enjoined and to those who abused or struck them they were to respond with meekness.[12] A comprehensive report prepared by the Inspector General of Police at the end of 1867 acknowledges the high ideals of the Kukas. Having sampled the opinions of 'the Native officers of one of our frontier regiments', he concluded:

They all seem to have a great respect for the tenets of the sect, and agree that it is an effort to restore the Sikh religion to its original purity, and to do away with the innovations which have crept into it, such as consulting Brahmins as to the proper day for marriages, &c. from what they say, the belief of the sect appears to be a pure dissension. They hold that God is one, not made or born, but existing by himself, and they appear to hold in utter reprobation the Hindoo belief of various incarnation of the deity. They inculcate a very strict morality, condemning most strongly lying, theft, and adultery, and appear anxious merely to revive the Sikh religion in its original state of purity and to eradicate the errors which have from time to time, defiled it.[13]

To this extent Ram Singh sought nothing more than a revival of the Guru's teachings and it is scarcely surprising that at this stage the sample of Sikh opinion taken by the police should have been generally favourable towards the Kukas. Even the vigour with which the Kukas urged the cause of cow protection brought no serious objections until it led to the murder of Muslim butchers in Amritsar and Raikot. Although the Gurus had not attached any evident importance to the issue the ancient tradition died hard and Sikhs who supported it would not thereby mark themselves out as deviants.

It was, of course, inevitable that distinctive beliefs and practices should soon emerge within the sect, but initially even these did not alienate the Kukas from the bulk of the orthodox Sikh community. At first they were regarded as little more than the harmless peculiarities of religious enthusiasts, and protests against them appear to have been largely confined to those members of the Sikh community who were the particular targets of Ram Singh's reforming strictures.[14] The most prominent of these differences was evidently responsible for the appearance of the word Kuka. On important occasions members of the sect would assemble for a ceremony called *Chandī kā Pāṭh*, literally 'A Reading of the Epic of Chandi'.[15] The ceremony was not, strictly, a reading in the literal sense, although passages from the epic were evidently recited as a part of it. Recitations of this and other passages from the Sikh scriptures were conducted antiphonally around a slow-burning bonfire. Gradually enthusiasm would mount amongst the participants until eventually ecstasy would overtake some of them. In this condition they would cry out,

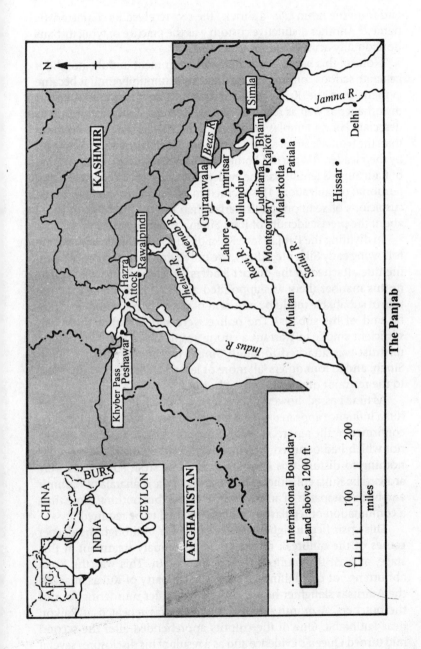

The Panjab

and from the noun *kūk*, 'a shriek', the sect received its characteristic name.[16] Another distinctive custom was the practice of tying turbans horizontally across the forehead.[17]

None of this bothered the Panjab Government unduly, nor did it generate serious concern within the Sikh community until it became evident that the Kuka movement could be an agent of social disturbance as well as religious reform. Even the Kuka disposition to desecrate Hindu temples and Muslim tombs seemed to be no more than the iconoclasm of a few fanatics whose activities were disowned by their leader.[18] What did bother the British from the very beginning of Ram Singh's tenure was the evidence which they soon perceived of territorial organization. This seemed to add substance to their vague suspicions of sedition, particularly when they began to learn more about the precise identity of Ram Singh's subordinates.

In dividing the Panjab into Kuka districts Ram Singh was merely following early Sikh precedents, the only significant difference being the title attached to the district leaders. To each district designated in this manner there was appointed a trusted disciple bearing the title of subah. He might be innocent of sedition, but could the same be said of his subahs? The police were satisfied that there was sufficient smoke to warrant a strong suspicion of fire. A particular mistrust was attached to Sahib Singh, the heir-apparent of Ram Singh, and to four others 'all more or less truculent and ill-disposed to the restraint of constituted authority'.[19]

As time passed, however, their fears subsided. By the end of 1868 Kuka influence appeared to be waning,[20] a trend which seemed to be confirmed by the reports received during the following year.[21] A Kuka riot which had occurred in Ferozepore District during that year did nothing to disturb this confidence.[22] Some fresh suspicions were aroused by Kuka enlistments in the army of the Maharaja of Kashmir and by the despatch of an emissary to Nepal, but nothing more than a continuation of regular surveillance seemed to be required.[23]

This crisis began eighteenth months later. Although the deeper causes of the outbreak must defy any summary treatment at this stage, at least the immediate issue was plain. This was the Kuka abhorrence of cow killing. In June 1871 a party of Kukas attacked the Amritsar slaughter-house and escaped after murdering four of the butchers. A month later the incident was repeated at Raikot, near Ludhiana. One of the culprits apprehended after the second raid turned Queen's Evidence and as a result of his disclosures several arrests were made. All were Kukas and three of them were subahs.[24]

At once the tone of the police reports changed. No serious outbreak was yet envisaged, but the growing tendency to treat the Kukas simply as harmless religious fanatics came to an abrupt end.

The climax followed soon after. On 14 January 1872 a party of Kukas from Bhaini attacked the obscure fort of Malodh in Ludhiana District and then, with augmented numbers, attempted to force their way into the town of Malerkotla.[25] Having failed in their objective, the dispirited party retreated into Patiala territory, where sixty-eight of them surrendered at the village of Rurr. Meanwhile, Mr L. Cowan, Officiating Deputy Commissioner of Ludhiana District, had hastened to Malerkotla, and when the prisoners arrived there he proceeded to blow forty-nine of them away from guns without trial. This he did in spite of an earlier caution which he had received from Mr T.D. Forsyth, Commissioner of Ambala Division, and a second letter from Forsyth which arrived while the last batch of prisoners was being lashed to the guns. One other prisoner attacked him and was cut down. Two of the total were women, leaving sixteen whom Cowan proposed to execute the following day.

In the letter which arrived during the course of the executions, Forsyth had explicitly ordered Cowan to proceed according to legal requirements. Having received Cowan's report, however, he approved the action. He then proceeded to Malerkotla and after a summary trial blew the remaining sixteen prisoners away from guns. Four more prisoners captured during the earlier attack on Malodh were executed the following day.[26]

The result of this episode was a furore. Two separate issues had to be decided and one at least generated a considerable controversy. Cowan had plainly transgressed the bounds of established legal procedure by executing without a trial, and Forsyth had compromised his earlier rectitude by subsequently approving his action. The method of execution was, moreover, irregular and the manner in which Forsyth had tried the second batch of prisoners was not beyond suspicion. Cowan argued vigorously that dangerous situations require impressive remedies, and that because he had been prepared to act with such expedition 'a rebellion which might have attained large dimension was nipped in the bud'.[27] Forsyth supported this claim,[28] and so too did the Anglo-Indian press, with the notable exception of the *Friend of India*.[29] Many amongst the landed and the titled of Panjab society declared their appreciation of Cowan's action,[30] and even the Lieutenant Governor of the Panjab demonstrated an evident willingness to concur.[31] The Government of India did not, however, concur. Cowan was dismissed from the service and Forsyth was transferred to Oudh.[32] This decision was subsequently confirmed by the Secretary of State for India.[33]

The second major question concerned the treatment of Ram Singh and his surviving subahs. In this instance the primary issue was not one of guilt. It was assumed by the Lieutenant Governor and doubtless by many others that Ram Singh, as leader of the sect, must assuredly have been implicated in the attacks on Malodh and Malerkotla,[34] but it soon became clear that an accusation of complicity would stand little chance in a court of law. The available evidence actually pointed to his innocence. Ram Singh claimed that he had attempted to dissuade his headstrong followers from their rash course, but that they had refused to listen to him. Having failed to convince them of their folly he had immediately visited the Deputy Inspector of Police at Sahnewal and warned him of their intentions.[35]

Forsyth suggested that this action had been no more than 'a ruse on his part to try and escape the responsibility of the acts of his followers', that he merely had to wait until they were on their way in order to cover himself without affecting their chances of success.[36] This patently failed to provide evidence upon which a prosecution might proceed. The suggestion was alien to the known character of Ram Singh and had the police officer at Sahnewal acted promptly the entire episode might well have been averted. Ram Singh was probably innocent, and even if guilty of complicity there could be no chance of establishing the charge. The same result would obviously have followed an attempt to establish his complicity in the earlier murder of the Amritsar and Raikot butchers. The possibility of instituting proceedings against him had been given careful consideration at the time by the Lieutenant Governor, but had been reluctantly rejected.[37]

Against the subahs there appeared to be a strong case, for depositions had been obtained which, if sustained in court, would probably establish their guilt. The situation was reviewed by the Government of India and eventually it was decided not to proceed.[38] The principal objection of the Council was expressed in a note by Sir Richard Temple:

I am against trial if it can be avoided. I say this with great regret but there is no overlooking the fact that whenever a trial for political crimes takes place there are unhappily found English Barristers who not content with justly defending their clients (which is quite right) go beyond all legitimate bounds, and raise a sort of political excitement, very detrimental to the minds of native people.[39]

This decision did not mean that the Government of India was prepared to let Ram Singh and his subahs go free. There was an alternative, one which was speedily adopted in the case of Ram Singh and with greater reluctance in the case of his subahs. The Government's principal objective was to deprive the Kuka sect of its leadership 'until the movement has lost all vitality and has perished beyond all chance of resuscitation'.[40] An alternative method of securing this purpose was provided by the Bengal Regulation III of 1818, a measure which was designed to cover occasional circumstances which

render it necessary to place under personal restraint individuals against whom there may not be sufficient ground to institute any judicial proceeding or when such proceeding may not be adapted to the nature of the case or may for other reasons be unadvisable or improper.[41]

Indefinite detention could thus be imposed on the prisoners without trial. E.C. Bayley, Secretary to the Government of India, offered a justification.

The opinions expressed above may seem harsh and it may perhaps be deemed a strong measure to use Regulation III of 1818 to the extent contemplated. But it is to be remembered that almost beyond moral doubt all the prisoners have been concerned in crimes which would have subjected them to transportation for life if proved conspiring to wage war against the Queen, seditious preaching and teaching, abetment of murder and of rebellion with murder. These are the offences with one or more of which every one of the prisoners is at least on strong grounds charged. It seems probable now that if it were politic to bring them to trial, proof even for legal conviction (as for example against Burma Singh) could easily be obtained. There seems accordingly no practical injustice inflicting upon them under the Act, for reasons of policy, restriction of their liberty which they really deserved by their breaches of the criminal law. It seems only necessary to discriminate between those who as active leaders will be dangerous under any circumstances so long as inflammable marks of ignorance and fanaticism exist in the Panjab, and those who are dangerous only in connection with the present movement.[42]

Faced with a choice between Regulation III and freedom, the Viceroy's Council had already invoked the regulation in Ram Singh's case and despatched him to Rangoon.[43] Bayley's argument was accepted in the case of the subahs and, in October 1872, the eleven who were regarded as dangerous to peace and security were distributed to various British jails, most of them outside peninsular India.[44]

The subsequent history of the Kukas may be narrated very briefly. Religious preaching continued and a few members of the sect endeavoured to sustain a covert agitation against the Government. One of them, a subah named Gurcharan Singh, actually reached Samarkand where he established a fitful contact with the Russian governor of Turkestan.[45] The political phase was, however, soon to come to an end. Brief contacts with the restless Maharaja Dalip Singh marked its terminus.[46] Although the Kukas continued to look for the prophesied return of Ram Singh, their activities following the death of Dalip Singh in 1893 occasioned no further concern to the Government. During the present century they have been distinguished only by their continuing insistence upon reform of the Sikh religion, and notably by their refusal to permit lavish weddings or dowries. Their horizontal turbans are still to be seen in the Panjab and although their numbers are now few the message which issues from Bhaini and Jiwan Nagar remains a vigorous one.[47]

This summary narrative of the rise and decline of the Kuka sect must serve as a basis for our analysis of that rise and decline. The basic facts are clear. A sect which began as a religious reform movement within the Sikh community multiplied rapidly, came into conflict with the British administration in the Panjab, and then dwindled into insignificance. The questions which confront us concern the reasons which account for the sudden increase in Kuka popularity, for the sect's confrontation with the Panjab Government, and for the decline which took place thereafter.

Two theories have already been advanced, both of them based upon interpretations which stress the political motivation of the Kukas during the brief period of Ram Singh's leadership. The British administrators who had to deal with the Kuka disturbance quickly produced a theory which, they claimed, was justified by the decline which followed so closely upon the banishment of the Kuka leaders. The events of Malodh and Malerkotla were viewed in the setting of recent military history. Only a quarter of a century had passed since the might of British arms had destroyed Sikh rule in the Panjab. Sikh rule meant, above all, the glories of Maharaja Ranjit Singh and it was but natural that the Sikhs should look back to the recent past with an ardent longing. There was, moreover, the conviction amongst the Sikhs that their defeat in the Sikh Wars had been the result more of treachery than of British power and the events of 1857 had demonstrated the extent to which that power could be successfully challenged. And so the Sikhs, or many of them, dreamt of driving the British out of the Panjab. Ram Singh provided a focus for this ambition and with aid of his territorial subahs he set about preparing for the battle. Unfortunately for him, his headstrong subahs moved too soon and provoked a clash which was easily suppressed. The clash proved highly advantageous to the Government, for it provided it with sufficient grounds for suppressing the movement before it became a serious problem. Mr Cowan's methods were wholly irregular, but at least they succeeded and the name of British justice was redeemed by means of disciplinary action. All that was required in order to cripple the movement was to deport its leader. When this was done Kuka numbers and influence declined rapidly. The simple analysis had evidently been correct.[48]

The second theory is a modern nationalist interpretation, and specifically a Panjabi interpretation. During the uprising of 1857–8 the British had received welcome assistance from Sikh troops. This assistance subsequently proved to be an embarrassment to Panjabi participants in the independence struggle and prompted an effort to prove that the Panjab had been as loyal to the ideal of freedom as any other part of India. On the one hand it was claimed that the help had been rendered not by the people of the Panjab but by the princes; and on the other it was suggested that amongst the people, as opposed to the princes, independence movements were already afoot.

The Kuka episode has in recent years been advanced as proof of the second claim. Although indications of this theory appear as far back as 1913 in the propaganda literature of the revolutionary Ghadr Party,[49] the interpretation did not win instant acceptance. Fifty years later R.C. Majumdar, the historian of the Freedom Movement, could still dismiss Ram Singh with a brief comment.

He gave military training to his followers and organised the sect. There is, however, no adequate evidence to support the view that the Kuka movement ever aimed at the subversion of the British rule.[50]

In making this comment Majumdar had, however, noted a growing tendency to regard various local disturbances as freedom struggles.[51] The tendency eventually emerged in a coherent form when in 1965 two books appeared in support of the freedom-struggle thesis. M.M.

Ahluwalia's *Kukas* is significantly subtitled 'The Freedom Fighters of the Panjab', and Fauja Singh Bajwa is equally explicit in adding to his *Kuka Movement* the subtitle 'An important phase in Panjab's role in India's struggle for freedom'.[52]

Much of this modern nationalist interpretation is curiously similar to the earlier theory advanced by the British administrators, differing only in points of emphasis. There is, for example, a heavier stress upon the claim that the British owed their earlier victories to treachery within the Sikh ranks, and much attention is understandably devoted to the punitive measures taken by Cowan and Forsyth, and later by the Government of India. The principal difference derives from the attempt made by the two authors to relate the Kuka outbreak to the wider struggle for independence. According to their interpretation it was an early phase of the larger struggle, and because the struggle ultimately succeeded the Kuka sacrifice did not go in vain. Whereas the early British theory had treated the outbreak as an isolated, insignificant, and somewhat sordid failure, the modern interpretation regards it as a heroic setback on the road to ultimate triumph.

The primary purpose of this essay is to suggest a third interpretation, one which shifts the focus of attention away from the political aspects of the Kuka outbreak to the social conditions within which it developed. This is not to deny the existence of political issues, nor their importance. Clearly the Kuka outbreak must in some measure relate to the annexation of the Panjab by the alien British, and it has already been shown that its sudden emergence took the form of political action. There were, however, issues at once more important and more obscure. An examination of these issues raises the possibility that the Kuka movement may be interpreted as a distinctively Indian example of the millenarian pattern. The movement develops within a disturbed social environment; it gathers around the person of a religious leader; it generates a glorious vision of the future; and in pursuit of this objective it moves towards an ill-defined expression of political protest. These features prompt the suggestion that a comparison with characteristic millenarian processes may perhaps lead us to a deeper understanding of the Kuka outbreak.

Protest movements assuming a millenarian form normally pass through four distinct and successive phases of development. The first involves the spread of social discontent within a particular geographical area, with the consequent emergence of a substantial group of disoriented and frustrated people. This is followed by the appearance of a holy man, one regarded as inspired and perhaps as divine. The third phase results from a junction of the leader and the group, a connection which produces a fraternity fortified with a social myth adapted to their needs. Finally, the fourth phase issues in 'a frantic urge to smite the ungodly', an irresistible impulse to strike out at the person, the group, or the institution identified as the source of falsehood and oppression.[53]

The possibility that this pattern may enlarge our understanding of the Kuka movement arises from an obvious correspondence of three of these phases to the known pattern of Kuka development. Correspondence at three points suggests the possibility of correspondence at the fourth also. In the case of the Kukas it is the first of the four phases which is obscure, the phase which concerns the origins and motivation of the sect. As we have already seen, the causes of the sect's brief popularity have hitherto been interpreted in political terms as a conscious desire to shake off the British yoke. A comparison with millenarian movements elsewhere implies deeper causes. The political aspects of the sect's activities are not thereby denied, but are instead to be understood as essentially incoherent responses to an underlying social discontent.

The second of the phases outlined above is at once obvious in the case of the Kukas. Ram Singh of Bhaini was the holy man around whom a following rapidly gathered. The fact the Ram Singh evidently disapproved of the violence of his followers does nothing to disturb the pattern. A holy man can serve as a focus for discontent without necessarily sharing the discontent itself or participating in the actions which it provokes.

The third of the four phases is well illustrated by a document which the police acquired in 1863.

The Sākhī of Guru Govind Singh

I, Guru Govind Singh, will be born in a carpenter's shop, and will be called Ram Singh. My house will be between the Jamna and Sutlej rivers. I will declare my religion. I will defeat the Faringhis and put the crown on my own head, and blow the sankh. The musicians shall praise me in 1921 [1864]. I, the carpenter, will sit on the throne. When I have got one lakh and twenty-five thousand Sikhs with me, I will cut off the heads of the Faringhis. I will never be conquered in battle, and will shout 'Akāl Akāl'. The Christians will desert their wives and fly from the country when they hear the shout of $1^1/_4$ lakhs of Khalsas. A great battle will take place on the banks of the Jamna, and blood will flow like the waters of the Ravi, and no Faringhi be left alive. Insurrections will take place in the country in 1922 [1865]. The Khalsa will reign, and the rajah and ryot will live in peace and comfort, and no one shall molest another.

Day by day Ram Singh's rule will be enlarged. God has written this. It is no lie, my brethren. In 1922 [1865], the whole country will be ruled by Ram Singh. My followers will worship Wahaguru [God]. God says this will happen.[54]

The parallels with other millenarian movements are self-evident. Guru Gobind Singh (who died in 1708) has declared that he will be reincarnated in the person of Ram Singh the carpenter. To him the righteous of the Khalsa will flock. The enemy is identified (the Faranghi, i.e. the alien, Christian British). The final conflict is imminent, the battle will be bloody, and following its inevitably triumphant conclusion the Khalsa will rule a world transformed, an earthly paradise in which ruler and peasant will dwell together in perfect harmony. All this is expressed in terms derived from the Sikh past and specifically from the period of Gobind Singh, the warrior Guru. It is the Khalsa (the brotherhood founded by Guru Gobind Singh) which will fight the battle. Its forces will number one and a quarter lakhs (125,000), the figure traditionally associated with the triumph of Khalsa arms. The battle will take place on the banks of a river closely connected with the life of Guru Gobind Singh, and the warcry to be raised will be one of the Sikh names of God (*Akāl*, or 'the Eternal One').

Other characteristically millenarian features appear in later police reports. Discontent was directed against the privileged classes and found expression in an attempt to restore traditional values. The targets may have been Brahmans rather than bishops, and the most compelling of ancient traditions may have been the distinctively Indian reverence for the cow, but the pattern was essentially the same as elsewhere. Religious leaders who were attacked duly retaliated,[55] and so too did the larger landholders when they perceived the social implications of the movement.[56] Amongst the stock criticisms applied to Ram Singh and his followers, accusations of sexual immorality figure prominently.[57] Other resemblances are the more striking for being less predictable. The Kuka versions of the *Sau Sākhīs* offer a parallel to the Sibylline Books both in their actual usage and in their convenient mutations.[58] A Kuka equivalent of the Heavenly Letter appeared in 1876,[59] and in the claim that Ram Singh was a reincarnation of Guru Gobind Singh they produced their own version of the Sleeping Emperor legend.[60] Like many of their European counterparts the Kukas also attached a particular importance to the colour white.

The fourth stage is reached when the impulse to smite the ungodly issues in unplanned conflict and speedy repression. Two varieties of the ungodly served as targets for Kuka anger. The first to be attacked were the Muslim butchers of Amritsar and Raikot, enemies not merely because they were killers of kine (a most abhorrent crime) but also because they were Muslims. Enmity between Sikh and Muslim, greatly strengthened during the eighteenth century, had not been allayed and if a traditional opponent were to be identified the obvious candidate would be a Muslim. This enmity was also in evidence during the later outbreak. Malerkotla was not the most convenient of objectives for a party operating from Bhaini. One reason for selecting it may have been the fact that it was the only Muslim state in the Panjab. In this later episode, however, the second enemy was also involved. The new tyrant was the British *mlechchha*, the destroyer of the Khalsa dominion and a more obvious target for the socially discontented during the second half of the nineteenth century.

Three of the four phases can thus be identified in the case of the Kukas. Is it possible similarly to identify the remaining one, the first of the four? What emerges when, following the characteristic millenarian pattern, we look behind the actual incidents for evidence of people disoriented and frustrated? Is this a description which fits those who participated in the Kuka movement, or are they still to be seen as rebels/nationalists pursuing deliberate and coherent political objectives?

The answer must be that the Kukas did indeed represent, in distinctly millenarian terms, the measure of confusion and frustration which one would expect from parallel examples of the same responses. The two decades preceding the sudden surge in Kuka numbers had been for the Sikhs a period of dissolving religious values and slackening communal cohesion. This stood in marked contrast to the preceding century and a half. The eighteenth century had been a stirring period for the Sikh community, as its traditions so vividly demonstrate. This was the century in which persecution and martyrdom had been succeeded first by heroic struggles and ultimately by the triumph of the Khalsa. The triumphs of the eighteenth century were further extended by Maharaja Ranjit Singh, and when he died in 1839 Sikh glory was at its zenith.

This was a powerful myth, one which still retains much of its vitality today. Set against its grandeur, the decades which followed the death of Ranjit Singh presented a sorry spectacle of failure and decay. Treachery had destroyed the Khalsa army from within. The teachings of the Gurus had been forgotten. Worldliness and immorality consumed the community's leaders. Those who held power and influence had obtained it by unscrupulous means and used it to oppress the less fortunate. Sacred traditions were openly violated. The foreigner who had inflicted the indignity of defeat brought with him not merely his soldiers but also his missionaries. More and more Sikhs were casting aside the visible symbols of their loyalty to the community.

Thus was the myth extended. The brightness of the past was now matched by the darkness of the present. It is scarcely surprising that interpretations of this kind should issue in attempts to arrest the process of dissolution. Balak Singh's Jagiasi movement was one of the earliest of these attempts. For him the earlier glory consisted in the purity of the Gurus' religious teachings, and specifically in the devotional practice of *nām simraṇ*. Ram Singh evidently propounded the same message, but for many of his followers the glories of the past were primarily the military triumphs of the Khalsa. During the eighteenth century Mughal authority had been extinguished in the Panjab and Afghan efforts to invade the land had been resisted. Ranjit Singh had consolidated these successes and then pushed back the boundaries of the Panjab in three directions. Even the British, for all their strength, had drawn back from a confrontation. There had been unity and purpose, and for none more than those who were Sikhs. There had also been employment, for Ranjit Singh's army had been a large one.

The two decades following the death of Ranjit Singh were certainly a period of progressive disillusionment for the Sikhs, and the Kuka attempts to evoke the heroic traditions of Guru Gobind Singh suggest that the development of their sect must be related to this experience of disillusionment. This should not be the end of the analysis, however, for it is possible to proceed further in pursuit of the origins of the distress and disarray. The role of Ranjit Singh's army as an employer of many Jat Sikhs could conceivably imply that the overtly religious aspects of Kuka discontent derived from essentially economic sources. Here too the example of other millenarian movements may provide a guide. In such instances it is normally economic distress with its attendant social problems which creates the tension leading to distinctively millenarian responses.

At first sight the available evidence is unpromising. The Kuka movement drew practically all of its support from the rural areas of the Panjab and if we are to judge from the comments offered by the British administrators of this period, these areas were not economically depressed during the years which cover the sect's rapid ascent to its short-lived prominence. The evidence is best presented in the settlement reports produced towards the end of the nineteenth century. These record increases in cultivation and in the irrigation of areas already under cultivation.[61] Population increases are briefly noted, but without evident concern. At this stage it was believed that the agricultural resources of the fertile plains could cope with such increases.[62] The critical test of rural stability was taken to be the degree of willingness with which taxes were paid, and it was recorded, with obvious satisfaction, that revenue collection had generally involved little difficulty during the period preceding the writing of the reports.[63]

It is in just such circumstances that analyses of other millenarian movements can demonstrate their usefulness as guides. A survey of the evidence provided by the settlement reports would suggest that, whatever the reasons for the Kuka outbreak, economic distress was not to be numbered amongst them. The parallel pattern which can be observed in other millenarian situations should caution us against accepting this evidence without further analysis. Was rural Panjab really as contented as the British observers believed? There seems to be little doubt that most of the revenue-paying landholders must have been in relatively prosperous circumstances, but was this the group which provided the Kukas with the main body of their support? Other millenarian examples direct us to look elsewhere, not to the wealthier grain-producing landowners but rather to the humbler orders of Panjabi society. These are the people who characteristically provide a millenarian movement with its strength. They are also the people who figure prominently in reports concerning the constituency of the Kuka sect.

The dominant caste group within the Sikh community was (and remains) that of the Jats, a rural and agrarian people with strong martial traditions. Some Jats were landlords; others of lesser means cultivated small holdings as tenants. In undivided Panjab only a minority of the Jats were Sikhs (the balance being Muslims or Hindus), but within the Sikh community the Jat element has always retained a strong numerical preponderance. These were the people for whom the eighteenth century conditions had proven particularly advantageous and for whom the army of Ranjit Singh had subsequently provided congenial employment. Their poorer members were also the people who offered the strongest body of support to the Kuka movement. Others who joined it were drawn mainly from artisan and other depressed castes which stood in a client relationship to Jat patrons. The line of investigation which must now be pursued concerns these poorer members of the Sikh community. Is there any evidence which might suggest that theirs was a condition of unrest during the period leading up to the emergence of the sect?

A feature commonly associated with millenarian developments is increasing population pressure. This feature was certainly to be found in the Panjab of the middle and later nineteenth century. The eighteenth-century struggles which opened the way to Khalsa dominance had served, in the usual manner of military disturbances, to impose a check upon population growth. This condition was altered by Ranjit Singh's rise to power. All of his major battles were fought beyond the fertile tract of Central Panjab, and after 1824 they ceased altogether apart from some minor skirmishes. Warfare made a brief return during the fifth decade of the nineteenth century, but peace was reimposed in 1849 and was little affected by the events of 1857. By the time Ram Singh emerged as leader of the Kukas the Panjab had experienced five decades of relative tranquillity. But for the disturbances which followed Ranjit Singh's death the total would have been six. Indeed it can be argued that the span was even longer, for the more devastating disturbances of the eighteenth century were over well before the century concluded.

The result was an increase in the population of the Panjab. Although no figures exist for the period prior to 1855, it seems safe to assume that the trend which appeared in successive censuses from that year onwards will have been an extension of earlier increases during the preceding half century. Certainly there is no doubt about the trend during the years immediately preceding the Kuka outbreak. Between 1855 and 1868 the population of the Panjab increased by 16.1 per cent.[64]

The portion of the province which absorbed the greater measure of this rapid increase was the central tract, the area which already possessed the highest density. Whereas Jullundur District had a population of 513 per square mile in 1855, the corresponding figure for the potentially fertile but unirrigated Montgomery District was still only 55.[65] This in itself meant little, for Jullundur District in 1855 could obviously support a much higher density than areas which lacked either its fertility or its supply of water. A figure in excess of 500 was nevertheless a high one for a rural area to support and it was one which continued to rise in the years following 1855. During the brief period from 1855 to 1868 Jullundur District had to absorb more than 80 extra persons per square mile. Although the figure for Jullundur is one of the highest (only Amritsar District with an increase of 96 per square mile is higher), it is clear from a conspectus of the district totals that the major growth was concentrated in the central tract and that the rate of increase dropped away steadily as one moved outwards from it.[66]

These are impressive figures and they can be rendered even more impressive by the observation that during the middle decades of the nineteenth century urban areas absorbed relatively little of any population increase. An overwhelming proportion had to be accommodated within rural society. Against them must be set the statistics for agrarian extension provided by the settlement reports. Although these reduce the force of the demographic argument, they fall far short of destroying it. The situation which thus emerged did not in itself constitute a crisis, but it appears that it did involve a condition of considerable risk. Even the settlement officers perceived this.[67]

In such a situation a regular succession of adequate harvests was vital. For several years after the British annexation this succession was maintained, but eventually it was broken. Following a favourable year in 1857, the harvests of 1858 were much reduced, and during 1860–1 the Panjab experienced a serious famine.[68] This was followed by another period of acute scarcity in 1869–70.[69] In such a situation, those in possession of grain surpluses could secure a handsome profit from the inevitable increase in prices. Others, however, must suffer and, for some, this was the beginning of the road leading to indebtedness and eventually expropriation.

In such circumstances the poorer Jats would certainly have experienced distress, and in their case the experience of shared disaster will have been aggravated by two additional features. One was the Jat custom of fragmenting land-holdings at death. Large landholders, the heirs of substantial estates from the days of Sikh rule, might survive and flourish. Others must look elsewhere for alternative or supplementary means of support. Such means are usually available and the Jat has been characteristically prompt in utilizing them. The second aggravating factor was, however, a temporary blockage of the customary means of supplementary support. During the period of

Ranjit Singh and his successors there was the Army, an outlet which was soon to reopen under the British rule. Later there were the canal colonies, later still the Mercedes trucks and Calcutta taxis, and during recent years there have been opportunities for migration overseas.[70] The period immediately following the British annexation of the Panjab in 1849 was, however, a disastrous exception as far as the Jats were concerned. The British had insisted upon disbandment of the large Khalsa army, and although the Indian Army opened its ranks to the Sikhs with surprising speed there was inevitably an interval before this decision could provide a measure of aid sufficient to compensate for the economic problems of the Jat peasants.[71]

Discontent which afflicted the Jat peasants of the central tract would also have affected other rural caste groups of inferior economic status. In addition to the general problem of food shortages anything which affected the Jats could also be expected to affect those who were dependent upon them. If the Jat patrons suffered, the artisan and menial clients must suffer with them. If discontent were to develop within a distinctively Sikh group the vehicle of that discontent would predictably be a Sikh movement. Its origins might be religious, but the secret of its power to attract evidently lay in economic distress and in the threats to social stability which this involved. The Kuka sect evidently served as a convenient focus for rural unrest. Having won a generous measure of support, the sect was first transformed by its new converts and then shattered by their impulsiveness.

This analysis appears to be the only one which will take account of three fundamental aspects of Kuka history. The first of these is the lowly social and economic constituency of the sect. It was highly significant that Major Perkins should have observed that 'converts are chiefly made from Juts, Tirkhans, Chumars and Muzbees'.[72] Later police analysis of Kuka membership showed that of these four groups by far the strongest was that of the Jats,[73] and that this element was drawn largely from the ranks of the poorer Jats.[74] These were the people who would suffer extensively from conditions of economic deprivation while retaining memories of a more prosperous past.

Secondly, there is the close correlation between periods of food shortage and spurts in Kuka activity. The first serious famine took place in 1860–1, and the sect suddenly surges ahead in 1862–3. In 1868 and 1869 the police report a condition of general tranquillity amongst the Kukas. Another period of scarcity follows during 1869–70 and by the middle of 1871 the outbreaks of violence have begun.

Thirdly, there is the striking increase in the sect's strength which immediately followed the death of Balak Singh. When Balak Singh died in 1862 the focus of the sect's activities automatically moved away from his home in Hazro to Ram Singh's village of Bhaini. Hazro was a small town situated on the periphery of the Panjab in an area which still suffered little from population pressure or social dislocation. Within this area the Sikh population constituted only a fragment of the total population and within the Sikh community itself a majority belonged to mercantile castes.[75] Bhaini, in contrast, lay within the fertile central tract where Sikh traditions were powerful, where most members of the community were Jats, and where crop failure had so recently caused serious problems.[76] A religious leader appears within an area afflicted by famine and immediately attracts a substantial following from the poorer sections of the community. It seems impossible to resist the conclusion that the reason for the sudden growth of the sect must lie in the existing condition of economic distress. And this is precisely what the example of other millenarian movements would lead us to expect.

It thus becomes evident that the Kuka sect is best understood as a distinctively Sikh version of a common millenarian pattern. Social instability had produced discontent, and discontent had found the holy man to whom it could attach its aspirations. Out of this there emerged the myth which drew together past glories, present frustrations, and future hopes. Battle was joined, not with deliberation but impulsively, and the movement was quickly crushed. The leaders were imprisoned, adherents quickly fell away, and although a loyal remnant remained the discontent which had prompted the sect's rapid growth soon found outlets elsewhere. For many the armed forces and the canal colonies provided a sufficient answer. Others found a more convincing purpose in the Gurdwara Reform Movement or in the political channels which fed the Ghadr Conspiracy and eventually the Panjab Communist Party. It is, in many ways, a sad story. Like so many other millenarian movements it culminated in tragedy and slipped thereafter into a respectable insignificance. There was, however, more to the later Kuka experience than hopes deceived and fruitless intrigues with a Russian governor. The sect had begun a religious reform movement and to this exclusive concern it subsequently returned. The contribution of Sikh belief and custom to Panjab society is immense and voices which preach its reform have yet to be wholly ignored.

Notes

1. *Jagiāsī*, 'worshipper', from *jagya* or *yagya*, 'sacrifice', 'offering'. In some references the title used is Abhiasi (*abhiāsī*, 'student', 'one who meditates or devoutly repeats a sacred *mantra*', from *abhiās*, 'study, meditation, repetition').

2. According to orthodox Sikh belief the unbroken succession of ten Gurus extending from Nanak (1469–1539) to Gobind Singh (1666–1708) represented the embodiment of a single divine spirit in ten human bodies. Gobind Singh's sons had all predeceased him and according to Sikh tradition he had declared that at his death the spirit which had inhabited the ten bodies would thereafter dwell in the corporate community and in the sacred scripture. The belief which emerged amongst the followers of Balak Singh assumed a resumption of human form by the divine spirit. In Sikh usage the title 'Guru' signifies this divine spirit and within the community it could not be applied to a mere mortal however pious or enlightened he might be.

3. From a report dated 12 June 1863, included in *Memoranda regarding Gooroo Ram Singh, of a new sect of Sikhs, 'Jagiasis'*, compiled by J.W. Younghusband, Officiating Inspector General of Police, 28 June 1863, reproduced in Nahar Singh, *Gooroo Ram Singh and the Kuka Sikhs*, New Delhi: Amrit Book Co., 1965, I, p. 1. Nahar Singh's work is a comprehensive collection of government documents covering the period 1863 to 1881, most of them drawn from the National Archives of India in New Delhi. The other major depository of official documents re.ating to the Kuka sect (India Office Library, Judicial-Public files and Punjab Government records) largely duplicates the material provided by Nahar Singh. The collection consists of three volumes published by the compiler (vols I and II, New Delhi, 1965 and 1966; vol. III, Sri Jiwan Nagar, 1967). The collection is cited hereafter as *NS*.

4. Minute on Younghusband's *Memoranda*. *NS*, I, p. 10.

5. Ibid.

6. *NS*, I, p. 30. The Tarkhan, or carpenter caste, occupies a low ritual and economic status. Chamars are outcaste leather workers (known as Ramdasis when they become Sikhs). Mazhabis are members of the Chuhra (sweeper) outcaste group who have become Sikhs. Ram Singh was himself a Tarkhan.

7. Ibid.

8. *NS*, I, p. 11.

9. *NS*, I, p. 60.

10. Notably Dhian Singh, *Srī Satgurū Bilās* (Bhaini Sahib, 1942), Nidhan Singh Alam, *Jug Paltāū Satgurū* (Delhi, 1947), and Santokh Singh, 'Satgur Bilās' (unpub.). For quotations see Fauja Singh Bajwa, *Kuka Movement*, Delhi: Motilal Banarsidass, 1965, *passim*.

11. Fauja Singh Bajwa, *op. cit.*, M.M. Ahluwalia, *Kukas*, Bombay: Ganda

Singh, 1965. Ganda Singh, *Kūkiān dī Vithiā*, 2nd edn, Amritsar: Allied, 1946. Nahar Singh, *Nāmdhārī Itihās*, Delhi, 1955. Summary accounts of Kuka history and belief are given by Stephen Fuchs, *Rebellious Prophets*, Bombay: Asia Publishing House, 1965, pp. 192–7; and Khushwant Singh, *A History of the Sikhs*, Princeton, 1966, II, pp. 127–35. A brief notice appears in S. Gopal, *British Policy in India 1858–1905*, Cambridge, 1965, pp. 98–101.

12. *NS*, I, p. 26.
13. *NS*, I, p. 66.
14. *NS*, I, pp. 56–7.
15. *Chaṇḍī kī Vār*, or 'The Epic of the Goddess Chandi', is a work ascribed to the tenth Guru, Gobind Singh.
16. *NS*, I, p. 31.
17. Orthodox Sikhs wrap their turbans upwards from each ear to a central point of convergence immediately below the hair-line.
18. *NS*, I, p. 72.
19. *NS*, I, p. 77. The term 'subah' (or *sūbā*) designates a Mughal province. In Namdhari usage a subah was a missionary with the responsibility for a particular area corresponding to a province. Subahs were the same as the *mañjī* or preaching system established by Guru Amar Das, even to the extent of there being 22 which was the traditional number of the territorial *manjis*. The Mughal Empire under Akbar was divided into 22 provinces and Sikh tradition maintained that for this reason Guru Amar Das had appointed 22 *manjis*. Ram Singh in turn appointed 22 subahs.
20. *NS*, I, pp. 98–9, 102.
21. *NS*, I, pp. 111–12, 114.
22. *NS*, I, pp. 105–11.
23. *NS*, I, pp. 115, 119.
24. *NS*, I, pp. 123–7.
25. The number of attackers, originally estimated to have been 500, appears to have been at most 125, *NS*, II, p. 12.
26. A summary narrative of the episode is given in *NS*, II, pp. 57–72. This narrative, prepared in the Judicial branch, represents a collation of all relevant correspondence received up to 8 April 1872. For the documents upon which it is based see *NS*, II, p. 2 ff. One error in the summary narrative is the statement that Forsyth executed the batch of sixteen prisoners by hanging them. It was not until 21 May that the Punjab Government realized that Forsyth had followed Cowan's example and had the prisoners blown away from guns. *NS*, III, p. 75.
27. *NS*, II, p. 34. Also II, pp. 105, 168–9, 175 ff.
28. *NS*, II, p. 97. G.R. Elsmie, *Thirty-five Years in the Punjab*, Edinburgh, 1908, pp. pp. 163, 164.

29. *NS*, II, p. 227 ff.
30. *NS*, III, p. 164 ff.
31. *NS*, II, pp. 125, 151, 194–8.
32. *NS*, III, pp. 18 ff, 29–30, 30–1.
33. *NS*, III, p. 138.
34. *NS*, II, pp. 14–15.
35. *NS*, II, pp. 4, 134. Sahnewal is six miles from Bhaini.
36. *NS*, II, p. 50.
37. *NS*, II, p. 149.
38. *NS*, III, pp. 187–8.
39. *NS*, III, p. 115.
40. *NS*, III, p. 107.
41. *NS*, II, p. 111.
42. *NS*, III, p. 107.
43. *NS*, II, pp. 204, 226. In 1878 Ram Singh was transferred to Mergui when it was discovered that clandestine communications were being passed between Rangoon and the Punjab, *NS*, III, p. 368.
44. *NS*, III, pp. 156–68, 187–8.
45. For this episode see P.C. Roy, 'Gurcharan Singh's Mission in Central Asia', *Indian Historical Records Commission Proceedings*, XXXIV, 2 (December 1958); and 'Sikh Emissary in Russian Turkestan', *Indo-Asian Culture*, 3 (July 1968).
46. Fauja Singh Bajwa, pp. 167–70.
47. The present headquarters of the Namdhari sect are located in the village of Sri Jiwan Nagar, District Hissar, Haryana. The Guru continues to reside at Bhaini.
48. For an example of the British interpretation see David Ross, *The Land of the Five Rivers and Sindh*, London: Chapman and Hall, 1883, pp. 225–6. See also *Gazetteer of the Ludhiana District*, 1888–9, Calcutta, pp. 67–9.
49. N. Gerald Barrier, *The Sikhs and Their Literature*, Delhi: Manohar, 1970, p. 100. For the Ghadr Party see Khushwant Singh, II, pp. 181–92.
50. R.C. Majumdar, *History of the Freedom Movement in India*, Calcutta: Mukhopadhya, 1962, I, pp. 282–3.
51. Ibid., p. 282.
52. See above, n. 11.
53. Norman Cohn, *The Pursuit of the Millennium*, Paladin rev. edn, London, 1970, p. 60. For a summary of the characteristic pattern of millenarian belief in medieval Europe see ibid., p. 13, See also his essay 'Medieval Millenarianism' in S. Thrupp, ed., *Millennial Dreams in Action*, The Hague: Mouton, 1962, pp. 31–43. The literature dealing with millenarian movements in different parts of the world is now immense. One work which deserves particular notice is Peter Worsley, *The Trumpet Shall Sound*, London, 1957.

54. *NS*, I, p. 6. This document was supplied by an informer who had been sent to Bhaini by the Cantonment Magistrate of Jullundur in June 1863. The informer reported having received it from the leading Kuka subah, Sahib Singh. The word *sākhī* means 'testimony'. Guru Gobind Singh, the last of the personal Gurus recognized by orthodox Sikhs, died in 1708. The years 1921 and 1922 are dated according to the Indian Vikrami era. They correspond to A.D. 1864 and 1865.

55. *NS*, I, pp. 56–7.

56. *NS*, II, pp. 224–5. III, 164 ff.

57. *NS*, I, pp. 99, 144–45. Cf. Cohn, p. 49.

58. Fauja Singh Bajwa, pp. 22–3, 40, 184. Cohn, pp. 30–3. An English translation of the version of the *Sau Sākhīs* used by the Kukas was made by Sardar Attar Singh of Bhadaur and published under the title *Sakhee Book or the Description of Gooroo Govind Singh's Religion and Doctrine*, Benares: Attar Singh, 1873. See esp. pp. 38, 96. See also Attar Singh's *The Travels of Guru Tegh Bahadur and Guru Gobind Singh*, Lahore: Indian Public Opinion Press, 1876, p. v.

59. Fauja Singh Bajwa, pp. 160–1.

60. See above, p. 202.

61. W.G. Purser, *Final Report of the Revised Settlement of the Jullundur District in the Punjab*, Lahore: Punjab Government, 1892, p. 154. T. Gordon Walker, *Final Report on the Revision of Settlement (1878–83) of the Ludhiana District in the Punjab*, Calcutta: Punjab Government, 1884, p. 183.

62. Purser, p. 1.

63. Walker, p. 178.

64. *Census of India 1891: The Punjab and its Feudatories*, Calcutta, 1892, I, p. 76. The comparison was possible only in the case of the British territories, the actual figures being 15,161,321 and 17,609,518. It was, however, assumed on the basis of subsequent trends that the population of the princely states must have shown a corresponding increase. Ibid.

65. *Report on the Census of the Punjab taken on the 17th February 1881*, Calcutta, 1883, I, p. 92. (Cited hereafter as *1881 Census*.)

66. Ibid. It should be noted that these figures relate to the entire area of the district, uncultivated as well as cultivated. In 1881 the figure for Jullundur District based on the entire area was 597 per square mile. In the same year the figure for the cultivated areas was 762 per cultivated square mile. Purser, p. 2.

67. Purser, pp. 2–3.

68. S.S. Thorburn, *The Punjab in Peace and War*, Edinburgh and London: William Blackwood, 1904, pp. 232–3. Walker, pp. 123–4.

69. Walker, p. 124.

70. Four-fifths of the Indian migrants to the United Kingdom have been Punjabis, a large majority of them Jats.

71. Characteristically several Kukas enlisted in the army of the Maharaja

of Kashmir. (See above p. 194.) The emoluments were, however, negligible in comparison with those provided by British paymasters.

72. See above, p. 86.

73. A police list of prominent Kukas prepared in 1878 shows the following distribution:

Cultivator	109
Lambardar	18
Carpenter	14
Miscellaneous (occupations shown in each case)	74
None	38
	253

This is an occupational list, not a caste analysis, but it is possible to deduce from it an approximate figure for the Jat constituency of the sect. Almost all the cultivators will have been Jats and likewise the lambardars. Of the various persons grouped above under 'Miscellaneous' at least ten and perhaps as many as twenty, can be identified as Jats. The category 'None' presumably covers retired persons, and on the basis of the results shown by the other figures may be interpreted as including a majority of Jats. It seems safe to conclude that at least 150 of the Kukas listed by the police must have been Jats. I am indebted to Professors N.G. Barrier and R. Slater of the University of Missouri for the figures given above.

74. The only prominent Jat Kuka of elevated social or economic status appears to have been Mangal Singh, a relative of the Maharaja of Patiala. Mangal Singh subsequently claimed that he had never been a Kuka but that he had become 'a believer in Ram Singh' when the Kuka leader cured his ailing son. *NS*, III, p. 97. A few other landholders had attached themselves to the movement shortly before the outbreak. *NS*, I, pp. 143–4. At least some of these recanted as soon as the movement turned to violence and the Government to vigorous suppression. *NS*, III, p. 14.

75. Hazro is situated in Attock tahsil which, during the period covered by this essay, was one of the constituents of Rawalpindi District. In 1855 the population density of Rawalpindi District was 114 per square mile, rising to 146 by 1868, and 169 by 1881 (*1881 Census*, I, p. 92). In 1881 Sikhs accounted for 1.7 per cent of the total population of Rawalpindi Division. Of these Sikhs 68 per cent are classified as belonging to relatively wealthy mercantile castes (Khatri, Arora, and Banya). Ibid., p. 139. The population density of the area around Hazro will have been lower than the district average. Cf. the figures for Hazara District, immediately adjacent to Hazro: 1855 (98 per sq. m.), 1868 (122), 1881 (134). Ibid., p. 92. Balak Singh was himself an Arora by caste. (*Gazetteer of the Ludhiana District, 1888–9*, p. 68) Ram Singh was a Tarkhan.

76. Bhaini is located in Ludhiana District, a few miles from the boundary of the neighbouring Jullundur District. For the years 1855, 1868, and

1881 the figures for the population density of Ludhiana District were respectively 383, 429, and 450; and for Jullundur District respectively 513, 596, and 597. Ibid., p. 92. Sikhs constituted 6.2 per cent of the total population of Jullundur Division. (The division includes both districts.) Of these Sikhs, 72.7 per cent belonged to agricultural castes, more than 60 per cent of the total being Jats with the remaining 12 per cent distributed amongst Sainis, Rajputs, and Kambohs. 14.5 per cent belonged to artisan castes, notably Tarkhans (carpenters) and Lohars (blacksmiths). 11 per cent were outcastes and only 1 per cent came from mercantile castes. Ibid., p. 139.

13

AHLUWALIAS AND RAMGARHIAS: TWO SIKH CASTES

The eighteenth century was a period of considerable turbulence for the Punjab. It began with Mughal authority still to all appearances in full control of the area, and it terminated on the threshold of a return to firm rule under Maharaja Ranjit Singh. Between these two periods, however, there were rebellions, invasions, a fragmenting of authority, political confusion. By the middle of the century, following the final collapse of effective Mughal power, there were emerging the celebrated Sikhs *misls*, autonomous armed bands each under an acknowledged chieftain (*sardār* or *misldār*) and each asserting control over an ill-defined portion of central Punjab. During the period of their emergence a sense of unity was sustained, partly by the ties of a common allegiance to the Sikh faith but more effectively by the recurrent attacks of the Afghan invader, Ahmad Shah Abdali. Together with the preceding period of Mughal persecution these years constitute an interval of critical importance in the development of the Khalsa[1] and exploits associated with it have secured an enduring popularity in Sikh tradition.

With the removal of the Afghan threat in 1769 the precarious unity of the invasion years rapidly collapsed and for the remainder of the century political affairs in the Punjab were distinguished by inter-*misl* rivalry, leading on occasion to open war. Eventually one of the *sardārs*, Ranjit Singh of the Shukerchakia *misl*, by means of marital alliance,

*Originally published in *South Asia*, 4, 1974.

intimidation, and judicious use of force succeeded in eliminating almost all his rivals. The only major exception was the Phulkian *misl* which, because its territories lay in the Malwa region (south of the Satluj river), came within the ambit of the advancing British before Ranjit Singh could swallow it, and survived in consequence as a cluster of princely states. North of the Satluj Fateh Singh of Kapurthala managed to retain an empty title by accepting a thoroughly one-sided 'alliance' with Ranjit Singh. The fact that he succeeded in retaining his title was, however, important. We shall have reason to refer to the House of Kapurthala later in this essay.

Ranjit Singh belonged to a third generation of *misl* leadership. The first successful generation was the second (that of his father) and amongst the *sardārs* of this middle generation his father does not stand out as one of the most prominent. Two *sardārs* enjoy a particular prominence within this second generation, both of them bearing the name Jassa Singh. The older of the two first appears as Jassa Singh Kalal but subsequently Kalal was dropped and replaced by Ahluwalia. Similarly, his namesake abandoned his original name Jassa Singh Thoka in favour of Jassa Singh Ramgarhia. In accordance with these changes the groups which they led came to be known as the Ahluwalia and Ramgarhia *misls* respectively.

For the purposes of this essay both sets of names are important. In each case the change of name serves to represent the process which the essay discusses, and all four are names which must recur frequently during the course of the discussion. The original names Kalal and Thoka designate castes, both of them artisan and both low in the status hierarchy of the Punjab. The Kalals as brewers and distillers occupied a conspicuously low ranking. *Thokā* means 'carpenter' and indicates a member of the a Tarkhan caste.[2] The Tarkhan, or carpenter, caste ranked distinctively higher than that of the Kalals or indeed of any other Punjabi artisan caste, but artisan it remained and its actual status was in consequence comparatively low. Both ranked well below the Jats, who were the dominant caste within the Khalsa and who were, during the eighteenth century, establishing a much wider dominance over rural Punjab.

There seems little doubt that the obvious explanation for this abandoning of caste names must be the correct one. Both leaders sought to relinquish inherited names redolent of lowly status. This they did by appropriating names more in accord with the exalted status earned in each case by successful military enterprise. Jassa Singh Kalal followed the common practice of assuming the name of his native village. This was a small place near Lahore named Ahlu or Ahluval and he accordingly came to be known as Jassa Singh of Ahluval (Jassa Singh Ahluvalia).[3] Initially his namesake followed the same convention and, as a resident of Ichogal village (also near Lahore), was known as Jassa Singh Ichogalia as well as Jassa Singh Thoka. In 1749, however, he played a critical role in relieving the besieged fort of Ram Rauni outside Amritsar. The fort was subsequently entrusted to his charge, rebuilt and renamed Ramgarh, and it was as governor of the fort that he came to be known as Jassa Singh Ramgarhia.[4] Although the old caste appellation Thoka continues to appear in many later references, Ramgarhia is clearly regarded as a more elevated title and later heroic literature almost invariably refers to him by this name.

An understanding of the careers of the two Jassa Singhs is certainly relevant to what follows. Our concern, however, is not with two distinguished individuals of the eighteenth century, but rather with the caste groups to which they belonged—with the means whereby sections of both groups have subsequently endeavoured to enhance their corporate status, and the degree of success each has achieved. The scanty literature dealing with the two groups will be consolidated and, where possible, supplemented.[5] Particular attention will be directed to their common Sikh allegiance; the extent to which status ambitions have encouraged conversion to the Khalsa; and the degree to which the Sikh affiliation has encouraged and facilitated the continued pursuit of these ambitions.

From this declaration of intent it is obvious that the discussion must concern the issue of upward caste mobility. Does this necessarily imply that it must in consequence concern Srinivas's celebrated theory of 'Sanskritization'? The answer must be that, although a general correspondence may be discerned, the 'Sanskritization' formulations relating to caste mobility are more likely to confuse than to enlighten and that the term ought, in consequence, to be eliminated from the discussion. We are dealing with a comparatively simple process of emulation, one which in its essential rudiments was recognized and understood by the earliest of the systematic British observers of Punjabi society. In his treatment of Punjab castes in the 1881 census Ibbetson includes a section entitled 'Instances of the mutability of caste'. In this and the following section he gives several examples of castes which have moved up or down in status by means of adopting or abandoning particular customs or occupations.[6] Although Ibbetson produced no sophisticated theory to cover the phenomenon there can be no doubt that he and his colleagues were well acquainted with its more obvious features as they manifested themselves in Punjabi society of the late nineteenth century.

The case against retaining the terminology of the Sanskritization debate in this examination of the Ahluwalia and Ramgarhia communities can be illustrated by reference to the patterns of behaviour which have provided models for Punjabi Kalal and Tarkhan imitation. These can scarcely be described as brahmanical. In several respects they are distinctly anti-Brahman in sympathy and in actual practice. The overt model has been the Khalsa discipline, a pattern which represents the teachings of Nanak and his successors transformed and extensively supplemented by the culture of the dominant Jats. Neither Nanak nor his Jat followers betray a particular affection for Brahmans. Nanak frequently goes out of his way to denounce brahmanical pretensions and specifically the notion that real worth or salvation must necessarily relate to degrees of caste status. Although Jats still showed a residual respect for Brahmans during the eighteenth and early nineteenth centuries,[7] it has since dwindled to vanishing point as they secured an increasing dominance over rural Punjab. Because the principal Kalal and Tarkhan attempts come within this latter period it would be surprising to find in them a conscious imitation of brahmanical ideals, apart from such as have been retained within the Sikh faith or continuing Jat practice. This applies most strongly in the case of the Tarkhans who, as rural artisans dependent on landlord patronage, have been in particularly close association with Jats.

II

Before proceeding to discuss the Kalal and Tarkhan castes it is perhaps wise to clarify the meaning of the term 'caste' when used in a Punjabi context. Within the Punjab caste consciousness has comparatively little to do with the concept of *varna*, except for those at the upper and lower extremities of the classical hierarchy. For the bulk of the population the status hierarchy which really counts is one which takes slight account of the traditional fourfold *varna* distinction. It is in the Punjab a hierarchy which exalts the mercantile Khatri and agrarian Jat while tending to depreciate the Brahman. For the Jat the classical hierarchy has little relevance except perhaps to increase the condescension which nowadays he characteristically bestows upon

Brahmans. It has had relevance for the Khatris as a means of claiming Kshatriya status, but even here its importance has been only marginal. Khatri status obviously owes much more to commercial, industrial and administrative success than to a dubious etymological assertion.[8] As far as this essay is concerned the only relevance of the traditional *varṇa* theory derives from intermittent Kalal claims to Khatri status. The link is an exceedingly tenuous one, as the target has been the actual Khatri mode rather than the vague status of the warrior Kshatriya.

In Punjabi usage the term most commonly encountered is *zāt*, a cognate form and synonym of *jāti*. The word is, in practice, used very loosely and one must frequently construe its meaning from the context. It may refer to the larger endogamous unit of caste organization; to the smaller exogamous unit, or to the groupings of exogamous units. In some contexts it may even be used to signify *varṇa*.[9] A strict definition is, however, possible and it designates one of the two major units of caste organization in the Punjab. In its strict sense *zāt* connotes the larger endogamous unit and is thus properly applied to such groupings as Khatri and Jat. The smaller exogamous units which together constitute the *zāt* or *jāti* are called *got* (Hindi *gotra*).

In Punjabi society it is the *zāt* hierarchy which is most significant and it is upon his *zāt's* ranking that an individual's status will normally depend. Within each *zāt*, moreover, one can expect to find an internal *got* hierarchy of varying clarity and precision. Kalal and Tarkhan are both regarded as *zāts*, each containing its own *gots*. This much is clear and easily understood, and it retains its clarity as long as the discussion is confined to the Kalals. In the case of the Tarkhans, however, an interesting complication is introduced following the assumption of the title Ramgarhia by Sikh Tarkhans. Sikh members of other artisan *zāts*, notably the Lohar (blacksmith) and Raj (mason), have also claimed to be Ramgarhias and on the whole their claim has been accepted by Punjabi society in general. This has, in effect, created a new composite Ramgarhia *zāt* by an alliance of the Sikh segments of various artisan *zāts*. It should be added that the alliance has been an unequal one in most areas. In practice the Ramgarhia grouping has always been overwhelmingly dominated by its Tarkhan constituency.

One other term which will be encountered in any detailed investigation of caste relationships is *barādarī* (lit. 'fraternity'), the group responsible for making decisions which affect the members of any given *got*. In theory the *barādarī* embraces the entire membership of the *got*. In practice, however, *barādarīs* are much more restricted in size than the theory would suggest. The effective *biradari* is much more likely to comprise the members of a particular *got* within a single village or group of contiguous villages. Each *got* will thus have many *barādarīs* and the number of *barādarīs* in any given area will approximate to the number of *gots*. These *barādarīs* have been important in terms of caste mobility. Movement in either direction has only partly been the product of fortuitous changes in external circumstances. Positive decisions by *barādarīs* (as for example in such areas as education) have commonly produced significant local results, some of which will have spread by imitation to *got* members in other geographical areas. The action taken by many Sikh Tarkhans in returning themselves as Ramgarhias in the 1921 and 1931 censuses presumably represents *barādarī* decisions in most instances.

III

Having thus defined three of the key terms we can return to the Kalal and Tarkhan *zāts*, and specifically to the question of when they first entered the Sikh community in substantial numbers. This is a very difficult question to answer satisfactorily as there exist neithers statistics nor detailed reference for the entire period preceding the 1881 census. The earliest British observers, writing in the late eighteenth century, were plainly under the impression that the overwhelming majority of Khalsa Sikhs were Jats.[10] The impression is understandable as all the evidence (both from contemporaneous sources and from the censuses of a century later) confirm a strong preponderance of Jats. It seems likely, however, that there may have been some measure of exaggeration in their emphasis. Pre-Khalsa sources (notably the eleventh *vār* of Bhai Gurdas) point to a significant Khatri constituency, plus a sprinkling from several other diverse castes. Although the Khatri proportion failed to carry over in the same strength into the Jat-dominated Khalsa it is clear that the Khalsa has always included an indeterminate minority of non-Jats and that particular individuals from amongst this composite minority have achieved high rank in its counsels. The two Jassa Singhs testify to this general truth and to the specific presence of both Kalals and Tarkhans.

Beyond this observation we are, however, reduced to little more than cautious conjecture, much of its based upon the appreciably later evidence of the censuses. In the case of the Kalals we can assume that in terms of influence as well as numbers their pre-census representation was small. The same may also be posited with regard to the influence of the Tarkhans but not with reference to their numbers. The Tarkhans were, after all, tied to the Jats in an intimate *jajmānī* relationship and if the patron chose to follow a particular way it would scarcely be surprising if the client should do the same. This might be unlikely in the case of a lowly menial, but not for the higher ranks of the artisans. Scattered hints offer some small support for this assumption. There are, for example, the reference in police files concerning Baba Ram Singh, leader of the Kuka sect of Sikhs from 1862 until his deportation in 1872. Ram Singh was himself a Tarkhan Sikh and in a police report of 1867 on the Kukas it is claimed that 'converts are chiefly made from Juts, Tirkhans, Chumars, and Muzbees'.[11]

This is, however, essentially conjecture. With the appearance of the 1881 census light begins to break. A total of 1,706,909 persons were returned as Sikhs at this census. As everyone had expected the caste analysis of this figure produced a pronounced absolute majority in favour of the Jats (more than 66 per cent of the total community). The second-largest figure, however, produced a surprise. From the Jat total there is a spectacular drop to the second-largest constituent which, it turns out, is provided by the Tarkhans with 6.5 per cent.[12] Other constituents in excess of 2 per cent were the two outcaste groups of Chamar (5.6 per cent) and Chuhra (2.6), the Aroras (2.3), and the Khatris (2.2 per cent). The Kalals with 0.5 per cent emerge as one of the smallest of the remaining twenty *zāts* appearing in the census table.[13] Another table lends some support to the theory that Tarkhan adherence to the Khalsa will have derived its impulse from the *jajmānī* relationship with Jats. Abstract 55, 'Distribution of Male Sikhs by Caste for Divisions', shows a parallel area concentration of Jats and Tarkhans.[14]

Elsewhere in the 1881 Census analyses of religious affiliation are provided for each caste. Out of a total of 40,149 Kalals 22,254 were returned as Hindus (55.4 per cent), 8,931 as Sikhs (22.2 per cent), and 8,964 as Muslims (22.3 per cent).[15] Tarkhans totalled 596,941. Of these 219,591 were Hindus (36.8 per cent), 113,869 were Sikh (19 per cent), and 263,478 were Muslims (44.1 per cent).[16]

A similar range of figures are provided in the 1891 Census, but thereafter the Kalals are dropped from the tables which provide informative analyses. There is, however, no reason to assume that the Kalal trend will have been significantly different from that of the Tarkhans or of the Sikh returns as a whole. The Sikh Kalals do register a small proportionate drop during the decade 1881–91, but so too does the overall Sikh total. Thereafter both the Sikh total and that of its Tarkhan component register comparatively steep rises through to the 1931 Census (the last to incorporate caste returns) and it is probably safe to assume that the Kalal component also increased. The 1931 Census gives the following figures:[17]

Census	Absolute figures for Sikhs	Percentage increase	Proportion per 10,000
1881	1,706,909*	—	822
1891	1,849,371*	8.4	809
1901	2,102,813	13.7	863
1911	2,881,495	37.0	1,211
1921	3,107,296	7.8	1,238
1931	4,071,624	31.0	1,429

* Includes figures for Delhi.

The same Census also provides a table showing 'for each of the last six censuses the variations in the population figures of certain castes, which claim both Hindus and Sikhs among their members'. This table includes the following entry for Tarkhans:[18]

	1881	1891	1901	1911	1921	1931
Hindu	213,070	215,561	233,934	162,305	161,833	146,727
Sikh	113,067	134,110	146,904	180,447	139,327	158,446

Khan Ahmad Hassan Khan, author of the 1931 Census Report, explaining the apparent drop in the number of Sikh Tarkhans following the 1911 Census, indicates that the earlier pattern of increase had in fact continued through to 1931. He says:

Among occupational castes, such as Tarkhan and Lohar, Hindus have been decreasing since 1901, while the number of Sikhs has been rapidly growing, though of late it has had a downward tendency. This is merely due to the failure on the part of Sikh artisans to return any caste at all or to claim Ramgarhia as their caste instead of the traditional caste, Tarkhan.[19]

Although one must certainly treat these census returns with considerable caution it is obviously safe to conclude that the period from 1891 to 1931 is marked by a substantial movement within several castes away from a Hindu identity to a conscious Sikh identity. The Tarkhan *zāt* is on‹ such caste and given the nature of the general trend it would be extremely surprising if the Kalals were not another. Earlier in his report Khan explain the trend:

The main conclusion is that the varying strength of the population returned as Hindu or Sikh in the Punjab States is due to social causes that are at work in that section of the population from which both Hindus and Sikhs are drawn. The Akali movement during the last decade is mainly responsible for numerous persons being returned as Sikhs instead of Hindus. Such persons for the most part comprise members of depressed classes, agriculturalists and artisans in rural areas, who obviously consider that they gain in status as soon as they cease to be Hindus and become Sikhs.[20]

This comment, here restricted to the princely states, is subsequently extended to cover the bulk of British Punjab.

The main cause for the discarding of Hinduism by some of the agricultural and artisan classes in the central and eastern Punjab is the enhanced prestige gained by agricultural tribes in the countryside by their becoming Sikh ... . Similar influences are operative in the case of such tribes as *Tarkhan* (carpenter), *Lohar* (blacksmith), *Julaha* (weaver), *Sunar* (goldsmith) and *Nai* (barber).[21]

IV

Up to this point the Kalal and Tarkhan *zāts* have been considered together. This has been convenient insofar as they manifest a similar impulse and produce similar responses. There are, however, distinctive differences and each will now be treated separately.

Ibbetson's classic Report on the 1881 Census of the Punjab provides the first systematic description of the Kalal caste in general and Ahluwalias (Sikh Kalals) in particular. In this brief account he refers to Jassa Singh's assumption of the name Ahluwalia and indicates that the borrowing of the name by Sikh Kalals was already general by 1881. 'The caste', he adds, 'was thus raised in importance' and in consequence 'many of its members abandoned their hereditary occupation [as distillers].'[22] Ibbetson here implies as consequence what was probably a simultaneous process, directed towards the same objective. Moreover, he refers in the same description to an economic incentive for renouncing the traditional Kalal vocation. This was provided by British regulation of the distilling and sale of spirits. As a result of the restrictions thus imposed many Kalals, particularly Sikhs and Muslims, had 'taken to other pursuits, very often to commerce, and especially to traffic in boots and shoes, bread, vegetables, and other commodities in which men of good caste object to deal'. He adds: 'They are notorious for enterprise, energy, and obstinacy.'[23]

Ibbetson indicates that the Sikh Kalals (whom we must henceforth call Ahluwalias[24]) were in a period of transition during the late nineteenth century. Another British observer writing less than twenty years later accepts the fact of change but disagrees with regard to its direction. In his *Handbook on Sikhs for Regimental Officers* (Allahabad, 1896) R.W. Falcon claims that most Ahluwalias had become agriculturalists.[25] Falcon, however, writes from personal observation rather than from statistics and the claim which he makes probably amounts to an impression derived from experiences as a recruiting officer, an occupation which directed attention to rural rather than urban groups. His statement should probably be regarded as a supplement to Ibbetson's information. We thus retain the clear impression of a caste in transition, moving in response to both economic pressure and deliberate choice. By the end of the nineteenth century many Ahluwalias had taken up agriculture and many more had moved into petty commerce. Some were already securing positions of responsibility in the army or civil administration, and others were appearing as lawyers.[26]

This process has continued throughout the present century, with the result that although Ahluwalias may still be found in petty commerce this is scarcely the image they project. Ahluwalias are now to be found in more exalted commercial enterprise and particularly in government service where many have achieved notable success. Some have achieved prominence in the army. Others have done so in literature and the universities, earning for themselves an acknowledged reputation as intellectuals. One of the finest flowers of Punjabi literature was in fact of Ahluwalia origin, the result of a decision by the Ahluwalia *barādarī* of the Abbotabad area to send two of its young men to Japan for their education. One of these, Puran Singh (1881–1931), matured into a poet of considerable renown within the Punjab.

Ahluwalias' status today is unquestionably a high one in Punjab society and few would deny them an honourable rank. It is, however, by no means clear what specific status the Ahluwalias have aimed to achieve, nor what precise status they are accorded in modern Punjabi society. The target of the Kapurthala princely family (the descendants of Jassa Singh Ahluwalia) appears during the later nineteenth century to have been Rajput status.[27] For at least some

Ahluwalias there appear to have been Jat ambitions, but if so these have been frustrated by Jat unwillingness to intermarry. As a whole the community seems generally to have regarded Khatri status as the desired objective, a claim which once produced a short-lived 'All India Ahluwalia Khatri Mahasabha'.[28] Solid evidence is not available, but one will often encounter claims that increasingly Ahluwalias are marrying Khatris. For a group moving strongly towards urban residence and commercial or professional occupations the Khatri identity provides an appropriate target.

The details are imprecise, but of the general outcome there can be no doubt. A fair summary of current attitudes was probably provided by a conversation with three Sikh graduate students (all non-Ahluwalias) in 1972. When asked to identify the caste status of the Ahluwalias one volunteered the suggestion that they must be Jats, a second linked them with the Khatris, and the third did not know. None were aware of any links with the Kalals. Ahluwalia success is, it seems, assured. It can be attributed partly to the comparatively lengthy spread in temporal terms of their ascent to a respectable corporate status; partly to the relative smallness of the community; partly to its association with the princely house of Kapurthala; and partly to the intelligent determination of so many individual Ahluwalias.

V

The experience of the Ramgarhias has been distinctly different, notwithstanding the place of high honour accorded individual Tarkhans in Sikh history and tradition. Jassa Singh Thoka we have already noted. Even higher in the traditional estimation stands the figure of Bhai Lalo, a carpenter who plays a central part in one of the most popular of all *janam-sākhī* stories about Guru Nanak.[29] As we have already seen, however, their strength and status within the Sikh Panth remains generally obscure until we reach the later nineteenth century.

Ibbetson's brief description of the Tarkhan caste suggests that in 1881 there was little evidence of the conscious mobility he notes in the case of the Ahluwalias.[30] By 1891, however, the proportion returned as Sikhs was already rising[31] and in 1896 Falcon noted that Sikh Tarkhans were commonly called Ramgarhias,[32] a title earlier used only by the direct descendants of Jassa Singh Thoka.[33] In the 1901 census 4,253 Sikhs returned themselves as Ramgarhias. A particular concentration in Gurdaspur district (1,548) indicates the connection with Jassa Singh's descendants, most of whose estates were located in that area.[34] The usage had, however, ceased to be a family preserve and its incidence increased rapidly through the three succeeding decennial censuses. Today, if a caste label is to be used for a Sikh of Tarkhan origins, it will almost invariably be Ramgarhia.

This increasing popularity of the name Ramgarhia during the present century accompanies a steady increase in the economic status of many Sikh Tarkhans (for some a positively spectacular increase). In 1896 Falcon warned his readers that a Tarkhan Sikh 'can rarely be persuaded to enlist on a sepoy's pay as an average carpenter can make Rs. 20 a month in his village'.[35] This was but a small beginning for what was to follow. From their homes in rural Punjab numerous Ramgarhias began to travel increasing distances in response to a substantial British demand for their services. The development of communications and industry required in large measure precisely those skills which the Ramgarhias were able to provide. Carpentry in Shimla, railways in eastern India, contracting in Assam, and a combination of the same opportunities in East Africa progressively attracted the services of the willing Ramgarhia and brought him a mounting economic return. It need occasion no surprise that the largest section of East African Sikhs is still that of the Ramgarhias.[36]

The economic success achieved outside the Punjab has subsequently been repeated within the Ramgarhias' home state, much of it on the basis of profits repatriated from other parts of India and from East Africa. Two features distinguish this Punjab-based enterprise. The first is its specialization in small-scale industries which relate closely to the traditional Tarkhan vocation. Furniture-making and agricultural machinery are two prominent examples. The second distinctive features has been a concentration in particular towns, notably Phagwara (auto parts and other industries), Kartarpur (furniture), and Batala (foundries and agricultural machinery).[37] Concentrations also occur in Ludhiana and Goraya, and impressive fortunes have been made by Ramgarhia contractors in New Delhi.

These enterprises convincingly demonstrate a substantial economic achievement on the part of numerous Ramgarhias. Has their success in the economic area been accompanied by a corporate social rise of any significance? Although individual Ramgarhias of considerable wealth appear to be achieving a measure of success in terms of marriage arrangements the corporate status of the community still appears to be essentially unchanged. This failure has not been the result of complacence or inactivity. In addition to their Sikh affiliation and change of name the Ramgarhias have, during the past half-century, achieved a notable degree of corporate cohension and engaged in the kind of corporate activities which are believed to foster advancement under twentieth-century conditions. These include the formation of Ramgarhia *sabhas* (societies), the erection of Ramgarhia *gurduārās* (temples), the publication of a *Ramgarhia Gazette*, and above all the development of an impressive educational complex in Phagwara. This complex now includes a degree college, a teachers' training college, a polytechnic, an industrial training institute, and several schools.[38] It is, moreover, evident that Sikhs of other artisan castes have believed the corporate status of the Ramgarhias to be a desirable one, with the result that Lohars and Rajs have adopted the title and been accepted into the predominantly Tarkhan community. These factors notwithstanding it remains apparent that in terms of corporate status the Ramgarhia community has achieved a comparatively slight success. Certainly it is appreciably less than that of the Ahluwalias.

The future may, of course, produce change in corporate status corresponding to economic success; or it may simply provide for a progressive weakening of caste hierarchies, reducing the present corporate status to meaningless relics. The present provides, in the case of the Ramgarhias, an unusually interesting composite *zāt* grouping, built around a substantial core of Sikh Tarkhans but somewhat indistinct at its edges. In addition to Lohar and Raj accessions some Nais (barbers) and a few Gujars have also assumed the Ramgarhia mantle. Amongst its more prominent *gots* are the Kalsi (named after a village in Amritsar District), the Mohinderu (borrowed from the Khatris), and the Matharu. In spite of its impressive educational apparatus in Phagwara the community has produced few scholars and little evident willingness to use education (in the manner of the Ahluwalias) as a means of professional advancement. Very few Ramgarhias will be found in administrative positions and there seems little likelihood that this situation will change. There has, however, been an interesting tradition in many Ramgarhia families of providing *granthis* (or readers) for *gurduārās*. Another interesting specialization has been art. Much of the marble inlay and many of the frescoes in the Golden Temple are the work of Ramgarhia craftsmen.[39]

The current condition of the community in terms of coherence and solidarity is difficult to estimate. Saberwal suggests after a period of research in 'Modelpur' (Phagwara) that the Ramgarhia coherence in that particular area is now dissolving as *barādarīs* lose their authority and as Ramgarhias of elevated individual status increasingly seek marriage arrangements outside the community. Ramgarhia involvement in politics has, he maintains, been sparse in the past and for the future it is at once unnecessary and impossible.[40] A different impression emerges, however, from the Batala area. Informants in Batala (one of them a former member of the Punjab Legislative Assembly) claimed that locally the Ramgarhias are well organized (at least politically). In recent elections (Punjab state elections of March 1972) their support has been given to the Congress, not to the Akalis whom they identify with Jat interests.

A report from yet another area indicates a similar degree of local cohesion, but a different beneficiary. Nayar found that the Ramgarhias of the rural Sidhwan Bet constituency in Ludhiana District voted solidly Akali in the 1962 elections because 'they insistently wanted to prove that they are as good Sikhs as any other, and the act of voting for the Akali candidate becomes a form of self-assurance and a public demonstration of being a complete Sikh'.[41] The difference between Batala and Sidhwan Bet is perhaps explained by a contrast between comparative Ramgarhia affluence in the former and backwardness in the latter. Whereas the Ramgarhias of Sidhwan Bet were still seeking to secure the status associated with their Sikh affiliation, those of Batala are more concerned to maintain favour with the Congress party which, as the central Government, can so affect the fortunes of small industries. In a general sense it seems reasonable to conclude that whereas there is no uniformity of Ramgarhia political policy at the provincial level there are, in at least a few areas, evidences of effective local unity.

Amongst individual politicians two Ramgarhias have achieved notable prominence in recent years. The former Chief Minister of the Punjab, Giani Zail Singh was Ramgarhia and the first of the community to occupy a position normally held by a Jat. He was later President of India. The late Dalip Singh Saund, the first Indian member of the United States Congress, was also a Ramgarhia.[42] In each case the success should probably be regarded as essentially personal.

VI

Ahluwalias and Ramgarhias, both of them caste groups within the wider Sikh Panth, have thus had differing success in their common quest for higher status. We conclude with the questions raised at the beginning of this essay and since then treated only indirectly. To what extent has this quest for higher status encouraged conversion to the Sikh Khalsa; and to what degree has conversion subsequently favoured its pursuit?

Although the first question must defy a precise response, it can be easily answered in a general sense. The census figures alone, testifying as they do to extensive lower caste conversion over the course of at least half a century, demonstrate the appeal of the Khalsa to those dissatisfied with their inherited status. The Sikh Gurus had preached the religious equality of all castes and coinciding with the period covered by the censuses the Singh Sabha reform movement stimulated a significant recovery of this message. Within the Khalsa the customs of *sangat* and *pangat*[43] are meaningful conventions and all who join it share in the measure of equal status which they confer. The Khalsa was, moreover, an institution of acknowledged prestige and influence. Within it caste distinctions may have survived, but it offered a promise of equality which was by no means wholly belied. This applied to the Ramgarhias as well as to the Ahluwalias. Tarkhans they may have remained, but their status was plainly superior to that of their Hindu caste-fellows. Apart from the reputation of the Khalsa there appears to be no explanation to account for this difference.

This acknowledgement provides a part of the answer to our second question. In purely economic terms we can, however, proceed further with this question. Saberwal argues that the Sikh symbols, imposing as they do an outward uniformity, enabled Ramgarhias who moved beyond the Punjab to escape from the constricting status of menials.[44] The recognizably Sikh exterior could, in fact, achieve even more.

In the eyes of foreigners Sikhs belong to a single community, and qualities attributed to the community as a whole have frequently been ascribed *pari passu* to its individual members. This would mean that the Sikh reputation for freedom, vigour and initiative (a reputation largely earned by the Jats) might well be extended to all who bore the external symbols.

There is perhaps a degree of exaggeration involved in this as the instructions issued to army recruitment officers betray if anything an excessive concern for character differences allegedly based on caste distinctions amongst the Sikhs. At the same time there also appears to be a measure of truth in it, a measure which probably increased as one moved away from army circles. The same willingness to endow all Sikhs with a common identity survives today in such instances as the reputation accorded Sikh taxi drivers. To be visibly a Sikh commonly means receiving both the benefits and disadvantages conferred by the composite Sikh reputation.

Others have attempted to go still further in claiming particular qualities for the Sikh regardless of his caste. The Khalsa *rahit* (code of discipline) is said to bestow advantages in terms of a regular disciplined life; and the specific ban on tobacco effectively debars the Sikh from a deleterious habit. Here, however, we broach issues which are debatable to say the least. The *rahit* is unquestionably a powerful means of personal discipline if in fact it is rigorously observed, but there is little evidence to indicate a widespread contemporary rigour. Whereas it certainly applies to many individual Sikhs, few would allow the claim to cover the Panth as a whole. Although the ban on smoking is almost universally observed by Sikhs some might want to suggest that gains made here are lost on liquor.

The most one can claim is that the Sikh way of life offers a possibility of temporal success and the certainty of enhanced personal respect for those individuals who strictly observe its precepts. To castes as a whole it offers the same benefits, but to an appreciably diminished degree. The varying success of the Ahluwalias and Ramgarhias suggests that for substantial gains in status other means are also required.

Notes

1. The Sikh order, with its distinctive symbols and discipline, instituted by Guru Gobind Singh in 1699.
2. The Punjabi *thokā* and Hindi *tarkhāṇ* are synonymous. The latter, however, is almost invariably used as the caste designation.
3. Hari Ram Gupta, *History of the Sikhs 1739–1768* (Simla: Minerva Book Shop, 2nd rev. edn, 1952), I, p. 50n.; Kanh Singh Nabha, *Guruśabad Ratanākar Mahān Koś* (Patiala: Bhasha Vibhag, 1960), p. 372.
4. Gupta, *op. cit.*, pp. 61, 90–1; Kanh Singh Nabha, *op. cit.*, p. 372; Teja Singh and Ganda Singh, *A Short History of the Sikhs* (Bombay: Orient Longmans, 1950), pp. 138–9, 141n.
5. The principal sources are the successive Punjab censuses from 1881 to 1931. Ibbetson's important Report on the 1881 census was subsequently reissued under the title *Panjab Castes* (Lahore: Punjab Government, 1916). R.W. Falcon, *Handbook on Sikhs for the use of Regimental Officers* (Allahabad: Pioneer Press, 1896) offers a conspectus of Sikh castes, but adds little to Ibbetson with regard to Kalals and Tarkhans. The only extended treatment of either caste provided by a modern authority is Satish Saberwal's valuable contribution on the Ramgarhias, 'Status,

Mobility and Networks in a Punjabi Industrial Town', *Beyond the Village: Sociological Explorations*, ed. Satish Saberwal (Simla: Indian Institute of Advanced Study, 1972). More can be expected from this author. Both groups are briefly and usefully described in their nineteenth-century context by P. van den Dungen in D.A. Low (ed.), *Soundings in Modern South Asian History* (Canberra: Australian National University Press, 1968), pp. 64–5, 70–1.

6. *Census of India 1881*, (Lahore: Her Majesty's Stationery Office, 1883), I, Book I, 174–6, Also Ibbetson, *op. cit.*, pp. 6–9.

7. Avtar Singh, *Ethics of the Sikhs* (Patiala: Punjabi University, 1970), p. 161.

8. The words *kṣatriyā* and *khatrī* are cognate terms, the latter Punjabi form apparently assumed as yet another example of upward mobility by means of caste titles.

9. Cf. André Béteille, *Castes Old and New* (Bombay: Asia Publishing House, 1969), pp. 146–51.

10. Ganda Singh (ed.), *Early European Accounts of the Sikhs* (Calcutta: Indian Studies Past and Present, 1962), pp. 13, 56, 105. The impression was still abroad in the mid-nineteenth century. Cf. W.H. Sleeman, *Rambles and Recollections of an Indian Official*. Rev. edn Annotated by Vincent A. Smith (Karachi: Oxford University Press, 1973), p. 476n.

11. W.H. McLeod, 'The Kukas: a Millenarian Sect of the Punjab', *W.P. Morrell: A Tribute*, eds G.A. Wood and P.S. O'Connor (Dunedin: University of Otago Press, 1973), p. 86. See above, p. 190.

12. Ibbetson comments: 'The [numerically] high place which the Tarkhans or carpenters occupy among the Sikhs … . is very curious'. *Census of India 1881*, I, Book I, p. 108.

13. Ibid., p. 107.

14. Ibid., p. 139.

15. Ibid., II, table VIIIA, p. 26.

16. Ibid., p. 8. A small discrepancy between the totals for each religion and the grand total appears in both Kalal and Tarkhan figures because of returns made by Jains and Buddhists.

17. *Loc. cit.*, XVII, Part I, 304. To this table an important qualification was added: 'Apart from the facts set forth in the extracts quoted above, the number of Sikhs since 1911 has greatly risen on account of the changed instructions about the definition of Sikhism. Prior to that year only those were recorded as Sikhs, who according to the tenets of the tenth Guru, Gobind Singh, grew long hair and abstained from smoking, but since then any one is recorded as a Sikh who returns himself as such whether or not he practices those tenets.' (Ibid., p. 306.) It is, however, a qualification which almost exclusively concerns Khatris and Aroras. Neither the Ahluwalias nor the Ramgarhias have observed to any significant degree the practice of calling themselves Sikhs without observing the outward forms of the Khalsa. For them this would have

destroyed any social advantage implicit in the title of Sikh. Indeed, the title would not have been accepted as valid.

18. Ibid., p. 308.
19. Ibid., p. 309.
20. Ibid., p. 293.
21. Ibid., p. 294. On the specific case of the Tarkhans see also pp. 337, 346.
22. Ibbetson, *op. cit.*, p. 325.
23. Ibid.
24. This is sometimes abbreviated to Walia in modern usage.
25. *Loc. cit.*, p. 78.
26. P. van den Dungen, *op. cit.*, p. 71.
27. *Punjab District Gazetteers*, XIVA *Jullundur District and Kapurthala State 1904* (Lahore: Punjab State Government, 1908), Kapurthala section, p. 3.
28. Dev Raj Chanana, 'Sanskritization, Westernization, and India's North-West', *The Economic Weekly* (Bombay), 4 March 1961, p. 410.
29. W.H. McLeod, *Gurū Nānak and the Sikh Religion* (Oxford: Clarendon Press, 1968), p. 86.
30. Ibbetson, *op. cit.*, p. 313.
31. *Census of India 1891* (Calcutta: Government of India, 1894), XIX, 335 and Appendix C, p. xcviii.
32. Falcon, *op. cit.*, pp. 29, 77.
33. It is used in this sense early in the nineteenth century by Murray in a document posthumously published in 1834 as an appendix to H.T. Prinsep's *Origin of the Sikh Power in the Punjab*. 'Intermarriage between the Jat Sikh Chiefs and the Aluwaliah [*sic*] and Ramgarhia families do not obtain, the latter being *Kalals* and *Thokas* (mace-bearers and carpenters) and deemed inferior.' *Loc. cit.* (1970 edition), p. 164n.
34. *Census of India 1901*, XVII, Part I (Simla: Government of India, 1905), 137, 183.
35. Falcon, *op. cit.*, p. 77.
36. Teja Singh Bhabra, 'The African Sikhs', *The Sikh Sansar* (California), Vol. II, No. 3, 78. The economic expansion is well described and acutely analysed by Satish Saberwal, 'Status, Mobility, and Networks in a Punjabi Industrial Town', *Beyond the Village*, ed., idem.
37. Saberwal convincingly relates the Phagwara concentration to the development of industry in the town with its consequent demand for skilled or semi-skilled workers. Industry, he suggests, was attracted partly by road and rail connections; and party by the town's pre-1947 location within a princely state (Kapurthala). This latter feature meant freedom from British Indian tax scales. Ibid., pp. 128–30. Kartarpur (Jullundur District) presumably owes its popularity, in part at least, to the first and third of these factors; and Batala (a post-1947 development) to its early

Ramgarhia connections. Situated within Gurdaspur District it has a substantial Ramgarhia population.

38. Ibid., pp. 155–6.
39. 'Historical Notes on the Ramgarhias: Record of Interviews with Sardar Gurdial Singh Rehill', unpub. MS. prepared by Satish Saberwal. The popular Sikh artist Sobha Singh is also a Ramgarhia: ibid.
40. *Beyond the Village*, pp. 157, 161.
41. Baldev Raj Nayar, 'Religion and Caste in the Punjab: Sidhwan Bet constituency', *Indian Voting Behaviour: Studies of the 1962 General Elections*, ed. M. Weiner and R. Kothari (Calcutta, 1965), p. 138.
42. A brother of Dalip Singh Saund, Karnail Singh, has achieved considerable personal eminence as a builder of railways in Assam and subsequently as chairman of the Railways Board. Both positions, it will be noted, are entirely congenial to Ramgarhia traditions.
43. *Sangat:* lit. association, congregation. In Sikh congregations all must sit together regardless of caste. *Pangat:* lit. a row of people sitting to eat. In the Sikh *langar* (the communal kitchen attached to each gurdwara) no caste distinctions are permitted with regard to seating. All dine together.
44. Satish Saberwal, 'On Entrepreneurship: Everett Hagen and the Ramgarhias' (unpublished paper read at National Seminar on Social Change, Bangalore, Nov. 1972), p. 10.

PART VI

SIKH MIGRATION

14

THE FIRST FORTY YEARS OF SIKH MIGRATION: PROBLEMS AND SOME POSSIBLE SOLUTIONS

There are at least four reasons why Punjabi migration deserves special discussion. One of the four may reflect sentiment rather than real need, but the other three offer sound justification for a close and careful examination of the subject. Two of them are accompanied by a hint of urgency, strongly implying that we shall be guilty of culpable neglect if we allow the subject to drift any longer.

The sentimental reason is that the present decade presumably marks the centenary of foreign migration by Sikhs. Overseas travel as soldiers or policemen had begun before the 1880s, but if Sikh civilians were leaving the Punjab for foreign destinations prior to that decade they must have been very few in number. It will do no harm if we remind ourselves that we are dealing with a century-old phenomenon.

In itself this observation and the centenary which it notes may be totally inconsequential. It nevertheless leads directly to one of the three sound reasons for academic attention. If the history of Punjabi migration were well served by archival resources, the need to work on it might perhaps be regarded as persuasive rather than pressing. It is my clear impression that the subject is poorly served by archival or published records and, as I shall later be arguing, this

*Originally published in Barrier & Dusenbery, eds, *The Sikh Diaspora: Migration and Experiences beyond the Punjab*, Chanakya Publication, Delhi, 1989.

confers a certain urgency for research in this area. If documentary sources are in short supply we shall have to depend on oral enquiry to some extent. That should surely spell immediate action. Most of the participants in the early phase of Punjabi migration are already dead or otherwise removed from effective participation in the enquiry. If this volume should serve to remind us of this situation, it will be useful; and if it prompts effective action, its value will be very considerable indeed.

That covers one of the urgent reasons. The other is the obvious one, the one which everybody understands without any need of hint or reminder. Recent events have repeatedly brought the Sikhs into the world news, and much of the media attention has focused on the activities of Sikhs overseas. None of us needs to be told how misinformed much of the comment and analysis has been. To that awareness we need only add that the academic community should accept a large share of the blame for the current misunderstanding of the Sikhs. Those of us who pursue an interest in overseas Sikhs should surely recognize that a greatly enlarged responsibility has suddenly been thrust upon us.

The third reason is one which alone would justify our discussion, regardless of what may be taking place back in the Punjab. Several studies of Sikhs (or Punjabi) migration have now been published and it is high time that we attempt to draw these different approaches together. The earlier contributions of Karnail Singh Sandhu (1969) and Kenneth Gillion (1962, 1977) dealt with Sikhs in a larger Indian context. In recent years they have been followed by Arthur Helweg (1979) on the Sikh community in Gravesend, Marie de Lepervanche (1984) on the old-established Australian settlement, and Parminder Bhachu (1985) on Ramgarhias who moved from East Africa to Southall. For Canada as a whole we have a recent book by Norman Buchignani and Doreen Indra (1985); and for Vancouver we have one by James Chadney (1984), with more to come from Verne Dusenbery. We should also note the important work of Roger and Catherine Ballard (1977), Joyce Pettigrew (1977), and Bruce LaBrack (1982, 1983, 1987) together with the developing contributions of a small number of graduate students. There has even been a study of Sikh migrants to New Zealand (McLeod, 1986).

An obvious reason for comparing these various contributions is to discover points of convergence, and we should expect that some of these points will become evident in this set of collected essays. Another purpose should be to reveal issues which have so far been inadequately treated or which suggest that there may be areas of disagreement as well as convergence. The general topic has not been so thoroughly examined that all problems have been identified and solved. Uncertainties still persist and the principal purpose of this paper is to elicit some of those which relate to the history of Sikh migration.

The first issue must surely be the question of why Sikhs chose to emigrate late in the nineteenth century, and why they have continued to do so as opportunity has afforded. For this particular question the answer may seem obvious, at least in general terms. The question of personal motive was one which I put to all my informants during the course of my New Zealand survey and the usual answer was the single word *garībī*. Literally translated the word means 'poverty' and it was poverty (so I was regularly assured) which accounted for the decision to emigrate.

In reality the issue seems to have been rather more complex than the single-word answer might suggest. If for 'poverty' we substitute 'economic need' as a translation of *garībī* we shall obtain a better sense of the actual situation, yet even with its wider coverage the replacement fails to communicate an adequate impression of the impulse behind emigration. We shall require a more diffuse explanation if that impulse is to be adequately understood.

A second issue follows from the first. If we are able to construct a reasonably convincing explanation for emigration in general, we shall still be confronted by the fact that some particular questions are inadequately covered by that general explanation. An important example concerns the differential distribution of the migrants' homes and specifically the question of why such a heavy concentration is evidently to be found in three adjacent tahsils of eastern Doaba. It is possible that the basic impression is actually mistaken and that the concentration is much less marked than some of us have assumed. If, however, the impression proves to be generally accurate it will call for an appropriate explanation.

A third line of enquiry leads us away from the geography of the Punjab back to Punjabi society. Here we encounter a cluster of questions, some of which may have been noted when dealing with the problem of basic causes but none of them likely to have received adequate treatment in that context. A consideration of basic causes is bound to introduce information and theories relating to the traditional occupations of the migrants. This inevitably leads on to the question of caste origins, and we can expect most analyses to make pointed reference to Jat cultivators. We can thus anticipate some awareness of the caste/occupation nexus. Occasionally, as in Parminder Bhachu's recent work (1985), it may become a primary focus. In other analyses, however, the input may be largely based on assumptions, and although these assumptions may ultimately prove to be sound there can be no justification for accepting them as such without offering evidence which support them.

Caste does at least offer the prospect of clear-cut categories, plainly distinguishing one migrant from another. We enter a much hazier area when we endeavour to identify individual migrants in terms of religious tradition. In the case of Muslims the task of actual identification is comparatively simple, though there may still be serious difficulties ahead if we seek to describe the manner in which they practise their Islam in various and usually inhospitable circumstances. When we attempt to distinguish Sikh from Hindu, however, we can expect to encounter a problem which is sometimes difficult to solve and occasionally quite impossible. We need to be aware that when we talk about Sikh migration we are choosing to use an imprecise adjective. A certain book which was originally planned as _Sikhs in New Zealand_ eventually appeared as _Punjabis in New Zealand_ (McLeod, 1986). It was no mere whim or fancy which prompted the change of title.

A final cluster of question carries us beyond the Punjab and into the world which was to receive the emigrants. It is a dates and sequence cluster. We all know that the early destinations included Malaya, Australia, and the west coast of North America; and we also have a general impression of an early move to East Africa. It is when we endeavour to identify actual dates and precise sequences that the problems emerge. One does not need to probe very deeply to discover that there are considerable uncertainties associated with the early phase of Punjabi migration.

It is, for example, rare to encounter solid evidence of the kind incidentally supplied by Kessinger in the course of his Vilayatpur study, and even this falls short of the ideal. Kessinger reports that approximately twenty men left Vilayatpur for Australia in the 1890s (Kessinger 1974: 90). This is certainly useful evidence and it is supplemented by his subsequent comment that by 1903 approximately thirty-five Vilayatpur men had departed for Australia, there to work as labourers or hawkers (Kessinger 1974: 92). What it does not tell us is when Punjabi migration to Australia actually began, nor how many Punjabis (or Sikhs) visited Australia before the door was shut. It seems safe to assume that entry probably began during the 1880s, but we are unable to extrapolate total figures from the Vilayatpur sample. Thirty-five men constituted almost one-third of the village's adult male population. If Vilayatpur were in any sense typical the Australian authorities are unlikely to have kept their anxious watch so largely confined to arrivals from Canton.

The nature of this cluster of problems becomes even more evident when we consider what lies between Malaya and Australia. If Singapore was indeed the staging-post which led onwards to Australia, what of the nearer and equally accessible destinations supplied by the Dutch East Indies and the Philippines? There were certainly Punjabis in these colonies (Darling 1934: 104–6) but when did they arrive, and how many were there, and what did they do, and how long did they stay? We should also look beyond Southeast Asia and Australia. The ripples from Singapore certainly spread as far as New Zealand and Fiji, and the two Sikhs from Garhshankar tahsil who were in Tonga early this century (McLeod 1986:103) should serve to remind us that few territories were so remote as to be beyond their range.

There are actually several general questions involved in this particular cluster of issues. The following four questions certainly deserve our attention. First, have we identified all the destinations to which Sikh migrants travelled late in the nineteenth century or early in the twentieth? Secondly, have we accurately identified (or at least plausibly deduced) the first arrival of Sikhs in any particular territory? Thirdly, what routes were established? Fourthly, what numbers were involved? Having thus, as it were, followed our travellers to their various destinations we immediately encounter yet another range of questions. Did they encounter entry problems, and if so how did they deal with them? What employment did they typically seek? What reception did they receive, and how did they cope with hostility whenever they encountered it?

The list will continue to grow if we choose to let it. That is not my intention, for there is little to be gained from mere question-posing. Having threatened to let the list-making get out of hand I shall now abandon it and turn to the task of attempting a few preliminary answers, dealing in the process with five of the issues already mentioned. In each instance I shall rely extensively on material gathered during the course of my New Zealand research and on conclusions indicated by that material. Whether or not the analysis can be generalized to any extent remains to be seen.

I begin with the first and most basic of all the questions noted above. Why did emigration from the Punjab begin during the second half of the nineteenth century? The first answer must be that Punjabi emigration (including the Sikh variety) did not begin at that time. It had begun centuries earlier, and the earlier pattern continues to the present day. The earlier pattern involved individuals and small groups from the trading castes of the Punjab (particularly the Khatris). Travelling to other parts of India they developed and maintained an extensive trading network, one which also served to establish a Nanak-panthi or Sikh presence in the various centres to which they travelled. A portion of the overseas migration which has followed World War II can legitimately be regarded as a continuation of this old tradition.

What we must obviously do at the outset is identify, at least tentatively, the distinctly different pattern which develops during the decades immediately following the British annexation of the Punjab in 1849. We are evidently dealing with a movement which largely derived from rural Punjab, which was initially based on police or military service, which offered hard work by generally unskilled labourers, and which assumed that the migrant would return to the Punjab after attaining the purpose for which he had left home. It was also a movement which consisted overwhelmingly of active males (most of them young adults when first they emigrated). Very few women were involved.

It will be apparent that we have already built a substantial battery of assumptions into our enquiry, and if we remain alert to our own ignorance we shall watch for indications that some of these assumptions may require modification. With that cautionary reminder we press on, seeking now to identify the dominant purpose of those who left the Punjab during the early phase of overseas emigration.

For our first answer to the question of motive we turn to Sir Malcolm Darling. During the course of his travels through the Punjab more than fifty years ago Darling reflected upon the reasons for Punjabi emigration, and he came up with the following explanation. The fundamental cause was (he claimed) the Jat custom of subdividing each patrimony, a practice which inevitably left some sons with uneconomic holding. Fortunately the Punjab environment delivers an answer to the problem thus created. A vigorous climate and a healthy diet nurture the kind of enterprise which will actively search for a solution to such a problem. The sturdy peasant will seek a supplement or an alternative in the army, in the canal colonies, or overseas. Eventually he will return to his village with funds sufficient to purchase what his inheritance had failed to bestow on him (Darling 1925, 1930).

Although Darling's simple answer is inadequate his stress on land division correctly identifies one essential element in the total explanation. There appears to be no doubt that the desire to purchase land prompted much of the emigration which took place during this early period. In the context of rural Punjab, however, that indicates something other than simple poverty. The truly poor would seldom, if ever, seek such an adventurous solution to their dire condition. It required a particular range of aspirations, together with access to the limited capital which was needed to finance overseas travel. Emigration, it seems, was typically a strategy adopted by those who might traditionally expect to be small land-owners but who needed financial supplements in order to attain this objective. Neither the truly affluent nor the truly poor are likely to figure prominently amongst overseas emigrants.

This renders the explanation somewhat more complex and a number of scholars have shown why it should be diversified still further. Kessinger, having acknowledged the acquisition of land to be a prime target, indicates that a brick house was also perceived as a normal feature of the emigrant's purpose (Kessinger 1974:155–6). Even today brick houses are not necessarily superior to the traditional mud-built variety, though they do withstand monsoon floods rather more effectively. In terms of comfort a mud-built house was usually superior to the *pakkā* brick construction, both cooler in summer and warmer in winter. This, however, misses the essential purpose of the latter. A brick house spelt prestige, and the quest for prestige (*izzat*) must also be incorporated within any sufficient explanation of overseas emigration from rural Punjab (Pettigrew 1977:66–9; Helweg 1979:11–33; McLeod 1986:22–3).

Brick houses are merely one means of acquiring or sustaining prestige. Conspicuous hospitality and expensive wedding settlements for daughters were also regarded as standard tests. For all three examples access to finance was the essential pre-requisite and overseas employment proved to be one means of gathering the necessary funds. The twin purposes (land and prestige) were, of course, closely linked. Land was itself a primary source of *izzat* (for Jats the most important of all) and those who owned land could use it as collateral if additional expenditure should be required. If we were to set the two purposes in order of priority it could well be argued that the fundamental value was *izzat*. Land might be more valuable to Jat cultivators than any other commodity, but in an ultimate sense it too was a means to an end rather than an end in itself.

It should also be noted that in such circumstances the decision to emigrate would typically be a family decision, often taken in anticipation of a patrimonial division rather than after the actual event. *Izzat* attached to the family as a whole rather than to its individual members.

It thus becomes evident that the simple answer is not an adequate answer. To the perceived need for land one must attach status objectives, and the latter should be perceived as primary in any analysis of basic motives. This, moreover, is the comparatively simple pattern of the early days, for with the passing of time the causes became even more complex. As early migrants returned and stories began to circulate in Punjabi villages some young men were evidently attracted to the possibility of emigration largely for the interest and the adventure which it promised. This, at least, was the message communicated by some of the Punjabis who entered New Zealand immediately after World War I, and there is evidence in the New Zealand material to suggest that it was a factor even earlier.

This attitude was one which influenced young men of moderate means and moderate education, men who could obviously have led a reasonably comfortable life in their home villages yet chose the rigours of emigration as a preferred alternative. Such decisions were, of course, encouraged by the expectation that the period spent overseas would be of limited duration. Ironically these were precisely the people who tended to remain in New Zealand. Better equipped than others to cope with New Zealand conditions they were able to purchase their own farm and put down permanent roots.

Though the result may be more complex than Sir Malcolm Darling anticipated the process of identifying general causes seems to be reasonably manageable. When we move to the second of our questions the task becomes rather more difficult. How are we to explain the unusually large numbers of emigrants from three tahsils in eastern Doaba?

As with first of our questions we should begin by ensuring that the actual area has been correctly identified. It is not correct to identify it as Jullundur District, nor is the expression 'eastern Doaba' strictly accurate. In terms of geographical regions the area which concerns us comprises the territories known locally as Manjki and Dhak (McLeod 1986:14–15). In administrative terms it embraces three of the four tahsils situated within the loop of the Satluj river. If all four tahsils were involved the area would indeed coincide with eastern Doaba. The furthest east of the four (Balachaur tahsil in Hoshiarpur District) has, however, been much less affected by emigration than its neighbours. One of the three remaining tahsils (Garhshankar tahsil) is likewise in Hoshiarpur District, and the other two occupy the eastern sector of Jullundur District (Nawanshahr and Phillaur tahsils).

Having thus identified this limited portion of the Punjab we should acknowledge that the identification may not be as firm as we seem to believe. It is certainly an accurate identification as far as migration to New Zealand is concerned, but that may not always prove to be the case when the migrants to all other major destinations have been satisfactorily analysed in terms of origins. Even in the case of the New Zealand figures the earliest arrivals evidently came from Malwa rather than from Doaba, and the fact that only one of the early immigrants entering New Zealand came from Ludhiana District suggests that its figures may not be altogether representative in this respect.

Malwai emigration may be more substantial than we have been encouraged to believe, and if this eventually proves to be the case our analysis will change accordingly. In the meantime there appears to be general agreement that the villages of three tahsils in eastern Doaba have been unusually well represented in the flow of emigrants, and it is legitimate to ask why this should have been the case.

Sir Malcolm Darling asked himself this question and having done so he suggested two answers, both of them seeming to reinforce his general explanation. In the case of eastern Doaba, he maintained, there was greater pressure on the available land than one encountered elsewhere in the Punjab. The general shortage of land in the area, he continued, was further aggravated by a falling water-table (Darling 1930:28, 42–3, 160–1, 173–4).

The first of these claim receives only limited support from the available figures (McLeod 1986:28–9). It is indeed true that Nawanshahr tahsil had an unusually high rate of population pressure, but it is also true that the same did not apply in the case of Phillaur tahsil. The analysis is, in reality, a difficult one to pursue because appropriate figures are not available for all the tahsils which would need to be scrutinized if the task were to be adequately performed. From the figures which are available, however, it is certainly not safe to assume that population pressure was significantly higher in the three tahsils than in all other comparable areas of the Punjab.[1]

The water-table claim was also offered by one of my elderly informants from Phillaur tahsil, but it too is open to some question. It receives no support from the settlement officers of both Jullundur and Hoshiarpur districts (McLeod 1986:29–30), and if a lively anxiety was felt by the cultivators of the area their fears seem to have attracted little official concern. As with the population pressure claim we should probably allow it as a contributing factor, but neither separately nor together do they seem adequate as explanations for the eastern Doaba phenomenon.

At least three other possible reasons might be added to these two. First there is the question of accessibility, relevant both for the flow of information concerning overseas opportunities and also for the possibility of utilizing those opportunities. This feature applied as much to Ludhiana District and presumably to other areas along the Grand Trunk Road, but it may nevertheless have conferred an advantage on eastern Doaba as opposed to some of the remoter tracts in the Punjab (including Balachaur tahsil). It is, however, an uncertain argument and it is weakened by the comparative remoteness of Garhshankar tahsil.

A second possibility derives from the preference of British recruitment officers for men from the Malwa region. It is impossible to measure the results of this policy with any precision, but if Malwais found it easier to enlist in the army they would presumably be less likely to seek employment further afield. This feature may perhaps account for the prominence of Malwais in Malaya, a territory which received many of its early immigrants as ex-soldiers or ex-policemen. Doabis, ill-favoured by the recruiters but equally aware of overseas possibilities may have chosen the latter because the former was unavailable.

A third possibility may be traced to the *baṛā piṇḍ* or 'big village' network of eastern Doaba (McLeod 1986:25–26; Hershman 1981: 232). The villages which traditionally belonged to this informal grouping were thereby subjected to much stronger *izzat* requirements, particularly with regard to marital arrangements. This evidently prompted a higher incidence of female infanticide in the Jat families belonging to such villages, a practice which would explain the distinct disparity in the sex ratio which appeared during the early decades of census-taking. A shortage of girls drove the price up, increasing the strength of a bride's family and reducing the asset transfer required for a high-prestige marriage. Disadvantaged families within the *barā piṇḍ* network were confronted with two options. They could either settle for wives from the lower status *choote piṇḍ* (small villages); or they could postpone marriage and send their sons in search of the supplementary resources needed in order to establish an enhanced standing.

If we draw these several reasons together we may perhaps have a plausible explanation for the strong representation of eastern Doaba in the early emigration movement. Personally I find it less than wholly convincing, and I look forward to hearing or reading a more persuasive analysis.

Moving to the two identity issues we encounter difficulties of a very different kind. The first concerns the caste identity of the early migrants, an aspect of the enquiry which has proved very simple to document. In many instances an individual's sub-caste appears as a surname, and when this convention is not followed the individual or his descendants will usually supply the information without hesitation.[2] Many other cases can be determined by tracing marriage networks. If, for example, an individual is named Sarwan Singh Bains, we can safely assume that Sarwan Singh is a Jat. We may further deduce that Jagdev Singh of unknown caste is likewise a Jat because his mother's sister was Baldev Singh's brother's mother-in-law. This may sound fearsomely complex, but in reality it is exceedingly simple and it is based on the single well-established fact that the early Punjabi migrants came from families which almost invariably observed the standard *zat* and *got* prescriptions for marriage.[3]

During my own research I found that most informants were unhesitating in their answers to questions concerning caste identity, particularly those from Jat families and also (and interestingly) Chamars. If there has been a problem it has usually involved one of the lower-status upwardly aspiring groups. In the New Zealand situation this principally concerned Sainis and Mahtons, and only in the latter instance was a conscious attempt made to conceal a caste identity. In New Zealand, as in the Punjab, the Mahtons have claimed to be Rajputs (McLeod 1986: 138n). In my own experience I have found the present generation perfectly willing to acknowledge the true nature of the stratagem, but that would have been most unlikely during the early decades of the present century. If Doabi and Malwai migrants claim Rajput status one should enquire carefully before accepting the claim as accurate.

Caste identities and the constructing of general caste profiles should thus present comparatively few challenges to those who research Punjabi migration.[4] When we enquire into the relationship which subsisted between the various caste groups the task becomes rather more complex, yet even in this regard both the gathering of the material and its interpretation seem to match expectations. This certainly has been the case in New Zealand. Distance from home and the threat of the unfamiliar encouraged mixing and fraternity, yet never to the point of blurring the traditional lines. Chamars generally worked in Chamar gangs and although some strong cross-caste friendships were reported the awareness of difference remained. It still remains today.

The real problem of identity only emerges when we seek to distinguish Sikh from Hindu amongst those who migrated over-seas. I have already referred to the change which produced *Punjabis in New Zealand* as the title of a recent book, and it will have become evident from the present paper that I still prefer the less specific term. My original schedule on Punjabis in New Zealand contained a question designed to elicit religious identity, but it soon became evident that this apparently simple question was causing serious problems. 'Was he a Sikh or a Hindu?' I would naively ask of someone who was remembered as Munshi or Nama or some such inexplicit name. 'Both', was the answer, or perhaps it might be an uncertain shrug of the shoulders. 'Call him a Hindu-Sikh', I was sometimes advised. That is what I eventually did in some cases, recognizing that if a category was essential this was sometimes the only appropriate one to use (McLeod 1986:129–31). Munshi, it turned out, was sometimes known as Munshi Ram and sometimes as Munsha Singh. I was encountering precisely what I should have anticipated, namely that the Punjabi village of the early twentieth century was no place to go looking for clear-cut normative identities.[5]

The problem was one which largely concerned the Jats. Individuals from lower-status castes were more likely to assert an unambiguous Sikh identity. Amongst the Chamars I encountered some uncertainly, but the dominant preference in their case remains the Ad Dharm identity.[6] Few of the Chamars were identified as Sikhs, and of the few one had evidently shown Kuka sympathies.

The fact that the identity problem is largely confined to a single caste group does not mean, however, that it should be treated as insignificant. If it applies to the Jats it will apply to a majority of those who emigrated. This raises the serious question of whether or not we actually encourage misunderstanding by insisting on such terms as Sikh migration. The usage becomes increasingly defensible as we move towards the present, yet even today it may still raise legitimate questions except when applied to a particular group with an explicitly Sikh identity.

In the pre-1920 period of migration its accuracy is dubious, and if used in its customary sense it must surely encourage misunderstanding.

The problem concerning religious identity suggests another reason for caution when seeking to analyse the pattern and practice of emigration from the Punjab. It is obvious that if we rely on data and comment supplied by the host society, we shall receive a very partial impression of the migrants' true identity. This particular problem is not necessarily eliminated by adding Punjabi sources to European. Punjabi sources can also be misleading if we fail to recognize their distinctive perspective.

There are in fact two problems to be noted at this point. The first is that if we are not cautious we shall be unduly influenced by the recorded actions and interpretations of an unrepresentative minority. We should always remember that very few of the migrants possessed the formal skills or the opportunity to participate in community leadership or to record their experiences. A substantial majority were village men for whom such activities would have been truly alien. The result is that a small minority, functionally literate and socially active, supplies much of the information which we use, and there is a strong possibility that the same informants will mould the impressions which we derive from the records which they have left. Oral interviews can reduce this risk without necessarily eliminating it. Those with clearly-formed theories are likely to be as articulate in speech as in writing, and their influence is liable to dominate both forms of enquiry.

The second problem, closely related to the first, is one which has affected all Sikh studies during the present century. A dominant interpretation of Sikh society and religion emerged from the Singh Sabha period, an interpretation which still informs most analyses of Sikh identity. Most western scholars have been preconditioned by this interpretation and so too were many of the Sikhs who assumed leadership roles or commented on the migration experience. This dominance of the Singh Sabha interpretation can easily prompt misunderstanding. The majority of early migrants were little affected by its ideals, and we shall misconstrue their identity and their responses if we persist in viewing them through the Singh Sabha prism.[7]

The final issue concerns the actual timing and sequence of Sikh emigration during the half-century preceding 1920. A general pattern seems to have emerged, one which could probably be regarded as a consensus as far as its broad outline is concerned. It runs as follows.

Overseas migration dates from the post-Mutiny period when the British, having decided to encourage Sikh enlistment, posted some of their Sikh troops in Singapore and Hong Kong. Having served their time as soldiers or policemen most returned home but a minority, noting the possibility of civilian employment elected to remain in Malaya or an adjacent territory. During this early period Punjabi servicemen heard of two large islands over the horizon. These were *Ṭeliā* (Australia) and *Miṭkaṇ* (America). It was *Ṭeliā* which first attracted the adventurous and the earliest of them evidently arrived in the 1880s. From there a few found their way across the Tasman Sea to New Zealand and eventually (during the first decade of the present century) some of them also discovered Fiji. This final phase of the South Pacific discovery coincided with the beginnings of Punjabi migration to *Miṭkaṇ*. In 1903 or 1904 the first group arrived in Vancouver, initiating the most important of all the early ventures. As each territory was discovered, word was passed back to the Punjab and the standard migration chain soon delivered additional workers to the new-found location.

It is easy to make this unfolding pattern of discovery sound consistent and altogether believable. Before we write it in stone, however, we should remind ourselves that it is much stronger on plausible assumption than on established fact, and that it passes over some obvious possibilities without acknowledging their existence. The actual beginnings of emigration are exceedingly dim, the transformation of soldier into migrant labourer is poorly documented, the Punjabi presence in China and Southeast Asia (apart from Malaya) is obscure, the date of arrival in Australia is uncertain, and the means whereby *Miṭkaṇ* was actually discovered has yet to be definitively explained.

The danger of relying on a sensible, plausible assumption can be illustrated by reference to the New Zealand material. Until recently it was generally assumed that apart from some servant retinues and a Goan gold-miner called 'Black Peter', Indians did not start arriving in New Zealand until the period of World War I. Some elementary research would have brought this date nearer to the beginning of the century, but certainly not 1890 which is where (give or take a year) the date of the first Punjabi arrival now stands. This fact emerged only because the daughter of one of the two original arrivals is still alive. By showing me the wedding certificate and bills of sale still in her possession she was able to establish that her father (Phuman Singh Gill of Moga tahsil) was already established in a small business by 1895 (McLeod 1986:51, 165–7).

Ideally, of course, one should not have to depend on aged survivors as essential sources. What are government archivists meant to be doing if not collecting documentation for historians? Archives are selective at the best of times, and when all the immigration records go up in flames (as happened in New Zealand in 1952) their usefulness can be very limited indeed. The few relevant records which do survive raise other problems, one being the inability of shipping agents to elicit appropriate information or spell names correctly. Newspapers can sometimes help, but here too we should expect disappointment. Interest is raised only when there are troubles, and when this happens the need is seldom met by informed or impartial reporting.

What this suggests is that here is an urgent need for oral enquiry. The actual results can await processing if necessary, but if the information is to be gathered the final opportunity is now upon us. There remain very few whose memories can accurately recall the early period of Punjabi migration and a decade from now there will be none at all. Archival and newspaper sources may be better in some countries than they are in fire-swept New Zealand, but that is not necessarily a safe assumption and it is certainly not a sufficient one.

Problems abound, but then whoever heard of a field of academic enquiry which lacked them? There are, moreover, reasons for hope and there are messages of encouragement which those of us who work on Sikh or Punjabi topics have never previously received. Perhaps the clearest of all these messages is the one coming from the Sikh communities now established in various countries outside India. What are they to make of their past history, their present circumstances, and their future prospects? Helping them find answers must surely be one of our major priorities.

Notes

1. Roger Ballard has pointed out that the crucial factor was not population pressure as measured against the total area of the three tahsils, but

rather the pressure which resulted from a serious reduction in the common lands attached to villages.

2. It should, however, be noted that when A *List of Punjabi Immigrants in New Zealand, 1890–1939* (McLeod: 1984) was being prepared for publication I was specifically asked to omit caste identities. Entering the *got* (sub-caste) name for each individual proved to be acceptable on condition that it was called a 'family name'.

3. *Zāt* (Hindi jāti) designates the endogamous unit of caste society and *got* (Hindi *gotra*) the exogamous unit within the *zāt*. For a more detailed description of both conventions as observed within Sikh society, see W.H. McLeod, *The Evolution of the Sikh Community* (Oxford: Clarendon Press, 1976), pp. 89–90.

4. An exception to this rule is supplied by the Bhatras who settled in the United Kingdom between the two World Wars. Although their numbers may have been comparatively small their importance in the history of Punjabi migration to the United Kingdom is very substantial. If effective research is not undertaken in the near future, contact with the early arrivals will be lost forever.

5. This fundamental fact is enunciated with striking clarity and a wealth of relevant detail in Paul Hershman, *Punjabi Kinship and Marriage* (Delhi, 1981).

6. For a detailed study of the Ad Dharm movement see Mark Juergensmeyer, *Religion as Social Vision* (Berkeley, 1982).

7. The nature and influence of the Singh Sabha interpretation of Sikh doctrine and identity is discussed in W.H. McLeod, *Who is a Sikh? The Problem of Sikh Identity* (Oxford: Clarendon Press, 1989). Reprinted in W.H. McLeod, *Sikhs and Sikhism* (Delhi: Oxford University Press, 1999) For an excellent survey of the Singh Sabha movement see N. Gerald Barrier, 'The Roots of Modern Sikhism', in N. Gerald Barrier and Verne A. Dusenbery, *Aspects of Modern Sikhism*, Michigan Papers on Sikh Studies No. 1 (Center for South and Southeast Asian Studies, University of Michigan, Ann Arbor, 1986).

References

Ballard, Roger and Catherine. 'The Sikhs.' J.C. Watson, ed. *Between Two Cultures: Migrants and Minorities in Britain*. Oxford: Blackwell, 1977.

Bhachu, Parminder. *Twice Migrants*. London: Tavistock, 1985.

Buchignani, Norman, and Doreen M. Indra. *Continuous Journey*. Toronto: McClelland and Stewart, 1985.

Chadney, James G. *The Sikhs of Vancouver*. New York: AMS, 1984.

Darling, Malcolm L. *The Punjab Peasant in Prosperity and Debt*. London: Oxford University Press, 1925.

_____*Wisdom and Waste in the Punjab Village*. London: Oxford University Press, 1934.

Gillion, K.L. *Fiji's Indian Migrants: A History to the End of Indenture in 1920.* Melbourne: Oxford University Press, 1962.

_____*The Fiji Indians: Challenge to European Dominance, 1920–1946.* Canberra: Australian National University, 1977.

Helweg, Arthur. *Sikhs in England.* Bombay: Oxford University Press, 1979; rev. edn 1986.

Hershman, P. *Punjabi Kinship and Marriage.* Delhi: Hindustan, 1981.

Juergensmeyer, Mark. *Religion as Social Vision: The Movement Against Untouchability in 20th Century Punjab.* Berkley: University of California Press, 1982.

Kessinger, Thomas. *Vilayatpur, 1848–1968.* Berkley: University of California Press, 1974.

LaBrack, Bruce. 'Occupational Specialisation among Rural California Sikhs.' *Amerasia Journal, 9* (1982), 29–56.

_____Bruce. 'The Reconstitution of Sikh Society in Rural California.' In George Kurian and Ram P. Srivastava, eds *Overseas Indians: A Study in Adaptation.* New Delhi: Vikas, 1983. pp. 215–40.

_____Bruce. *The Sikhs of Northern California, 1904–1986.* New York: AMS Press, 1989.

Lepervanche, Marie M. de. *Indians in a White Australia.* Sydney: George Allen and Unwin, 1984.

McLeod, W.H. *The Evolution of the Sikh Community.* Delhi: Oxford University Press, 1975.

_____*A List of Punjabi Immigrants in New Zealand 1890–1939.* Country Section of the Central Indian Association, Hamilton, New Zealand, 1984.

_____*Punjabis in New Zealand.* Amritsar: Guru Nanak Dev University, 1986.

Pettigrew, Joyce. 'Socio-Economic Background to the Emigration of Sikhs from Doaba.' *Punjab Journal of Politics,* 1 (1971), 18–81.

Sandhu, K.S. *Indians in Malaya: Immigration and Settlement 1786–1957.* Cambridge: Cambridge University Press, 1969.

PART VII | BIOGRAPHY

15

MAX ARTHUR MACAULIFFE
(September 29, 1837–March 15, 1913)

'I bring from the East what is practically an unknown religion.' With these words Macauliffe began his famous and enduring work *The Sikh Religion*, published in six volumes by the Clarendon Press in 1909. 'The Sikhs,' he continues, 'are distinguished throughout the world as a great military people, but there is little known even to professional scholars regarding their religion.' Macauliffe's mission was to remedy that lack of knowledge and understanding. *The Sikh Religion* was a work which had involved for him more than fifteen years of labour, most to it carried out at his residence in Amritsar. It had also produced a series of disappointments, as his persistent efforts to gain patronage from the Punjab government met with either a parsimonious response or by the total rejection. Macauliffe died four years later, an impoverished and bitter man, recognition denied and his objectives unrealized.

Yet had his objectives been frustrated? He may have died without recognition, but, *The Sikh Religion* is still widely read almost one hundred years later. The group of Sikhs with whom he was closely associated, and whose ideals he reflected in his writing, propounded an interpretation of the Sikh religion and community which has ever since steadily gained ground. Today it commands the allegiance

*Originally published in *British Associations for the Study of Religions Bulletin*, No. 78, 1996.

of most Sikh scholars and the implicit acceptance of most members of the Panth (the Sikh community). It is also the view of the Sikh religion and Panth which most foreign observers assume to be the correct one. The Sikh religion is a completely independent religion in its own right; and Sikhs of the Khalsa are the only orthodox and sufficient representatives of that faith. Macauliffe's work has played a considerable part in this process. He may have died unfulfilled, but fulfillment in abundance has certainly followed his death.

This being the case the paucity of scholarly studies of Macauliffe's contribution comes as a surprise. Harbans Singh has contributed a study of his life, very admiring and very brief.[1] The respectful nature of the treatment is entirely understandable, for Harbans Singh comes from the school of scholars who were raised on Tat Khalsa principles and who had learnt to cherish the contribution of Macauliffe. The Tat Khalsa (the 'pure' Khalsa) was the radical section within the Singh movement, the reformist group which during the latter decades of the nineteenth century and the first two of the twentieth succeeded in imparting a new spirit and a new interpretation to the Panth. It was with members of the Tat Khalsa that Macauliffe had been particularly associated and it was entirely natural that his memory should be greatly venerated by its later descendants.

This veneration makes it difficult for those who have been raised on Tat Khalsa principles to critically evaluate his work, though it can produce a lively account of his life story. Harbans Singh produces just such an account. It means, however, that we are left with only one brief work which digs deeply into the sources relating to Macauliffe's career and which produces an accurate assessment of his contribution. This is a chapter by N.G. Barrier in a collected work, the chapter entitled 'Trumpp and Macauliffe: Western students of Sikh history and religion.[2] Professor Barrier is currently working on a book dealing with Singh Sabha period in Sikh history and we can expect that his highly perceptive insights concerning Macauliffe will be contained within it.

Macauliffe was born in Ireland in 1837 and received his schooling in Limerick, followed by Queen's College, Galway. In 1862 he joined the Indian Civil Service and was posted to the Punjab. None of the sources which I have seen mentions a wife. In 1882 he became a Deputy Commissioner and two years later was appointed a Divisional Judge. There is no evidence that he was interested in the work of the orientalists located in Lahore, though he may well have nutured a curiosity in the beliefs of the people for whom he was responsible. His one published work from this early portion of his career was a description of a visit to the major shrine of the semi-legendary saint Sakhi Sarvar in the Suliman Mountains. This produced an article in an 1875 issue of the *Calcutta Review*,[3] a descriptive work which indicated the author's interest in his subject but seemed well removed from his later fascination with the Sikhs.

In 1880-1, however, there appeared a series of articles in the same journal which indicated that the fascination had now gripped him. The first of these articles was 'The Diwali at Amritsar', followed soon after by 'The Rise of Amritsar and the Alterations of the Sikh Religion' and 'The Sikh Religion under Banda and its Present Condition'. These marked an important stage in Macauliffe's development, though all the views which they expressed were not yet those which characterized his later life.

In some senses though they were indeed the same. Macauliffe had become aware of the importance of the Sikh people and these articles manifested a desire to understand them which was never to leave him. They were a people who were not understood by their British rulers and Macauliffe was concerned to impart an understanding to them and to other westerners who shared an interest in these remarkable people.

Macauliffe also showed both the strengths and what may by regarded as the weaknesses of his approach. Possessing a fluent pen he was able to present his material in a very attractive manner. He was not particularly strong in terms of linguistic ability, though later he was able to overcome this to a considerable extent by circulating his translations amongst a group of traditional Sikhs whom he had gathered to help him in Amritsar. At this stage there was no pretence at original scholarship. Macauliffe utilized the contributions of other writers on the Punjab (men such as M'Gregor and Cunningham) and set down for the enlightenment of his readers what he believed to be the truth concerning these inadequately understood people.

In these respects he was generally in accord with the approach which was to underlie his later work. In other respects, however, his views differed from what they were to become. In his early opinions Macauliffe shared the current view that Nanak was strongly influenced by his Hindu background and that the Gurus were not endeavouring to separate the Sikhs from their Hindu roots. This was a view that he was later to renounce, but in the early 1880s he still held it. He still regarded Sikhism as evolutionary, with the decision of Guru Gobind Singh to establish the Khalsa being a response to the physical dangers confronting his people. It represented a belief which the Brahmans regarded as heretical. Just as they had succeeded in swallowing up Buddhism, so too the Brahmanical boa constrictor was winding its coils around Sikhism and would eventually squeeze it to death. The boa constrictor proved to be a favourite symbol for Macauliffe, though the nature of the intended victim was to undergo significant change.

This was the condition in the early 1880s. Macauliffe's opinions however, were rapidly changing, and the principal cause was his association with a group of Sikhs who firmly believed that the conventional interpretation of the Sikh religion was altogether mistaken. These Sikhs, as we have seen, belonged to the Tat Khalsa. In 1873 some Sikhs had become alarmed at what they regarded as the threatened status of the Panth and had met in Amritsar to form the Singh Sabha. The dominant group within Amritsar comprised those who wanted reform but reform along the inclusive lines which characterized the Sikhism of earlier days. The Sikhism which they favoured was one which drew inspiration from the Vedas and Hindu epics, and no clear difference between Sikhs and Hindus was recognized. Even the worship of idols was acknowledged if people who called themselves Sikhs wished to practise it.

These were the group which came to be called the Sanatan Sikhs, conservative in their views and harking back to the Sikhism they had known. They were soon to be confronted by the Tat Khalsa, radical Sikhs centred in Lahore and influenced by western education. Sikhism was for them not an inclusive faith. It was definitely exclusive. Guru Nanak had founded the faith as an entirely separate and independent one, in no way dependent on Hindu tradition. One of the most prominent members of the Tat Khalsa, Kahn Singh Nabha, compiled a book of proof texts and in 1898 issued it under the title *Ham Hindū Nahīn*, 'We are not Hindus'.[5] Kahn Singh was not only a prominent member of the Tat Khalsa. He was a also close friend of Macauliffe's and an intimate adviser as Macauliffe's opinions of the Sikh religion took final shape.

In 1893 Macauliffe resigned his position with the ICS, resolving to devote his labours to a reliable translation of the Adi Granth (the Guru Granth Sahib, the sacred scripture of the Sikhs). A translation had earlier been commissioned by the Punjab government and the task had been entrusted to the German missionary and linguist Ernest Trumpp. In 1877 Trumpp's partial translation appeared as *Adi Granth or the Holy Scriptures of the Sikhs*, together with five lengthy prefatory essays. Partly because of the wooden nature of his translation, but more particularly because of his outspoken and insulting comments, Trumpp's work never won acceptance among the Sikhs. To the Tat Khalsa it was anathema in that it laid firm stress on what Trumpp regarded as the clear evidences of Hindu influence. A reliabie translation would have to be provided in its place and this Macauliffe set himself to do.

He gathered around him a selection of traditional scholars of the Adi Granth and set to work, circulating portions of his translations to his informants and revising his drafts in accordance with their suggestions. As the work proceeded Macauliffe widened the scope to include narratives to the lives of the ten Gurus, together with those of the Bhagats.[6] For these he also relied upon the interpretation of those with whom he was closely associated, with the result that his final work mirrors exactly the views of the Tat Khalsa reformers. Sikhism was no longer to be seen as an outgrowth of Hindu tradition. There were certainly features within it which Hindu India also acknowledged (notably a belief in transmigration), but the Sikh faith should be viewed as an entirely new religion, distinguished be superior beliefs and a high ethical content.

Macauliffe issued the results of his work to date in a brief essay which he published at the turn of the century. In *The Holy Writings of the Sikhs* he produced the form which he would later be following in *The Sikh Religion*, presenting Guru Nanak as the founder of a new religion.[7] This was followed by more essays. In the first of these he commended the Sikhs to the British as potential allies;[8] and in the second presented the Tat Khalsa concept of a heroic determination to fight as the safeguard of the faith against Mughal intolerance.[9] Meanwhile he also published selections of the translations which he was making from the Adi Granth and also the life of the ninth Guru.[10]

Finally the great work which Macauliffe had been preparing was ready for the press. In 1908 the manuscript of *The Sikh Religion: Its Gurus, Sacred Writings and Authors* was delivered to the Clarendon Press and Kahn Singh Nabha, his close associate, accompanied him to England to help check the proofs. The work was finally published in 1909 as six volumes bound in three.[11] In Professor Barrier's words, 'Macauliffe gave Sikhs and the world a readable, popularized, but very uncritical account the early evolution of Sikhism'.[12] It may have been very uncritical (it undoubtedly was), but its influence has been profound. No other work has so effectively instructed western readers about Sikhism, with the result that the Tat Khalsa interpretation of the Sikh faith and community has been firmly fixed in the western understanding. The Sikh religion is a unique religion and the Khalsa represents its true form. Any attempt to demonstrate that the situation is rather more complicated than this must expect to encounter rugged opposition.

For Macauliffe the publication of *The Sikh Religion* marked the latest in a catalogue of little help or outright rejection. The Punjab Government and the Government of India refused to sanction the work and the latter's offer of a contribution of Rs. 5,000 was indignantly rejected as paltry in the extreme. Sikhs were loud in their praises, but fearing the loss of government patronage the wealthy amongst them held back from financial donations. The result was that Macauliffe had to spend a considerable sum from his own pocket in order to see the work through publication.

Macauliffe died at his London home at Sinclair Gardens in West Kensington on 15 March 1913, a disappointed man. His hopes and purpose had been clearly expressed in the words with which he closed the essay on 'How the Sikhs became a militant people':

Such are the deeds that have been done, the prophecies that have been uttered, and the instruction that has been imparted by that great succession of men, the Sikh Gurus. In them the East shook off the torpor of ages, and unburdened itself of the heavy weight of ultra-conservatism which has paralysed the genius and intelligence of its people. Only those who know India by actual experience can adequately appreciate the difficulties the Gurus encountered in their efforts to reform and awaken the sleeping nation. Those who, removed from the people and dwelling in the lofty and serene atmosphere of their own wisdom and infallibility, deem Sikhism a heathen religion, and the spiritual happiness and loyalty of its professors negligible items, are men whose triumph shall be short-lived, and whose glory shall not descend with the accompaniment of minstrel raptures to future generations. I am not without hope that when enlightened nations become acquainted with the merits of the Sikh religion they will not willingly let it perish in the great abyss in which so many creeds have been engulfed.[13]

Notes

1. Harbans Singh, 'English Translation of the Sikh Scriptures—An Arduous Mission of a Punjab Civilian' in K.S. Bedi and S.S. Bal eds, *Essays on History, Literature, Art and Culture*, (Delhi: Atma Ram & Sons, 1970), pp. 139–44.

2. *Historians and Historiography of the Sikhs*, ed. Fauja Singh (New Delhi: Oriental, 1978), pp. 166–85.

3. 'The Fair at Sakhi Sarvar', *Calcutta Review*, Vol. LX (1875), pp. 78–101. For an account of Sakhi Sarvar and of the importance of the cult in the late nineteenth century see Harjot Oberoi, *The Construction of Religious Boundaries: Culture, Identity and Diversity in the Sikh Tradition* (Delhi: Oxford University Press, 1994), pp. 147–60.

4. *Calcutta Review*, Vol. LXXI (1880), pp. 257-72; Vol . LXXII (1881), pp. 48-75; and Vol. LXIII (1881), pp. 155-68.

5. For an excellent account of the division within the Singh Sabha see Harjot Oberoi, *The Construction of Religious Boundaries*, particularly Part II.

6. The Sant poets whose works also appear in the Adi Granth.

7. *The Holy Writings of the Sikhs* (Allahabad: Christian Association Press, 1900), p. 30.

8. *A Lecture on the Sikh Religion and its Advantages to the State* (Simla: Superintendent, Government Central Printing Office 1903), p. 28. Reprinted in M. Macauliffe, et. al., *The Sikh Religion: A Symposium* (Calcutta: Susil Gupta, 1958), pp. 1–53.

9. *How the Sikhs became a Militant People* (Paris: Ernest Leroux, 1905). Reprinted in *The Panjab Past and Present*, Vol. XVI-II (October 1982), pp. 484-504.

10. The portions which were published were *Japji, Rahiras or the Evening Prayer of the Sikhs, Anand and the Sabd of Guru Amar Das, The Arati and Sohila of the Sikhs*, and *Asa di Var*, published between 1897 and 1902. His *Life of Guru Teg Bahadur* (Lahore: author) followed in 1903.

11. The same Gurmukhi font, apparently fashioned in wood, which was used for the Adi Granth quotation on the title page was later used on the dedicatory page of my *Gurū Nānak and the Sikh Religion*, published by the Clarendon Press sixty years later. In 1968 the font presented a dated but thoroughly satisfying impression.

12. N.G. Barrier in *Historians and Historiography of the Sikhs*, ed. Fauja Singh (New Delhi: Oriental, 1978), p. 184.

13. Macauliffe, 'How the Sikhs became a Militant People', in *The Panjab Past and Present*, Vol. XVI-II (October 1982), p. 504.

PART VIII | HISTORIOGRAPHY

16

CRIES OF OUTRAGE:
HISTORY VERSUS TRADITION IN THE
STUDY OF THE SIKH COMMUNITY*

'Sir', writes a correspondent to the May 1994 issue of *The Sikh Review*, 'This refers to the Editorial in the January '94 issue. I am inclined to agree that McLeod were best ignored. I wish he would thus pass into oblivion. But will he? One cannot imagine if anyone has done so much damage to the Sikh image at so high an academic level as Dr Hew McLeod.' The letter continues: 'What McLeod has done will perhaps be pardonable if it were inspired by objective scholarship' and then cities an incident which, he believes proves that the scholarship is anything but objective. 'One cannot get rid of "McLeod" by making up with McLeod. He has affixed a most damaging brand on Sikh "academics".'

And so the letter continues, only admitting at the very end that because this person McLeod admits that his study of Sikh history 'can never be adequate' the Sikhs should 'shed all resentment and bear him no malice'.

The letter is one of the more moderate ones to appear in the last few years. The less moderate ones I hesitate to quote. Comments which have been made to me orally indicate that what one finds published in the popular press is considerably more restrained than what passes in private conversation. Obviously I have touched an exceedingly delicate nerve in the Sikh community, at least as far as many of the more devout and loyal members of the Panth are

*Originally published in *South Asia Research*, Vol. 14, No. 2, 1994.

concerned. Cries of anguish and outrage are continually raised and although there is no evidence that anyone wants me to be actually harmed the news that I had decided to remain silent would be greeted with considerable relief. The news that I had gone further and publically renounced all the fruits of my research would be the occasion of profound thanksgiving.

I am not planning to remain silent, much less to renounce my published work, but obviously I have considerable cause of soul-searching. Venturing further on a career of teaching and research from (of all places) the School of Oriental and African Studies, I certainly did not anticipate the degree of indignation and resentment that I have encountered. Others of course have experienced the same hostile response, two of them in particular. Harjot Singh Oberoi is one who is very much in the line of fire, particularly since his book *The Construction of Religious Boundaries*[1] appeared earlier this year. And my former student, Pashaura Singh of the University of Michigan, has been particularly targetted for the University of Toronto Ph.D. dissertation he presented in 1991.

Oberoi and Pashaura Singh have both been associated with me, and much of the blame for their scholarly careers (particularly that of Pashaura Singh) has been visited upon me. They may be Sikhs but (so the argument runs) they have bent to my will in order to ensure employment in some prestigious western universities. Would that the claim were true, I often reflect! And yet perhaps in retrospect I can perceive that the reaction which my work has raised has been entirely predictable and entirely understandable. One cannot expect to engage in scholarly analysis of any living religion (including one's own religion, if any) without encountering the most vigorous rebuttal. It is absolutely certain to come.

Note here that we are talking about scholarly analysis. If one chooses to reflect the piety of believers and simply repeat what they hold dear the chances are immeasurably reduced. In fact they virtually disappear. And that is a perfectly respectable thing to do, one that may considerably enlarge our understanding. But it is not what I mean by scholarly analysis. This involves asking questions and seeking answers which, however true, may not be entirely to the liking of the believers. At times they will disconcert and at others they are liable to create serious dismay. This is what I meant by saying that the response is entirely predictable and entirely understandable. I was going to engage in scholarly analysis of this kind and I would be seeking answers to questions which, for at least some Sikhs, would cause alarm and consternation.

If one is a historian (and this is what I have tried to be) one is required to apply a certain range of techniques which will qualify for the description of scholarly analysis. Most insistently I would maintain that Sikhism must be studied from an historical point of view, the Sikh faith today being plainly the product of five hundred years of history. It is here that a crucial difference opens up between two kinds of historians, the two kinds we find ranged against each other in this battle for understanding of the true nature of the Sikh Panth. On one side we find arrayed the historians who put their trust in tradition. These defend the traditions of the Panth and, as a result, have a large and well-integrated version of the Panth's history set out before them. Opposed to the traditionalists are the sceptics, historians who maintain that every fact requires believable evidence to support it and who in consequence find the established history of the Panth much more restricted.

The disagreement here covers a whole range of historical method, but in the last analysis it comes down to the simple difference between these two approaches. On one side stands the historian who trusts traditional sources, on the other the one who views such sources with scepticism. It really is as simple as that. Within each camp one finds differences of opinion of course. Some of the traditionalists impart a degree of rigour to their research, while others view the traditions as true in all essential respects. Likewise, one expects degrees of scepticism from the other side, some giving traditional sources a measure of cautious trust while others are thoroughgoing in their criticism of them. But almost all fall within the territory marked out as either traditional or sceptical. The historian who can claim to have a foot in both camps is a very rare person indeed, though certainly that person may exist.

How does one explain this difference between the approach of the two varieties of historian? Here one's biases obtrude. If one belongs to the traditional school the difference is normally the certainty of belief as opposed to the insecurity of doubt. That is what explains the difference. If, however, one belongs to the sceptical school it is seen more in terms of the closed mind as opposed to free intelligence, the latter uninhibited by the constraints which shackle the understanding of the traditionalist. These are held to be the two extremes, with varying proportions of the two attitudes lying between. Take your pick, or combine them in what seems to you to be a reasonable mix. The argument here does not really concern the origins of the two attitudes. The fact seems to be that they certainly do exist and that one must come to terms with their separate existences.

In what I have just been saying the words 'tradition' and 'scepticism' have been central and it is perhaps worth pausing for a moment to ensure that I have made their meanings clear. It is perhaps difficult for me to sound absolutely fair in offering a definition of 'tradition', but I can at least try. I have a definition which makes sense, at least to me, and the definition is as follows.

With reference to Sikh history, 'tradition' means that which is handed down within the Panth. The material thus handed down has not been subjected to rigorous scrutiny, but for a traditionalist historian that is not necessary. It is known to be true because it is said to be derived from sources which are known by the Panth to be absolutely secure. The janam-sakhis, for example, are traditionally known to be generally accurate because they deal with matters concerning the life of the first Guru and (this is the important part) they have been recorded by faithful followers of the Guru. Occasionally they may err with regard to detail, but they are substantially accurate. When the material derives from the Gurus themselves, or is intimately associated with them, it is treated as wholly and absolutely beyond reproach. This means that the Sikh scripture (the Adi Granth) is beyond research and investigation. The Adi Granth is clearly perfect because it comes to us through perfect men. As such there can be no possibility of any research concerning it, at least with regard to its text and its meaning.

Not all adherents of the traditional school would carry the definition as far as that, but essentially they would agree with its substance. The general tenor of their interpretation makes this clear. And opposed to it are historians of the opposite camp—the historians who embrace the sceptical view with its rigorous examination of sources. In an extreme form this approach requires everything to be questioned and nothing to be affirmed unless there is evidence satisfactory to the researcher to support it. A more moderate view accepts a limited amount as accurate without subjecting it to the full battery of investigation. After all, Gurū Nānak was born in the Punjab. Surely no one would question this.

Some prefer the word 'critical' to 'sceptical', believing that the latter term implies doubt in too extreme a form. Personally I prefer 'sceptical'. The word certainly does imply doubt and is meant to do so. Its meaning however, is not limited to doubt, and the questioning it involves should not always leave one in a condition of uncertainty. Positive conclusions as well as negative ones should assuredly emerge from a sceptical approach. 'Critical' may perhaps serve as a synonym, but it is not as explicit in terms of the attitude which the historian should adopt. A sound critical historian is, above all else, a sceptical historian.

I make no secret of the fact that I belong to the sceptical camp— or, at least, I aspire to membership in it. The fact that I am not a member of the Panth leads to strong suspicions that mine is an attitude governed by a lack of belief in what the Panth upholds, but this is clearly not the case. Historians within the Panth are also to be numbered amongst those of a sceptical view. Professor Oberoi would certainly want to be regarded as one such historian and there are several more.

Let us take three prominent examples from Sikh history to illustrate the difference between the traditional historians on the one hand and the sceptical variety on the other. The three episodes are the life of Gurū Nānak, the development of the Sikh Rahit (the Khalsa code of belief and conduct), and the Singh Sabha movement. I am fully aware that in treating these three I will at once manifest my own particular bias. That is inevitablé, for there is no such thing as an unbiased historian. Indeed I have already been guilty of it, referring a moment ago to 'the development' of the Rahit instead of 'the bestowal of the immutable Rahit'. But I shall try to be as fair as possible and rigorously to restrain the temptation to present only that which I conceive as the truth.

The first example is the life of Nanak and here the analysis focuses on the hagiographical narratives of his life called the janam-sakhis. And once again my bias shows in referring to these narratives as hagiographical. The difficulty is that I cannot possibly (like the traditional historians) call them biographies. Let us call them instead just narratives.

By the middle of the nineteenth century the story of Nanak's life was related according to the so-called *Bālā* janam-sakhis, evidently pre-eminent because of their presentation of the many miraculous deeds wrought by the Guru. In the later nineteenth century, however, the *Bālā* janam-sakhis caused growing uneasiness amongst educated Sikhs, not only for the grotesque nature of many of the miracles but also for their lack of order. Baba Nanak could, it seemed, transfer himself to any part of the sub-continent (or beyond) by *tai-i-safar* (that is, by simply closing his eyes).[2] In 1872, however, Trumpp discovered a manuscript in the India Office Library which he believed to be the one from which all other janam-sakhis had originated. This came to be called the *Purātan* or 'Ancient' janam-sakhi. *Purātan* certainly had its fair share of miracles, but they were (on the whole) less bizarre than those of *Bālā*. The critical difference, though, was that *purātan* introduced order into the lengthy travel period of Nanak. Four *udāsīs* (missionary journeys) were followed to the four cardinal points of the compass, followed by a fifth within the Punjab.

Traditional historians have accepted the *Purātan* account of the life of Nanak as generally accurate. A varying number of miracles are either rationalized or completely abandoned, depending on the author's conception of what is or is not possible. To this limited extent the *Purātan* testimony is set aside. Certain incidents are, however, brought in from the *Bālā* or other janam-sakhis (incidents such as how Baba Nanak stopped the boulder pushed down the hill by Vali Qandhari—the story of Panja Sahib). To this extent *Purātan* is (to varying degrees depending on the historian) both diminished and supplemented. In essence, though, it is still *Purātan*. It is still the four journeys plus one which Baba Nanak undertakes and it is thus the *Purātan* pattern which is accepted by traditional historians. There may not be evidence of the kind demanded by the sceptical historian, but the account is essentially possible. The account is therefore accurate.

This the sceptical historian is unable to accept. The sceptical historian insists on analysing both the nature of the janam-sakhis and the details of the various anecdotes they record. The analysis of the various janam-sakhis produces a complicated pattern of growth and overlap. One work derives from a particular range of sources and is directed to a particular intention. Another uses a different range of sources and seeks to communicate a rather different emphasis. No janam-sakhis are close to Nanak in terms of composition, and their true value is therefore to show how he was perceived by later groups within the Panth. The analysis also reveals that the organization of *sakhis* into a more coherent structure is actually a product of the janam-sakhis growing to maturity, and that the *Purātan* pattern is accordingly a later rather than an early development.

And the individual anecdotes are required to answer historical questions of time, place and probability. Goraknath, for example, lived much earlier than Nanak and the sceptical historian is bound to exclude him from the authentic life of Nanak. The more cautious kind of traditional historian replies that the person concerned is not intended to be the historic Gorakhnath but merely a Nath yogi of the same name. To this the sceptical historian replies that the janam-sakhis clearly intend him to be the historic Gorakhnath—and so the debate continues. With regard to the life of Nanak the difference between the traditional and the sceptic is perhaps best seen in the oft-repeated comparison between the book-length account of the former and my own version which covers less than a page.[3] In less than a page (so I maintain) it is possible to record everything which can be positively affirmed concerning the Guru's life.

The second example is provided by the Rahit, the code of belief and behaviour which the Khalsa Sikh is required to obey. According to the traditional historian the Rahit was delivered in essentially its modern form by Guru Gobind Singh at the founding of the Khalsa in 1699. It is true (so most traditional historians believe) that during the next century and a half the Rahit was corrupted, but during the Singh Sabha revival (late in the nineteenth century and early in this century) the essential components were recovered and the Rahit was eventually published as *Sikh Rahit Marayādā*. Some features were never lost nor corrupted. The 'Five Ks' were certainly an absolutely central part of the Rahit as delivered by Guru Gobind Singh, and ever since 1699 this particular feature has been upheld by all who regard themselves as true Sikhs of the Khalsa.

The sceptical historian has to disagree. Even if the Khalsa was founded in 1699 (a fact which is open to some dispute) there can be no doubt (so the sceptical historian maintains) that the available sources make it clear that the Rahit delivered by Guru Gobind Singh at the inauguration of the Khalsa was appreciably shorter than that which is current today. The earliest sources (for example Sainapati's *Gur Sobhā*) make it clear that the Guru required his Khalsa to leave their hair uncut and to carry arms.[4] In other words there is explicit authority for the *kes* and implicit authority for the *kirpān*. That, however, falls short of the Five Ks.

But, says the traditional historian, what about the *hukam-nāmā* which Guru Gobind Singh addressed to his followers in Kabul? This was dated S. 1756, the very year of the founding of the Khalsa (1699 CE), and in it he refers to the necessity of bearing the Five Ks. This *hukam-nāmā* cannot be genuine, replies the sceptical historian. It lacks the Guru's seal and it is in direct contradiction to other early sources which make it perfectly clear that the Five Ks were not among the Guru's instructions.[5] He may well have commanded his followers to carry five weapons,[6] but these are not the Five Ks. And what about the testimony of Chaupa Singh? The first version of his *rahit-nāmā* makes no reference at all to the Five Ks. A later version does include them, but it names two of the five as *bāṇī* and *sādh sāngat*.[7]

But, replies the traditional historian, who can trust the *Chaupa Singh Rahit-nāmā*? It is precisely the kind of *rahit-nāmā* which was so corrupted that it had to be purged by the scholars of the Singh Sabha. Is it not the *Chaupa Singh Rahit-nāmā* which allows a special status to Brahman Sikhs? Obviously the Guru could never have uttered a Rahit which included such an instruction. Divergences of this kind, responds the sceptical historian, are a general feature of all these *rahit-nāmās*. They all represent not the words of the Guru but of the people who wrote them and the circumstances in which they were living.

And so this debate also continues. The traditional historian maintains that the Rahit has descended unchanged. The sceptical historian replies that it has evolved in response to historical circumstances, particularly those of the eighteenth century. Many items in the early *rahit-nāmās* reflect the fact that the Khalsa was fighting with Muslims. There is, for example, the commandment that Khalsa Sikhs should not have dealings with Muslim women.[8] Kahn Singh Nabha was a prominent member of the Singh Sabha movement and his interpretation of this particular item was that Khalsa Sikhs were being warned to steer clear of prostitutes, most of whom were Muslims.[9] The interpretation is distinctly strained, but later still the item was reinterpreted to mean that Sikhs should not engage in adultery. It appears in this form as one of the four *kurahits* in the modern *Sikh Rahit Marayādā*.[10] An interesting survival of these anti-Muslim items in the Rahit today is the instruction that Khalsa Sikhs must eat only *jhaṭka* meat (i.e. killed with a single blow), never *kuṭṭha* meat (i.e. halal meat where the animal has bled to death). This too is one of the *kurahits*.[11]

But I am taking advantage of my position as the speaker and using it to propound arguments acceptable only to a critical or sceptical historian. I must make it clear that they are arguments which would certainly not be acceptable to a traditional historian and the attempt would assuredly be made to rebut them.

The third example involves the Singh Sabha period of Sikh history (the period from 1873 to 1920). For the sceptical historian this period involves a wholly different approach to questions which it raises from the standard interpretation. Whereas the traditional historian will conduct research on the basis of a general acceptance of the truth of the Singh Sabha interpretation, the sceptical historian

will assume the reverse. Or (to put it a little differently) the Singh
Sabha interpretation will be treated as the product of scholars who
were themselves a part of the Singh Sabha movement (men such as
Vir Singh or Kahn Singh Nabha) and will be set aside. Research is
then conducted on the basis of modern historical research, with
such skills as sociology and linguistics employed, and although some
of the results may agree with earlier interpretations others assuredly
will not. An elementary difference will be to break open the Singh
Sabha movement and show that it was the result of at least three
major factions, one of which (Tat Khalsa) was eventually to carry
the day and assume the title of the whole Singh Sabha movement.
This awareness makes an enormously important beginning to the
task of interpreting the period.[12]

As an aside one may note that those whom I have called traditional
historians could also be termed Singh Sabha historians. This is because
their approach to Sikh history and religion has been shaped by the
philosophy of the Tat Khalsa. The historiography of the Tat Khalsa
has so permeated the world of Sikh history that the person who wishes
to challenge any aspect of it must expect stiff resistance. The life of
Gurū Nānak provides an excellent example of this.

These are but three examples from a lengthy list. All produce the
same result, with the traditional historians defending tradition and
the sceptical historian attacking those elements of it which are not
supported by evidence which they regard as acceptable. My own
view, as I say, is emphatically on the side of the sceptics.

But let us pause for a moment. Have we not omitted an essential
component? We are discussing a religious faith, yet we are doing
so merely from one direction, from one perspective. All that we
have said so far views Sikhism from the perspective of history. It
may be maintained (and certainly I would maintain this to be
true) that for the study of Sikhism history is absolutely essential.
But is it enough? Many Sikhs say—and say with emphasis—that
indeed it is *not* enough. To study Sikhism, they maintain, one needs
more than the approach of history, regardless of how important
that approach may be. Inder Jit Singh poses the question 'why' in
his recent book *Sikhs and Sikhism* and he answers the question as
follows: 'Because religion is a reality to which historical intellectual
analysis alone is ill-suited. Only in part can history and intellect
measure the intuitive reality that transcends both.'[13]

But what is that other perspective which is required? From an
academic point of view one could reply that the necessary discipline

is Religious Studies, yet so many teachers of Religious Studies are in fact historians. They pursue their discipline as historians, its definition as Religious Studies being provided by the actual subject they are studying. If they are not historians the chances are that they are philosophers, and one suspects that Philosophy would be laid under the same condemnation as History by those who regard the study of Sikhism as being inadequately served.

Perhaps the truth is that it is not so much History as such which is regarded as inadequate, but rather the academic approach. I.J. Singh indicates that this is indeed the case by saying that history *and intellect* can only partially *'measure the intuitive reality that transcends both'*. But what is this intuitive reality that transcends both history and intellect? It is presumably something which cannot be explained to those who do not already possess it, an experience which cannot be comprehended except by those who have already experienced it. It is that which is called 'religious' (without the word 'studies' being added) or perhaps 'spiritual'. Dr. Gurdarshan Singh Dhillon of Chandigarh expresses what is regarded as this crucial need in the following terms:

A proper study for religion involves a study of the spiritual dimension and experiences of man, a study which is beyond the domain of Sociology, Anthropology and History. Any materialistic interpretation of religion, which does not of [go ?] beyond the physical reality perceived by the senses, is bound to be lop-sided, limited and partial. Religion has its own tools, its own methodology and principles of study which take cognisance of higher level of reality and a world-view which is comprehensive and not limited. The study of religion requires sharp insights into the totality of life including transcendental knowledge concerning God, the universe and the human spirit.[14]

But what does this mean? What is imparted by such expressions as 'the spiritual dimension', 'a higher level of reality', and 'transcendental knowledge'? The terms are not explained and indeed cannot be explained to anyone who lacks the pre-requisite perception to understand them. According to Dr. Dhillon those of us who offer only a 'materialistic interpretation of religion' must unavoidably have a view which is 'lop-sided, limited and partial'. One must assume that this materialistic interpretation will prevent us from understanding the expressions he uses, whereas those who possess transcendental knowledge need no explanation. For them the meaning will already be clear.

For those of us who are largely devoid of this religious or spiritual experience no amount of explaining can ever succeed in communicating just what is meant by the terms. And so (the argument follows irresistibly) the person who lacks a sense of the numinous will never be able to explain the religion of the Sikhs—or any other religion for that matter. It seems that we have reached an impasse. The fact that unnumbered others have reached the same impasse with regard to the study of religion ought to have prepared us for this.

There are certain features, which have become axiomatic in all that I say about the Sikhs, their history, and their religion. The Sikhs are, to my mind, an open and a generous people, and in my seeking to communicate with a western readership this awareness is always present. This much can, I most sincerely hope, be taken for granted. Moreover, I can appreciate something of the awe and solemnity which, for example, is created by the ceremony of *amrit sanskar* (initiation into the Khalsa). But I approach Sikhism as a historian, one who is devoid of any pretence to that spiritual sense which many Sikhs (and many Christians too) assure me is vital to its understanding. I simply do not possess it, neither in relation to the Sikh religion nor to any other faith. At the same time I am most anxious that my efforts at understanding should not be construed as a covert intention to subvert the Sikh faith. Such a conclusion would be far from the truth, as far as it is possible to get. I am, I suppose, a genuine academic, much as I dislike that word. The intention which I uphold is to understand, and to understand simply for its own sake. Others may choose if they wish to use what I write for their own purposes, and some of these purposes will give me much pleasure. This they are certainly entitled to do, but I would hope that those who are Sikhs will never assume that those works represent any kind of hidden agenda. Everything, assuredly, is out in the open.

But this requires charity and forbearance on both sides. It certainly requires the sceptical historian to be ever aware that he or she is handling material which many Sikhs hold to be sacred and to proceed with a reverent disposition and extreme care. 'Tread softly' must ever be the motto of such a person, and not so that destruction can be wrought once reputations are established. The objective must *never* be destruction for its own sake, but always a strictly impartial understanding.

And just as caution is required of the sceptical or the critical historian, so too a corresponding response is also needed from the traditional historian. Sceptical historians, after all, are not in the business of burning and pillaging. They are not trying to suppress inconvenient evidence, they do not engage in fallacious reasoning (at least not consciously or deliberately), and they certainly do not foster disinformation campaigns. Positively the reverse is true. The traditional historian needs to recognize this and to address the sceptical historian in terms and in tones which recognize the latter's honesty. Rivals they may be, and the findings of the sceptical historian may sometimes run counter to the deeply-held beliefs of the traditionalist, but at least the sincerity of the former should be acknowledged. Truth and understanding should be the objectives of the sceptical historian. Although the two may diverge widely as far as method is concerned the traditional historian can at least accept that these are the purposes of the discipline perused by the sceptical historian.

In conclusion let me sum up what I believe to be the necessary features of any outsider's research into the religious faith of any people. This particularly applies when one is seeking to understand a faith which is different from that in which one was raised. In the first place, the researcher must comprehensively cover the sources. This obviously requires the learning of other languages where this is necessary—in the case of the Sikhs competence in at least Punjabi. Secondly, there must be a willingness to listen patiently and to carefully evaluate all that the researcher is told. Thirdly, he or she must avoid all argument— at least argument in the argumentative sense. Discussion can certainly be undertaken—it *must* be undertaken—but never at the cost of being drawn into an argument, much less into an open quarrel. Fourthly, there needs to be careful expression and an unfailing courtesy in making it. I acknowledged this in the first paragraph of the preface to my first book, *Gurū Nānak and the Sikh Religion*. And finally there needs to be an acknowledgement of one's limitations.

I have already spoken of one of my own primary limitations (or at least what many see as a serious limitation), namely the inability to comprehend the need for a spiritual interpretation in research on the Sikh religion or for that matter in anything else. But this is not the same thing as saying that the research should not be done, nor that I should want to apologize for its results. That certainly is not my intention. I was trained to be a historian in the School of Oriental and African Studies and I seek to perform the work of a historian in a manner which seems to me to be honest. It was, I suppose, something of an accident that I came to be involved in Sikh Studies, but having become involved I have tried to do the job as I learned to do it. I developed, if you like, into a sceptical historian, and that has set me in competition with the traditional variety. Most assuredly I hope that the competition continues, but at the same time I would want it to be a competition which observes the rules of decency and fair play. It should be a friendly competition and it should be a mutually instructive one.

Notes

1. *The Construction of Religious Boundaries: Culture, Identity and Diversity in the Sikh Tradition* (Delhi: Oxford University Press, 1994).
2. The method of locomotion commonly adopted in Sufi hagiographies.
3. W.H. McLeod, *Gurū Nānak and the Sikh Religion* (Oxford: Clarendon Press, 1968), p. 146.
4. Sainapati, *Gur Sobhā*, dhiau panjvan: *bachan pragās*. Ganda Singh, samp., *Sri Gur Sobha* (Patiala: Panjabi Yunivarasiti, 1957), pp. 20 ff.
5. Swaran Singh Sanehi, 'Rahitnamas of the Sikhs', *Journal of Sikh Studies* VOL. XI, No. 1 (1984), p. 80.
6. Ganda Singh, samp., *Hukamanāme* (Patiala: Panjabi Yunivarasiti, 1967), pp. 179, 194.
7. W.H. McLeod, trans., *The Chaupā Singh Rahit-nāmā* (Dunedin: University of Otago Press, 1987), pp. 58, 150.
8. Ibid., pp. 59, 150.
9. Kahn Singh Nabha, *Gurumat Maratand* (Amritsar: Shiromani Prabandhak Kameti, 1962), p. 546n. Idem, *Guramat Sudhākar* (Patiala: Bhasha Vibhag, 4th edn 1970), p. 307n.
10. *Sikh Rahit Marayādā* (Amritsar, 16th edn, 1983), p. 26. W.H. McLeod (trans. and ed.), *Textual Sources for the Study of Sikhism* (Chicago: University of Chicago Press, 1990), p. 85.
11. Ibid.
12. The task of analysing the early Singh Sabha period has been admirably performed by Harjot Oberoi, *The Construction of Religious Boundaries* (Delhi: Oxford University Press, 1994).
13. I.J. Singh, *Sikhs and Sikhism: A View With a Bias* (Columbia: South Asia Publications, 1994), p. 78.
14. Gurdarshan Singh Dhillon in a review of Harjot Oberoi's *The Construction of Religious Boundaries* in *Sikh Press* 4.33 (May 1–15, 1994), p. 4. Also in *The Sikh Review* 42.7 (July 1994), p. 59.

INDEX

Abbotabad 225
Abchalnagar 113, 120
Ad Dharam 159, 248, 252
Ādi Granth, sacred scripture 7, 23–5, 31–2, 40–42, 44–5, 53, 55, 57, 63, 94, 105, 106–7, 110, 122, 152–4, 165, 166, 169–70, 175, 184, 260–1, 270 Banno recension 170 Damdama recension 170 Kartarpur recension 169–70 *See also* guru Granth Sahib.
Ahlu (Ahluval), village 218
Ahluwalia (Sikh caste) 181, 219–26, 228, 230–4
Ahluwalia *misal* 217
Ahluwalia, M.M. 199–200
Ahmad Shah Abdali 78, 216
Akali Party (Shiromani Akali Dal) 67, 87–8, 158, 173, 224, 229
Akal Purakh (god) 81, 202
Akbar, Emperor 211
Akhand Kirtani Jatha *see* Bhai Randhir Singh da Jatha
Amar Das, third Guru 53–5, 211

amrit-dhari Sikh 178, 179, 186
Amritsar 55, 81, 92, 93, 111, 168, 181, 192, 194, 196, 203, 259, 260
Amritsar District 207
Anandpur 77, 81, 83, 84, 90, 104
Anand *Sāhib* 150
Angad, second Guru 53–4
Anglo-Sikh wars 92, 199
Ardās, Sikh prayer 62, 74, 81
Arjan, fifth Guru 31, 55–6, 57, 76, 115, 152–3, 170
Arora (mercantile caste) 144, 168, 178, 181, 214, 222, 232
Arya Samaj 65
Assam 40, 227
Attar Singh of Bhadaur 117, 120, 124
Attar Singh of Mastuana, Sant 158
Aurangzeb, Emperor 57, 80
Australia 238, 240–1, 250
Avtar Singh, Bhai 117, 131

B40 janam-sakhi 153
Babur 40

Bachitar Nāṭak 80
Baghdad 33, 39
Bagrian, town 158
Bagrian sants 158, 161
Baha al-Din Zakarya 28
Balachaur tahsil 245, 246
Balak Singh, Namdhari Guru 165, 190, 204, 209, 210, 214
Baldev Singh Share 98
Ballard, R. and C. 238
Banda 71, 77, 83, 259
Bania, Banya (trading caste) 87, 190, 214
barādarī (fraternity) 220–1
baṛā piṇḍ (big village network) 246–7
Barrier, N.G. 258, 261
Batala 149, 150, 227, 229, 233–4
Bathwal, P.D. 26
Bayley, E.C. 197–8
bazaar posters 75
Beas river 53
Bengal Regulation III 197–8
Bhachu, Parminder 238, 240
Bhagats of Adi Granth 105, 106, 122, 153, 261
Bhagvan Singh, *rahit-nāmā* compiler 110
Bhaini (Bhaini Raian) 165, 190, 191, 195, 198, 201, 203, 209, 212, 213, 215
Bhai Randhir Singh da Jatha 167–9, 180, 181, 185
bhakti tradition 12, 15, 30
Bhangali Kalan 150
Bhatra (pedlar caste) 252
Bhindran, village 158
Bible 164, 175
Bījak 23–4
Bir Singh, Bhai 155
Bouquet, A.C. 3
Brahman, Brahmans 24, 42, 87, 92, 129, 143, 144, 179, 190, 191, 202, 219–20, 260
Brahman Sikhs 274
British administration 79, 92, 154, 165, 190ff, 262
British annexation 92, 130, 198, 199, 200, 207, 242
Buchignani, Norman 238
Bulhe Shah 6

calendar art *see* bazaar posters
Canada 67, 238
Canton 241
caste 50–1, 52, 60–3, 66, 92, 94, 139, 141–5, 147, 181–2, 190–1, 206, 214, 217ff, 239–40, 247–9
Ceylon 40
Chadney, J. 238
Chamar (leather-working outcaste) 190, 208, 210–1, 222, 247–8
Chamkaur, fort 90
Chaṇḍī charitra 86
Chaṇḍī kā Pāṭh see Chaṇḍī kī Vār.
Chaṇḍī kī Vār 192, 211
Chaupa Singh Chhibbar 111–12, 125, 129, 273
Chhabra, G.S., historian 79
chhoṭe piṇḍ (small village) 247
Chief Khalsa Divan 66, 93, 118, 124
China 250
Chopra, Harinder Singh 97
Chuhra (sweeper outcaste) 211, 222
Congress Party 173, 229
conversion 20, 22, 26
Cowan, L. 195–6, 199, 200, 211
cow protection 192, 194–195, 202–3
Cunningham Joseph 79–80, 259

Dabistān-i-mazāhib 61
Dadu-panth 50
Dalip Singh, Maharaja 198

Daljeet Singh 170-1
Damdami (Bhindranwala) *ṭaksāl*
161, 169, 179, 185
Dariai, Bhai 113
Darling, Malcolm 242-5
Dasam Granth 32, 105, 106, 107, 166
Daya Singh, author of *rahit-nāmā*
111
de Lepervanche, Marie 238
Delhi 85, 223
ḍerā (camp) 151, 155-6, 157, 159
Dera Baba Nanak 50
Desa Singh, author of *rahit-nāmā*
111, 130
Devi cult 129
ḍhāḍhī, village bard 157
Dhak region 245
Dhariwal, town 149
dharma 145
Dhillon, Gurdarshan Singh 276
Dhir Mal 55
diaspora 67, 213, 238ff
Dip Singh, warrior 75, 83, 86, 89
Dit Singh, Tat Khalsa leader 93
Doaba region 53, 239, 244-7
Dumont, Louis 141-5, 147
Dusenbery, Verne 238
Dutch East Indies 241

East Africa 67, 227, 238, 240

Falcon, R.W. 225, 226, 227
Faridu'd-din Ganj-i-Shakar 6-7, 16,
28
Fateh Singh of Kapurthala 217
Fateh Singh, Sant 158
Fauja Singh Bajwa, historian 200
Fiji 241, 250
Five Ks 98, 104, 122, 168, 272
Forsyth, T.D. 190, 195-6, 200, 211
fundamentalism 162-86

Galway 258
Ganda Singh, historian 79
Gandhi, Indra 73
Garhshankar tahsil 241, 245, 246
Ghadr Party 199, 209
Ghazali 6
Ghumani, village 149-50, 157
Gillior, K., historian 238
Gobind Singh, tenth Guru 31—2,
57-9, 63-4, 69, 70-1, 76-7, 79,
80, 81-2, 83-5, 86, 90, 94, 98,
103ff, 127ff, 140, 155 165, 167,
170, 177, 202, 203, 204-5, 210,
213, 231, 232, 259-60, 273-4
God, doctrine of 10, 11, 12, 13-14,
17, 25, 26, 28, 133, 159, 192
Godavari river 113
Goindval *pothīs* 55
Golden Temple 92, 161, 175
invasion 1984 73, 88, 158, 178,
185
Gopal Singh, author 71, 79, 80
Gorakhnath 272-3
Goraya 227
got (*gotra*), exogamous group 220-
1, 228, 247, 252
Gujar (agrarian caste) 228
Guramat Prakāś Bhāg Saṅskār 118-
19, 112, 132
Guramat Sudhākar 117-8, 132
Gurbachan Singh, Baba 169
gur-bilās literature 109, 110, 121,
125
Gurcharan Singh, subah 198
Gurdas, Bhai 43, 60, 61, 106, 107,
160, 170, 221
Gurdas district 227, 234
Gurdwara Reform Movement 66-7,
87-8, 182, 209
Gurmukh Singh, Tat Khalsa leader
93
Gur Sobhā see Srī Gur Sobhā.

Gurū Granth (doctrine) 63-5, 84, 105, 175-6, 210

Gurū Granth Sahib 55, 63, 64, 66, 94, 105, 114, 133, 150, 165, 166, 175-7, 179, 181, 260 *See also* Ādi Granth.

Gurumat Mārtaṇḍ 110

Gurū Nānak and the Sikh Religion 27, 29, 278

Gurū Nānak Chamatkār 42

Gurū Panth (doctrine) 63-5, 84, 105, 210

Guruśabad ratanākar mahān koś 95, 110

Habib, Irfan 52

haj, pilgrimage to Mecca 25

halāl meat 62, 274

Ham Hindū Nahīn 87, 260

Handbook on Sikhs for Regimental Officers 225

Hans Rai 113

Hans, Surjit 97

Harbans Singh, writer 258

Harchand Singh Longowal 158, 161

Hargobind, sixth Guru 55-6, 61, 70, 76, 107-8

Har Krishan, eighth Guru 56

Harnam Singh, Sant 150, 159, 161

Har Rai, seventh Guru 56

Hasham 6

Hazara Singh, Sant 149-50, 157

Hazro 165, 190, 209, 214

Helweg, A. 238

Hindu domination 87, 90, 92-4, 260-1

Hindu tradition, Hinduism 3, 11, 13, 16, 27, 29, 44-5, 70, 92, 192, 224, 240, 248, 259-60

historians: critical 270-1 sceptical 269ff traditional 269ff.

historiography 71ff, 94, 98, 174, 267ff

Hong Kong 250

Hoshiarpur District 245-6

hukam-nāmā, letter of command 107-8, 121, 183, 273

Ibbetson, Denzil 218-9, 224-5, 226

Ibrahim, Shaikh 7

Ichogal, village 218

Inder Jit Singh 275-6

Indian administration 87, 179, 182

Indra, Doreen 238

Iran 162

Ishar Singh, Sant 157

Islam 3-18, 19-20, 22, 24-35, 39, 44-5, 62, 70, 240

izzat (prestige) 243-4, 246-7

Jagiasi movement 190, 204, 210

Jagraon, town 156, 157

Jahan Khan 86

Jaintipur, town 150

Jalal al-Din Rumi 6

Jamna river 202

janam-sākhīs 8, 16, 17, 28-9, 32-3, 35, 38-45, 51, 53, 68, 73, 85, 95-6, 107, 110, 115, 117, 123-4, 143, 151, 160, 226, 229, 270, 271-3, *Bālā* janam-sakhis 42, 45, 95-6, 271-2 *Miharbā Janam-sākhī* 39, 40, 45 *Purātan* janam-sakhis 39, 43, 45, 96-7, 272

Japjī 13

Jarnail Singh Bhindranwale 158, 163, 168, 173, 174, 179, 185

Jassa Singh Ahluwalia 217-8, 221, 224, 225

Jassa Singh Ramgarhia 217-8, 221, 226-7

Jaṭ (agrarian caste), Jats 52, 60-3, 67, 144-5, 161, 167, 168, 178,

181, 182, 190, 205–9, 213–5, 217, 219–22, 226, 240, 242–4, 246–7, 248–9
Jatpura, village 84
Jawahar Mal 190
Jehl Chiṭṭhīan 167
Jiwan Nagar, village 198, 212
Jodh Singh, Bhai 169–70
Jogindar Singh, Sant 150–1, 154, 157
Julaha (weaver caste) 24, 25, 26, 224
Jullundur District 207, 213, 244–6
Junaid 6

Kabir 17, 19–20, 23–7, 31, 34, 106, 153
Kabīr-granthāvalī 23–4, 36
Kabir-panth 22, 24, 50
Kabul 273
Kahn Singh Nabha 87, 95, 99, 110, 117–8, 120, 131, 2, 260–1, 274, 275
Kalal (brewer caste) 217, 219–26, 232, 233
Kaleran 156–7, 161
Kamboh (cultivating caste) 215
Kanihya, Bhai 83
Kapurthala princely house 217, 225–6, 233
karma 11–12, 17, 29, 145
Karnail Singh 234
Kartarpur (Jalandhar district) 227, 233
Kartarpur (Sialkot district) 39, 40, 50, 53
Kashmir 189, 194, 214
kathā, homily 74, 169
Kes-dhārī Sikh 178
Kessinger, T. 240–1, 243
Khadur 53
Khālistān, Khalistanis 88, 162–3, 171–2, 174, 179, 180, 182–3

Khālsā 34, 35, 58, 64, 70–1, 74ff, 92ff, 103ff, 126ff, 140, 167, 169, 178, 189, 202, 203–3, 216–9, 221–2, 230–1, 258, 259, 262, 273–4 inauguration 58–9, 76–7, 89, 98, 103–4, 127, 131, 133, 140, 273 initiation (*amrit saṅskār*) 73, 133, 148, 168, 178, 179, 277
Khalsa College, Amritsar 117
Khālsā Dharam Śastr Bāgh Saṅskār 117, 131
Khan, Ahmad Hassan Khan 223–4
khaṅḍe dī pāhul. Khalsa initiation 104
Khatrī (mercantile caste), Khatris 60, 61, 65–6, 69, 144–5, 161, 168, 178, 181, 182, 190, 214, 219–22, 226, 232, 242
Khem Singh Bedi 93
Khyber Pass 189
kīrtan, communal singing 49, 51, 152, 157, 158, 168
Kirpal Singh, artist 75
Kshatriya caste 220, 232
Kuka sect *see* Namdhari (Kuka) sect
kurahit, cardinal offences 104, 124, 168, 274
Kurukshetra 42

LaBrach, Bruce 238
Lahina *see* Angad, second Guru
Lahore 55–6, 82, 85, 131, 218, 258
Lakhmi Das 68
Lakhpat Rai 85
Lalo, Bhai 226
langar, gurdwara refectory 234
Limerick 258
Lingayat 143
liquor 231
Lohar (blacksmith caste) 215, 220, 223, 224, 228

Ludhiana 227
Ludhiana district 245-6

Macauliffe, M.A. 80, 95, 96, 99, 257-63
Madan, T.N. 163, 172-3, 176
Maharaj Singh, Bhai 154-5, 160
Mahimā Prakāś 42
Mahton (cultivating caste) 247
Majha region 53
Majumdar, R.C., historian 199
Malaya 240, 241, 246, 250
Malaysia 67
Malcolm, John 64, 139, 140-1
Malerkotla 83, 195-6, 198, 199, 203
Malodh, village 195-6, 198
Malwa region 53, 217, 245, 246, 247
Mangal Singh, Kuka 214
Mani Singh, martyr 83, 121, 125, 160
mañjī system 54, 194
manjki region 244-5
Mann, Jasbir Singh 170-1
'martial races' 67
martyrdom 56, 57, 76, 77, 82-3
masand system 58, 69, 155
Massa Ranghar 81, 86
Mazhabi (Sikh outcaste) 145, 190, 208, 211, 222
McLeod, Hew 267
meat-eating 43, 45-6, 168, 184, 274
Mecca 33, 39-40, 45
Medina 33, 39, 45
Mehtab Singh, warrior 81
Mehta Sahib (Mehta Chowk) 158
Mergui 212
M'Gregor, W.L. 259
migration 237ff
millenarian movement 200-9
Mir Mannu 82, 89

misal, misl (warrior band) 78, 86-7, 216-7
Moga tahsil 251
Montgomery District 207
Mughal administration 55-7, 69, 71, 77-8, 194, 204, 216
Multan 28, 189
Murray, Captain 97
Muslim influence *see* Islam.
Muslims, foes of Sikhs 85, 87, 114, 116, 203, 274
Muslim women 274
Mutiny 1857-58, 199, 206, 250
myth 72ff, 203

Nai (barbar caste) 224, 228
nām, the divine Name 51, 53, 54, 70, 92, 107, 112, 128, 165, 189, 190, 191
nām dān iśnān 112
Namdev 106, 153
Namdhari or Kuka sect 92, 124, 130, 159, 165-7, 180, 181, 184, 189-215, 222, 248 Namdhari *Rahit-nāmā* 166-7, 183-4
nām simaran 10, 13, 17, 28, 62, 92, 107, 152, 166, 168, 191, 204
Nanak, first Guru 3ff, 19ff, 37ff, 50-3, 54, 57, 62, 68, 70, 73, 93, 94, 95-6, 105, 107, 113, 133, 143, 151-3, 155, 159, 210, 219, 226, 259, 260, 270, 271-3, 275
Nanak-panth, Nanak-panthi 22-3, 50ff, 55, 59, 60, 62, 63, 68, 242
Nānak Prakāś 42
Nanaksar gurdwara 157
Nanded 113
Nand Lal, author of *rahit-nāmās* 111-12, 130
Nand Lal Goya, 111, 120, 129, 130, 131, 160
Nand Singh, Baba 156-7, 161

Narangabad, village 155
Narangwal, town 167
Nath tradition 4, 12, 15, 16, 18, 22, 26–7, 30, 33
Nath (Kanphata) yogis 9, 15, 159, 272
Naushehra Majha Singh, village, 150, 161
Nawanshahr tahsil 245–6
Nayar, Baldev Raj 229
Nepal 194
New Delhi 227
New Zealand 238ff, 250–1
Nihang Sikhs 167, 180, 181, 184
Nirankari sect 92, 180, 181
nirguṇa sampradāya 4
No Hindu, no Muslim 27, 104, 43–4
North America, west coast 240, 250

Oberoi, Harjot 1653, 170–1, 172, 174–6, 180, 268, 271

pāhul see khaṇḍde dī pāhul
Pakistan 35
Pak Pattan 7, 28
Panch Khalsa Divan 66, 124, 167, 184
Panjab *see* Punjab
Panja Sahib 272
Panth 23, 49–68, 127, 146–7
panth 21–3, 50–1
Param Sumārg see rahit-nāmā, manual of conduct: *Prem Sumārg*
Partition 1947 83, 88, 116–7, 120
Pashaura Singh 268
patit, renegade 104, 178
Perkins, Major 190, 208
Pettigrew, Joyce 238
Phagwara 227–9, 233
Philippines 241
Phillaur tahsil 245–6
Phulkian *misal* 217

Phuman Singh Gill 251
Piara Singh Padam, compiler 117
Pothī Sach-khaṇḍ 40
Prāchīn Panth Parkāś 97
Prahilad Rai *see* Prahilad Singh
Prahilad Singh 111, 113, 130
Prem Sumārg Granth 120
Prithi Chand 55
Punjab 19, 28, 38–9, 40, 42, 44, 45, 50, 52, 61, 64, 65, 68, 71, 77, 83, 87, 88, 117, 130, 151, 165, 189, 194, 198, 199, 204ff, 216, 217, 219, 239, 242, 245, 258, 259
Punjab Communist Party 173, 209
Punjabis in New Zealand 240, 248
Punjabi Suba 87, 158, 182
Purānas 32
Puran Singh, writer 225

qaum 146
Qaumī Ektā 146
Qur'an 9, 10, 14, 25, 30, 164

Rahit, Khalsa code of belief and discipline 34, 58, 62, 66, 67, 71, 73, 83, 85, 92, 94, 104–25, 126–35, 140, 166–7, 184, 231, 233, 271, 273–4
rahit-nāmā, manual of conduct 103–25, 126–35, 153, 177–8, 186
Chaupa Singh's *Rahit-nāmā* 111, 114–15, 116, 120–1, 129–31, 153, 273–4 Chaupa Singh/Nand Lal manuscript 117, 123, 131
Daya Singh's *Rahit-nāmā* 111, 116, 131 Desa Singh's *Rahit-nāmā* 111, 112 Nand Lal's *Praśan-uttar* 111, 117, 120, 125 Nand Lal's prose *rahit-nāmā* 111, 116, 131 Nand Lal's *Tanakhāh-nāmā* 111–12, 117, 120, 125 Prahilad Singh's *Rahit-nā,ā* 111, 113–14, 117, 120, 125 *Prem Sumārg* 111, 115–16,

117, 120–1, 125, 153 *Sau Sakhīān*
111, 115, 121, 130, 203, 213
Rahit-nāme 117
Rahit-prakāś 107
Rai Kalha 84
Raikot, town 192, 194, 196, 203
Raj (mason caste) 220, 228
Rajput (agrarian caste) 214–215,
226, 247
Ram Das, fourth Guru 55, 143
Ramdasia (Sikh outcaste) 145, 211
Ramgarhia (SIkh artisan caste) 161,
181, 219–24, 238, artists 228–9,
234 *granthī* (reader) 228
Ramgarhia *misal* 217
Ram Rauni (Ramgarh), fort 82,
218
Ram Singh, namdhari Guru 165–6,
190–99, 201–4, 206, 209, 211,
214, 222
Randhir Singh, Bhai 167–9, 180, 181
Randhir Singh, copyist 120–1
Rangoon 165, 198, 212
Ranjit Singh, Jathedar 169
Ranjit Singh, Maharaja 64, 65, 78–
9, 87, 92, 130, 165, 189–90,
204–6, 216–7
Ratan Singh Bhangu 97–8
Ravidas (Raidas) 153, 159
Ravi river 50, 202
*Rehat Maryada: A Guide to the Sikh
Way of Life* 119
Renan, E. 37
renouncer, definition 141–4
Rurr, village 195

Sahaj-dhari Sikhs 94, 133, 140, 178
Sahib Singh of Una 155
Sahib Singh, subah 194, 213
Sahib Singh, theologian 170
Sāhib-zāde, martyr sons of Guru
Gobind Singh 83, 84, 86

Sahnewal, village 196, 212
Sainapati 64, 109, 273
Saini (cultivating caste) 215, 247
Sakhi Sarvar 259, 263
Samarkand 198
sampradāya 21–3, 146
Sampuran Singh, Sant 117
Sanatan Sikhs *see* Singh Sabha.
Sandhu, Karnail Singh 238
sant 151ff
Sant Nirankaris 168–9, 181
Santokh Singh 42
Sants 149–61, 168
sant sipāhī 57
Sant traditiion, origins of Sikh faith
4–8, 10–12, 14–15, 16, 22, 26–
7, 30–1, 33–5, 49–51, 68, 70,
151ff, 263
Satluj river 53, 207, 217, 245
Saund, Dalip Singh 229
School of Oriental and African
Studies 268, 278
Schweitzer, Albert 37
sect, definitioin 141–5, 147
Shah Husain 6
Shahid Ganj 82
Shakti 32
Shamsher Singh Ashok, cataloguer
117
sharī'at, Muslim religious law 5
Sherpur, village 156
Shimla 227
Shiromani Gurdwara Parbandhak
Committee (SGPC) 67, 118,
120, 132, 173, 185, 186
Shivalik hills 56, 57, 71, 76
Shukerchakia *misal* 78, 216
Sidhwan Bet constituency 229
Sikh Gurdwaras Act 1925 173, 185
Sikh Rahit Marayādā 119, 133, 273,
274
Sikhs and Sikhism 275

silsilah, Sufi lineage 28
Singapore 241, 250
Singh Sabha 65–7, 87, 90, 91ff, 118, 119, 122, 131–3, 167, 169, 180, 230, 249–50, 252, 260, 263, 271, 273, 274–5 Amritsar *dīvān* 66, 184, 260 Lahore *dīvān* 66, 93, 184, 260 Sanatan Sikhs 90, 93–4, 169, 260 Tat Khalsa 90, 93ff, 169–70, 180, 182, 258, 260–2, 275
Sirhind 57, 77, 83, 84
Siri Chand 52, 68
Sobha Singh, artist 234
Southall 238
Southeast Asia 250
Srī Gur Sobhā 64, 109, 273
Srinivas, M.N. 218
Strauss, D.F. 37
subah 194–9
Sufis 4, 6, 7, 5–15, 16, 17, 18, 22, 27–31, 33, 35, 279
Sujanpur, village 149
Sukha Singh, warrior 81
Sumeru, Mount 40
Sunar (goldsmith caste) 224
Sundar Singh, Sant 158
syncretism 3–4, 20–21, 22–4, 26–35, 70

ṭaksāl, Sant institution 158
Tara Singh, Master 182
Tarkhan (carpenter caste) 60, 190, 208, 210–1, 214, 217, 219–24, 226–34
Tat Khalsa *see* Singh Sabha.
Tegh Bahadur, ninth Guru 57, 76, 77, 170, 261, 263
Teja Singh, historian 79, 170
Teja Singh of Bhasaur 167, 184
Temple, Richard 197
Textual Sources for the Study of Sikhism 127

The Construction of Religious Boundaries 268
The Fundamentalism Project 163, 170, 172
The Holy Writings of the Sikhs 261
The Sikh Religion 80, 95, 257, 261–2
Thoka (carpenter caste) 217–8, 233
tabacco 62, 231
Tonga 241
traditioin 269ff
transmigration 12, 261
Trilochan Singh, Dr 168
Trumpp, Ernest 96, 258, 260–1, 271–2

Udasi panth 52–3
Una sants 161
United States of America 67

Vahiguru 75, 89, 168, 184, 202
Vaishnava devotion 26–7
Vali Qandhari 272
Vancouver 238, 250
Varas 6
varṇa caste hierarchy 219–20
Vaudeville, Ch. 26
Vazir Khan of Sirhind 84–5, 86
Vedas 260
Vein river 27, 40
Vilayatpur 240
Vir Singh 42, 95, 97, 99, 167, 275

women 82–3, 127
World War I 244, 251
World War II 242

Zafar-nāmā 80, 86
Zail Singh, Giani 229
zāt (jatī), endogamous group 220–1, 247, 252